THE OFFICIAL

Arsenal

Yearbook 2006

Acknowledgements
The publisher would like to thank Julian Flanders, Kathie Wilson,
Joe Cohen, Jem Maidment, Ivan Ponting, Stuart MacFarlane and
Dan Brennan for their help throughout this project.

Produced for Hamlyn by Butler and Tanner

First published in 2006 by Hamlyn,
a division of Octopus Publishing Group Ltd,
2–4 Heron Quays, London E14 4JP

ISBN-13: 978-0-600-61494-4
ISBN-10: 0-600-61494-8

A CIP catalogue record for this book is available from the British Library

Printed and bound in the UK by Butler and Tanner

10 9 8 7 6 5 4 3 2 1

Executive Editor Trevor Davies
Senior Editor Jessica Cowie
Match Reports, 162–169 and 172–179 Jem Maidment
Additional Material   134–135 and 184–187 Dan Brennan
                        136–161 and 180–183 Ivan Ponting
Project Editor Julian Flanders at Butler and Tanner
Design Craig Stevens, Kathie Wilson at Butler and Tanner
Production Ian Paton
All images copyright © Arsenal Football Club Plc /Stuart MacFarlane
except the following: Colorsport 163 (bottom left), 171 (top left);
Empics 164 (bottom left and right, second from left), 165 (top left),
171 (middle left, bottom left and right)

All statistics are correct to 31 May 2006

CONTENTS

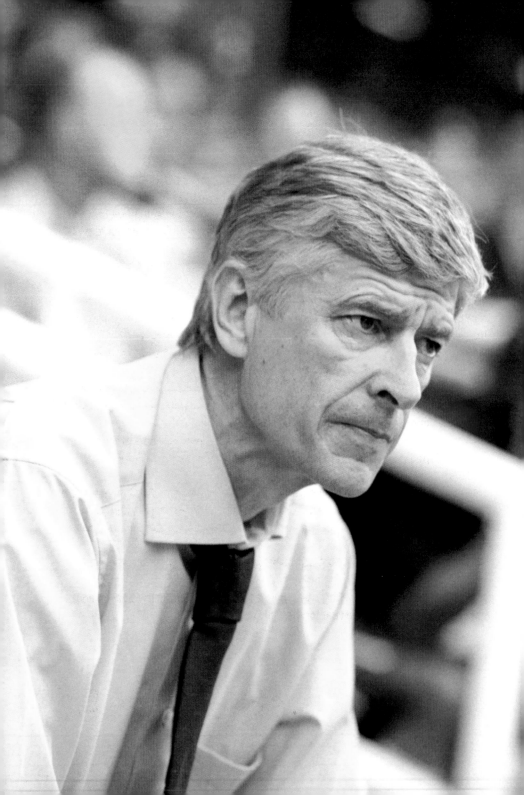

MANAGER'S MESSAGE

I feel immensely proud of what my team achieved in season 2005/06, the way the team responded after January was tremendous.

Of course, we were disappointed to lose the Champions League final, even more so because we feel we weren't afforded the chance to play a proper match against Barcelona. But we shouldn't forget the performances we put in during the European campaign. We were unbeaten until the final and the record of ten games without conceding – at the very highest level – is just remarkable, and full credit should go to the whole team for that.

I have full confidence and belief in this side, and after a difficult first half of the season they began to grow in self-belief in the new year.

We rounded off the league season in fitting style. It was very important that we all left Highbury for the very last time on a high. We would have felt guilty to walk out of the stadium on a low, after what has happened there for so many years.

Saying goodbye to Highbury and clinching that vital fourth place at the same time – it's a day that will live in my mind forever.

We all have a very positive feeling looking ahead to the new season. The young players have learned so much from the past 12 months, and I am convinced that many of them will benefit greatly from the World Cup too.

The young players, under the guidance of the experienced members of the squad, have developed week on week, and I personally believe there is a lot more to come from them.

Of course, Thierry Henry staying here will have a huge impact on the Club as a whole, and I always said the progression on the team would rely on Thierry signing again.

So we can look ahead to the new season, our first in Emirates Stadium, with great confidence.

Emirates Stadium looks fantastic, and we want to make it a fortress for us, and of course the fans will play a big part in that.

It's an exciting time for the Club, let's build on the positives from last season and make 2006/07 a memorable year for Arsenal Football Club.

ARSÈNE WENGER

Spanish Steps: Thierry Henry (right) is joined by Alexander Hleb after scoring the only goal of the game in Madrid.

CHAMPIONS LEAGUE

Arsenal gave a best-ever performance in Europe's premier club competition, reaching the Paris final only to narrowly lose 2–1 to Barcelona, despite playing with ten men for more than 70 minutes.

Wenger's side were outstanding from matchday one and entered the knockout stages as group winners. The highlight was a 2–0 win at Sparta Prague, which saw Thierry Henry beat Ian Wright's club goalscoring record.

The Gunners' outstanding defence also set a competition record with ten clean sheets in succession.

Henry fired a memorable winner at Real Madrid, while Patrick Vieira's return to Highbury in a Juventus shirt saw Arsenal put on an assured display to win 2–0 – Cesc Fabregas scoring one and setting up another – before drawing in Turin.

Villarreal were beaten at Highbury in the semi-final first leg and Jens Lehmann put Arsenal through to their first Champions League final when he saved Juan Riquelme's last-gasp penalty to earn a 0–0 draw in Spain.

However, heartache was to follow at rain-swept Stade de France when Juliano Belletti struck a late winner for the Catalans, although defeat in the final could not eclipse a sensational European campaign for the Gunners.

MATCHES

MATCHES PLAYED	13
PLAYERS USED	25

GOALS

SCORED	15
Per game	1.15
CONCEDED	4
Per game	0.3

ATTENDANCE

AT HOME	211,386
Average home gate	35,231

Memorable moments

- Henry scoring against Sparta Prague to become the Club's all-time record goalscorer
- Arsenal fans chanting for the squirrel that invaded the pitch during the home tie against Villareal
- Jens Lehmann's last-minute penalty save from Riquelme that sent the Gunners to Paris
- Sol Campbell's towering header in the Stade de France and the feeling that it just might be our night...
- Thierry Henry's superb individual effort that humbled the 'Galaticos' on their home turf

CHAMPIONS LEAGUE SEASON RECORD

BIGGEST WIN
3–0 v Sparta Prague (h) 2/11/05
Henry, van Persie 2

BIGGEST DEFEAT
1–2 v Barcelona 17/5/06

QUICKEST GOAL
Ljungberg – Two minutes
v Ajax (a) 26/9/05 (1–2)

ARSENAL 2
GILBERTO 51,
BERGKAMP 90

FC Thun 1
FERREIRA 53

DATE **WEDNESDAY 14 SEPTEMBER 2005**
VENUE **HIGHBURY**
ATTENDANCE **34,498**
REFEREE **GRZEGORZ GILEWSKI (POLAND)**

FORM	
D 0–0 (N)	FA Cup (won 5–4 on pens)
D 3–3 (A)	Friendly
W 2–0 (H)	Prem
L 0–1 (A)	Prem
W 4–1 (H)	Prem
L 1–2 (A)	Prem

OLD-TIMER DENNIS BERGKAMP produced an ice-cool winner two minutes into stoppage time to break the resistance of the Swiss minnows. The old ones, as one hack observed in the following morning's papers, are the best ones and that proved to be true for the Gunners when 30-year-old Sol Campbell lofted a long ball into the Thun box and the Dutch maestro, 36, used his strength to hold off defender Ljubo Milicevic and produce an assured finish while off-balance to win the game.

That famous old Arsenal spirit was needed after the side had dominated the game from start to finish, but had seen Robin van Persie sent off and Thun grab a fortunate equaliser after Gilberto had given the hosts a 51st minute lead.

The red was shown to van Persie on the stroke of half-time after he caught Alen Orman with a high boot as he attempted to control the ball. "It was not Robin's fault," argued Arsène Wenger after the game. "It was an accident." Thun manager Urs Schonenberger added, "He didn't do it on purpose."

The sending-off gave Thun a numerical advantage, but six minutes into the second half Gilberto headed home José Antonio Reyes's corner to give Arsenal a valuable lead.

Within two minutes the Swiss were level, though, when Nelson Ferreira lobbed the ball back over his shoulder and into the far corner, but with the clock ticking down it was substitute Bergkamp who popped up with almost Swiss-like precision to give Arsenal a winning start. It was his first European goal for three years.

Above Ashley Cole tests the Swiss defence with a right-foot shot.
Opposite, top Gilberto rises to head Arsenal into the lead.
Opposite, bottom Dennis Bergkamp coolly slots home the winner.

	P	W	D	L	F	A	Pts
ARSENAL	1	1	0	0	2	1	3
Ajax	1	0	1	0	1	1	1
Sparta Prague	1	0	1	0	1	1	1
FC Thun	1	0	0	1	1	2	0

MAN OF THE MATCH

GILBERTO

Mins on pitch	90
Tackles won	12
Passes completed	51 (86%)
Shots on target	2
Shots off target	0
Goals	1

"That was vintage Bergkamp for me and one of his best goals ever. The way he controlled it, used his strength and finished so well as he was falling over, showed all his talents in one small passage of play." DEAN PORTMAN, HORNCHURCH, ESSEX

"Dennis did very well, because it's a goal full of class, but not only of class, because we are used to that from Dennis, but full of fight and determination." ARSÈNE WENGER

"Bergkamp just beats the clock." DAILY TELEGRAPH

DID YOU KNOW?
This was FC Thun's first ever match in a major European competition.

GAME STATISTICS

ARSENAL		FC THUN
2	GOALS	1
0	1ST HALF GOALS	0
8	SHOTS ON TARGET	3
7	SHOTS OFF TARGET	3
5	BLOCKED SHOTS	2
10	CORNERS	2
12	FOULS	16
2	OFFSIDES	2
1	YELLOW CARDS	3
1	RED CARDS	0
84.2	PASSING SUCCESS	65.6
35	TACKLES	47
85.7	TACKLES SUCCESS	85.1
72.3	POSSESSION	27.7
57.1	TERRITORIAL ADVANTAGE	42.9

Ajax 1 ROSENBERG 70

ARSENAL 2 LJUNGBERG 2, PIRES 68 (PEN)

DATE TUESDAY 27 SEPTEMBER 2005
VENUE AMSTERDAM ARENA
ATTENDANCE 50,000
REFEREE LUIS MEDINA CANTALEJO (SPAIN)

A FIRST AWAY CHAMPIONS LEAGUE WIN in seven attempts saw off a lively Ajax side at the Amsterdam Arena. Fredrik Ljungberg gave Arsenal an early advantage and Robert Pires doubled the lead in the 68th minute, before Ajax set up a grandstand finish when Markus Rosenberg pulled a goal back.

Thierry Henry and Dennis Bergkamp were both missing through injury, while Robin van Persie was suspended after his red card

PERFORMANCE IN THE PREMIERSHIP YEARS		FORM		
Amsterdam Arena		L	0–1 (A)	Prem
		W	4–1 (H)	Prem
PLAYED	1	L	1–2 (A)	Prem
WON	0	W	2–1 (H)	CL
DRAWN	1	W	2–0 (H)	Prem
LOST	0	D	0–0 (A)	Prem
FOR	0			
AGAINST	0			

	P	W	D	L	F	A	Pts
ARSENAL	2	2	0	0	4	2	6
FC Thun	2	1	0	1	2	2	3
Ajax	2	0	1	1	2	3	1
Sparta Prague	2	0	1	1	1	2	1

against Thun. Ljungberg was thrown into attack as a makeshift striker and it took him just 80 seconds to open his Champions League account for the season.

Mathieu Flamini won possession and dispatched the ball to José Antonio Reyes, who delayed his final ball to dissect the Amsterdammers' defence. Ljungberg then timed his run brilliantly, before producing a delightful finish over Hans Vonk.

A sickening clash of heads between Kolo Toure and Angelos Charisteas saw both carried off. The Arsenal player returned to the pitch heavily bandaged, but a concussed Charisteas was forced out of the game – and Ajax were then dealt a further blow when the English side doubled their lead with 20 minutes remaining.

Reyes raced on to Sol Campbell's clearance only to tumble under Vonk's challenge – penalty. Pires got on with the job in hand and placed the ball past Vonk to make it 2–0. Ajax, though, were not finished yet and when Almunia could only parry Tomas Galasek's fierce 30-yard drive against a post, Rosenberg put away the rebound for an Ajax consolation.

GAME STATISTICS

AJAX		ARSENAL
1	GOALS	2
0	1ST HALF GOALS	1
7	SHOTS ON TARGET	2
8	SHOTS OFF TARGET	2
1	BLOCKED SHOTS	2
4	CORNERS	4
19	FOULS	15
1	OFFSIDES	1
4	YELLOW CARDS	2
0	RED CARDS	0
81.4	PASSING SUCCESS	74.1
40	TACKLES	23
92.5	TACKLES SUCCESS	73.9
59.9	POSSESSION	40.1
56.1	TERRITORIAL ADVANTAGE	43.9

FINAL THOUGHTS

"We needed that win away in Europe. It had been a while, but I thought we equipped ourselves brilliantly. There was two young sides out there, but it was the older hands of Ljungberg and Pires who made the difference. Ljungberg is brilliant at getting into those positions with well-timed, late runs. David Platt used to do it and Freddie is equally as good at it." JULIE-ANN LAIDLAW, EDINBURGH

"We are in a strong position, but it can change quickly. We were 1–1 against Thun, but won it in the last minute. Now we have six points after two games – and we take it in a cautious way. After a dodgy start we are getting a good run together." ARSÈNE WENGER

"Pires sparkles as Arsenal wipe the floor with Ajax."
THE GUARDIAN

MAN OF THE MATCH

SOL CAMPBELL

Mins on pitch	90
Tackles	3
Tackle success	100%
Passes completed	31 (74%)
Successful clearances	4

DID YOU KNOW?

Arsenal's first goal in this tie was their 100th in 70 UEFA Champions League games.

Opposite, top *Fredrik Ljungberg stuns Ajax with Arsenal's opening goal in the second minute.*
Opposite, bottom *José Antonio Reyes goes down under the challenge of Hans Vonk to earn Arsenal a penalty.*

Sparta Prague 0
ARSENAL 2 HENRY 21, 74

DATE TUESDAY 18 OCTOBER 2005
VENUE LETNÁ STADIUM, PRAGUE
ATTENDANCE 12,128
REFEREE WOLFGANG STARK (GERMANY)

PERFORMANCE IN THE PREMIERSHIP YEARS		FORM	
Letná Stadium		W 2–1 (H) CL	
		W 2–0 (H) Prem	
PLAYED	1	D 0–0 (A) Prem	
WON	1	W 2–1 (A) CL	
DRAWN	0	W 1–0 (H) Prem	
LOST	0	L 1–2 (A) Prem	
FOR	1		
AGAINST	0		

MATUSOVIC (PERGL 70)

BLAZEK

PERGL PETROUS LUKAS KADLEC

ZELENKA KISEL

POSPECH PETRAS POLACEK

SLEPICKA

VAN PERSIE REYES

FABREGAS FLAMINI GILBERTO PIRES

LAUREN TOURE CYGAN CLICHY

LEHMANN

HENRY (REYES 16) EBOUE (VAN PERSIE 73)

THIS WAS THE OCCASION when Thierry Henry surpassed Ian Wright's 185 goals to become the leading scorer in Arsenal's 119-year history.

The France international was inspirational in his first game since hitting the winner for his country in their 1–0 victory against the Republic of Ireland at Lansdowne Road in a Group 4 World Cup qualifier in September.

DID YOU KNOW?
Of the 186 Henry goals, 7 were headers, 31 with his left foot, 146 with his right and 2 from elsewhere on his body.

	P	W	D	L	F	A	Pts
ARSENAL	3	3	0	0	6	2	9
Ajax	3	1	1	1	4	3	4
FC Thun	3	1	0	2	2	4	3
Sparta Prague	3	0	1	2	1	4	1

FINAL THOUGHTS

"Thierry is everything to this Club. To do what he did tonight, coming on as a sub early on and not being fully fit, was just amazing. The boss always says he is the best striker in the world and who are we to disagree?" CLARE WILLIS, WEST KENSINGTON, LONDON

"I'm just over the moon about the record. Wright was a great player and will always be a legend at Arsenal. To beat his record is tremendous. I wanted to do it at Highbury, but if I get the chance to score I'll do it." THIERRY HENRY

"Henry a right cracker." DAILY STAR

GAME STATISTICS

SPARTA PRAGUE		ARSENAL
0	GOALS	2
0	1ST HALF GOALS	1
4	SHOTS ON TARGET	5
6	SHOTS OFF TARGET	3
7	BLOCKED SHOTS	3
8	CORNERS	3
16	FOULS	13
5	OFFSIDES	2
1	YELLOW CARDS	2
0	RED CARDS	0
70.4	PASSING SUCCESS	78.1
26	TACKLES	31
96.2	TACKLES SUCCESS	74.2
43.8	POSSESSION	56.2
57.6	TERRITORIAL ADVANTAGE	42.4

He picked up a groin strain in Dublin that day, but made a welcome return to the bench for this trip to central Europe.

Arsène Wenger had hoped to give Henry a half-hour run-out at the end of the game, but after just 16 minutes he was called into action when José Antonio Reyes was injured. Six minutes later he announced his return with a goal of stunning beauty.

Henry deftly controlled Kolo Toure's long pass, spun around the ball in an instant and curved a brilliant first-time shot with the outside of his right boot beyond Sparta goalkeeper Jaromir Blazek to haul himself level with Wright's 185 goals.

Sparta responded to their setback with several raids into Arsenal's penalty area, Jens Lehmann – returning after a two-match suspension – dealing with Slepicka's clever back-flick and later tipping Slovakian international Karol Kisel's long-range effort over the bar.

But it was to no avail and the moment finally came for Henry to make history with his 186th goal in his 303rd Arsenal match. With 16 minutes to go, he collected a sweeping Robert Pires pass, dummied two defenders and created enough space to nervelessly shoot past Blazek. His record breaking double strike put Arsenal five points clear at the top of Group B.

Opposite, top Arsène Wenger gives instructions to Henry before he replaces José Antonio Reyes, a welcome return for Thierry following injury in a France World Cup Qualifying match in September.
Opposite, bottom Thierry Henry curls in a stunning effort for his first of the evening.

MAN OF THE MATCH

THIERRY HENRY

Mins on pitch	76
Tackles won	2
Passes completed	18 (62%)
Shots on target	2
Shots off target	1
Goals	2

ARSENAL 3
HENRY 23,
VAN PERSIE 81, 86

Sparta Prague 0

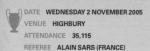

DATE WEDNESDAY 2 NOVEMBER 2005
VENUE HIGHBURY
ATTENDANCE 35,115
REFEREE ALAIN SARS (FRANCE)

FORM		
W 1–0	(H)	Prem
L 1–2	(A)	Prem
W 2–0	(A)	CL
W 1–0	(H)	Prem
W 3–0	(A)	C Cup
D 0–0	(A)	Prem

VAN PERSIE (HENRY 71) FABREGAS (PIRES 74) EBOUE (REYES 82)

ALMUNIA

LAUREN TOURE CAMPBELL CLICHY

REYES GILBERTO FLAMINI PIRES

HENRY BERGKAMP

MATUSOVIC

ZELENKA HASEK

PETRAS POLACEK POSPECH

PERGL PETROUS LUKAS KADLEC

BLAZEK

SLEPICKA (POLACEK 58) JESLINEK (PETROUS 80)

WHEN SUBSTITUTE ROBIN VAN PERSIE hit a late double to vanquish the Czech Republic champions and fire Arsenal into the last 16 it officially confirmed that Arsenal had now had their best ever start to a Champions League campaign with four straight victories.

A heavy downpour in north London prior to kick-off had left the conditions far from perfect, but Sparta made the early running and the Gunners nearly fell behind when Lukas Zelenka forced a tremendous one-handed save from Manuel Almunia.

However, it was only a minor glitch and after 23 minutes Arsenal nosed in front, with Thierry Henry finishing off a flowing move to give the stationary Jaromir Blazek in the Sparta goal no chance.

Frustrated Sparta, with a solitary point from their Group B campaign so far, conceded a succession of free-kicks, while

Above *Dennis Bergkamp is denied by Jaromir Blazek.*
Opposite, top right *Robin van Persie fires home his second and Arsenal's third.*

	P	W	D	L	F	A	Pts
ARSENAL	4	4	0	0	9	2	12
Ajax	4	2	1	1	8	5	7
FC Thun	4	1	0	3	4	8	3
Sparta Prague	4	0	1	3	1	7	1

MAN OF THE MATCH

ROBIN VAN PERSIE

Mins on pitch	25
Tackles won	0
Passes completed	4 (36%)
Shots on target	4
Shots off target	1
Goals	2

Blazek had to scramble across goal to repel one well struck Henry free-kick. Almunia was also called upon on a couple of occasions, but the visitors lacked any real punch up front.

Arsène Wenger waited until 19 minutes from the end to replace Henry with van Persie – and it would prove to be a masterstroke. Nine minutes remained when he collected Bergkamp's centre and opened up his body to swerve an accurate shot round Blazek to help Arsenal breath a little easier.

He then added the icing on the cake five minutes later – after Martin Petrous had hit the Arsenal bar – when he swept home a cross from fellow substitute Emmanuel Eboue.

FINAL THOUGHTS

"What I noticed tonight is that there is a growing maturity among our players when we play continental opposition. Sparta are a decent enough side, but they did try and disrupt our rhythm with niggly fouls. We coped well and just remained patient."
DOMINIC STACEY, CAMDEN TOWN, LONDON

"Van Persie is making big steps forward and he will get his chance. When you look at his goalscoring rate, with the number of minutes he has played, it is quite amazing."
ARSÈNE WENGER

"Arsenal do their talking on the pitch." DAILY MIRROR

GAME STATISTICS

ARSENAL		SPARTA PRAGUE
3	GOALS	0
1	1ST HALF GOALS	0
9	SHOTS ON TARGET	1
7	SHOTS OFF TARGET	9
1	BLOCKED SHOTS	2
11	CORNERS	4
3	FOULS	19
0	OFFSIDES	4
0	YELLOW CARDS	1
0	RED CARDS	0
84.2	PASSING SUCCESS	66.6
22	TACKLES	35
68.2	TACKLES SUCCESS	85.7
68.5	POSSESSION	31.5
53.9	TERRITORIAL ADVANTAGE	46.1

DID YOU KNOW?

This was the fifth successive season that the Gunners had reached the knockout stage of the Champions League.

FC Thun 0
ARSENAL 1 PIRES 88 (PEN)

DATE TUESDAY 22 NOVEMBER 2005
VENUE STADE DE SUISSE, BERN
ATTENDANCE 32,000
REFEREE LUCILIO BATISTA (PORTUGAL)

PERFORMANCE IN THE PREMIERSHIP YEARS	FORM	
Stade de Suisse	W 1–0	(H) Prem
This was Arsenal's first visit to this ground	W 3–0	(A) C Cup
	D 1–1	(A) Prem
	W 3–0	(H) CL
	W 3–1	(H) Prem
	W 3–2	(A) Prem

ARSENAL WERE CONFIRMED AS WINNERS of Group B when Robert Pires struck two minutes from time on a bitterly cold evening.

Thun's passage to the Champions League has shown that even in these multi-million pound days, miracles can happen and they started well with ex-Hibernian defender Alen Orman stinging Manuel Almunia's hands.

Thierry Henry was making his 70th appearance in the competition and tried his luck with a couple of long-range shots, although Robin van Persie had the best opportunity, only to be denied by Eldin Jakupovic.

The home crowd of 32,000 at Bern's Young Boys stadium (Thun's own 5,000-seat stadium was deemed inadequate for the game) were enjoying the visit of Arsenal in the biggest game in the Club's history. That was until Armand Deumi pulled down van Persie on the edge of the area and Portuguese referee Lucilio Batista didn't hesitate in producing a red card.

The fans were further incensed shortly afterwards when the ten-man side had a goal disallowed after Silvan Aegerter and Lustrinelli combined well for Nelson Ferreira to fire past Almunia.

As the second half progressed, Thun had the ball in the back of the net again, and again it was Ferreira who was left disappointed as Switzerland international Lustrinelli was deemed to be in an offside position, despite the fact that he wasn't touching the ball.

Henry was then sacrificed for Pires, but his colleague proved to be the matchwinner when he swept home the spot-kick after van Persie was fouled by Selver Hodzic.

	P	W	D	L	F	A	Pts
ARSENAL	5	5	0	0	10	2	15
Ajax	5	3	1	1	10	6	10
FC Thun	5	1	0	4	4	9	3
Sparta Prague	5	0	1	4	2	9	1

FINAL THOUGHTS

"Were we lucky? No, because we were composed and bided our time. You just get the feeling we have an inner-belief in Europe that we don't have in the Premiership."
CARSTEN HORSTMANN, COLOGNE, GERMANY

"The real competition starts now, because it is completely different with a direct knockout." ARSÈNE WENGER

"Rob-bery as Gun nick it." DAILY STAR

GAME STATISTICS

FC THUN		ARSENAL
0	GOALS	1
0	1ST HALF GOALS	0
3	SHOTS ON TARGET	3
4	SHOTS OFF TARGET	7
4	BLOCKED SHOTS	1
2	CORNERS	5
14	FOULS	18
11	OFFSIDES	10
3	YELLOW CARDS	3
1	RED CARDS	0
69.8	PASSING SUCCESS	78.1
21	TACKLES	15
81.0	TACKLES SUCCESS	73.3
40.4	POSSESSION	59.6
51.3	TERRITORIAL ADVANTAGE	48.7

DID YOU KNOW?
This was a Club-record sixth successive Champions League victory.

MAN OF THE MATCH

PHILIPPE SENDEROS
Mins on pitch	90
Tackles won	1
Tackle success	100%
Passes completed	8 (80%)
Successful clearances	4

Above Robert Pires (left) is joined by Sol Campbell and Cesc Fabregas after scoring his late penalty in Bern.
Opposite Emmanuel Eboue tries to find a way into a crowded penalty area.

ARSENAL 0
Ajax 0

DATE   WEDNESDAY 7 DECEMBER 2005
VENUE   HIGHBURY
ATTENDANCE   35,376
REFEREE   EDUARDO ITURRALDE GONZÁLEZ
(SPAIN)

FORM		
W 3–1	(H)	Prem
W 3–2	(A)	Prem
W 1–0	(A)	CL
W 3–0	(H)	Prem
W 3–0	(H)	C Cup
L 0–2	(A)	Prem

AN UNCHARACTERISTIC PENALTY-SPOT MISS by Thierry Henry denied Arsenal the opportunity of ending their Champions League Group B campaign with six wins out of six.

The France striker sent Ajax goalkeeper Maarten Stekelenburg the wrong way, but the ball flew wide of the upright. It was the final act of the first half and, as Spanish referee Eduardo Itturalde González blew his whistle for half-time, the closest either side got to scoring in the whole 90 minutes.

Above Young Dutch prospect, Quincy Owusu-Abeyie on the attack against his former employers, Ajax.
Opposite Emmanuel Eboue hurdles a challenge.

DID YOU KNOW?
Arsenal have not been beaten by Dutch opposition in their last eight matches.

Arsène Wenger changed his side to blood several youngsters, with Sebastian Larsson slotting into the midfield for his debut and exciting Dutch youngster Quincy Owusu-Abeyie partnering Henry in attack. There was also a special cheer for Alexander Hleb, who was returning to the line-up after nine weeks out with a knee injury.

Danny Blind's side had also qualified already, but were determined to avenge their 2–1 loss to the Gunners at the Amsterdam Arena in September and, as is characteristic with Ajax sides past and present, they enjoyed huge chunks of possession and played some delightful keepball, but with no end result.

	P	W	D	L	F	A	Pts
ARSENAL	6	5	1	0	10	2	16
Ajax	6	3	2	1	10	6	11
FC Thun	6	1	1	4	4	9	4
Sparta Prague	6	0	2	4	2	9	2

FINAL THOUGHTS

"Ajax are a decent side and this was not a bad result, especially as we had so many youngsters out. Larsson looks like he could make the step up soon and it was nice to see English lad Kerrea Gilbert given another run-out."
JASON PRIOR, FELTHAM, MIDDLESEX

"We were in some interesting situations, but we gave the ball too late, or we didn't give the ball at the right moment, or we didn't give the ball at all. However, overall I feel it was interesting to see some young players and many of them did well." ARSÈNE WENGER

"Arsenal have been awarded a remarkable nine penalties (this season). They have missed four." THE GUARDIAN

Henry's chance from the penalty spot came after José Antonio Reyes was felled in the area, but he failed to hit the target and Robin van Persie came off the bench to inject some life into a misfiring Arsenal attack.

In fact, he nearly silenced the vocal visiting fans, berating him for his Feyenoord connections, when he danced past two challenges, only to shoot straight at Stekelenburg's legs.

MAN OF THE MATCH

MATHIEU FLAMINI

Mins on pitch	90
Tackles won	4
Tackle success	100%
Passes completed	32 (82%)
Successful clearances	1

GAME STATISTICS

ARSENAL		AJAX
0	GOALS	0
0	1ST HALF GOALS	0
3	SHOTS ON TARGET	0
5	SHOTS OFF TARGET	8
5	BLOCKED SHOTS	2
3	CORNERS	3
12	FOULS	15
1	OFFSIDES	7
2	YELLOW CARDS	1
0	RED CARDS	0
77.8	PASSING SUCCESS	77.6
18	TACKLES	39
83.3	TACKLES SUCCESS	84.6
49.7	POSSESSION	50.3
51.0	TERRITORIAL ADVANTAGE	49.0

Real Madrid 0
ARSENAL 1 HENRY 47

DATE TUESDAY 21 FEBRUARY 2006
VENUE ESTADIO SANTIAGO BERNABEU
ATTENDANCE 80,000
REFEREE STEFANO FARINA (ITALY)

PERFORMANCE IN THE PREMIERSHIP YEARS	FORM		
	W 2–1	(H)	C Cup
Estadio Santiago Bernabeu	L 0–1	(A)	FA Cup
This was Arsenal's first visit to this ground in the Champions League	L 2–3	(H)	Prem
	W 2–0	(A)	Prem
	D 1–1	(H)	Prem
	L 0–1	(A)	Prem

Arsenal

PIRES (HLEB 76) DIABY (REYES 80) SONG (FABREGAS 90)

LEHMANN

EBOUE TOURE SENDEROS FLAMINI

FABREGAS LJUNGBERG
HLEB GILBERTO REYES

HENRY

Real Madrid

RONALDO

ROBINHO ZIDANE GUTI BECKHAM

GRAVESEN

CARLOS RAMOS WOODGATE CICINHO

CASILLAS

MEJIA (WOODGATE 9) RAUL (ROBINHO 63) BAPTISTA (GRAVESEN 76)

THIERRY HENRY scored one of his greatest goals in a Gunners shirt as Arsenal became the first English side to win in the Santiago Bernabeu in over 80 years.

Having recently had a rather wretched time, the Londoners gave their best performance of the season with an assured display against the nine-times winners of Europe's premier prize.

Henry's goal came just after the restart – and it is one to cherish for many years to come – after he seemed to take on most of the Real team before finding the net with a delicious finish. Picking the ball up just inside the hosts' half from Spaniard Cesc Fabregas, who was playing his first professional Club game in his own country, he skipped past Ronaldo. He then danced neatly away from substitute Alvaro Mejia and swatted aside Guti. As the France striker accelerated away, Sergio Ramos desperately attempted a last-ditch tackle, but it was too late and Henry finished brilliantly with a firm effort past Iker Casillas' left hand.

The travelling support, dotted all around the vast stadium, erupted and even a sizeable number of the notoriously demanding Madrid fans gently applauded a goal of stunning quality.

It was a fascinating, open game, one of the best in European competition for years, with Madrid showing more zest as the game wore on. David Beckham was a constant thorn in the side of

Other Results:		
PSV Eindhoven	0–1	Lyon
Bayern Munich	1–1	AC Milan
Benfica	1–0	Liverpool
Chelsea	1–2	Barcelona
Rangers	2–2	Villarreal
Ajax	2–2	Inter Milan
Werder Bremen	3–2	Juventus

emergency left-back Mathieu Flamini, but the young Frenchman, like his team-mates, refused to buckle and stood firm against the England captain. When the final whistle blew Arsenal were victorious, and deservedly so, because they were by far the better side.

FINAL THOUGHTS

"Where did that result come from? And what a performance. Everyone played superbly. It was a real team performance and I, for one, was so proud to be in the stadium. Fabregas was my man of the match – and the goal was just amazing. It's been emotional!" EDWARD ODARO, HARRINGAY, LONDON

"The most important thing is that when you play in the Champions League or any competition away from home you cannot be scared, you must play football. We were not scared tonight and we played football." THIERRY HENRY

"King Henry proves the Real deal as Arsenal come of age." THE TIMES

DID YOU KNOW?

Arsenal are the first English team since Lancashire amateurs Nelson, in 1923, to beat Real Madrid at the Bernabeu. It was also Henry's 40th European goal for the Club.

Opposite *Thierry Henry plays a cheeky backheel to the outstanding Cesc Fabregas.*
Above *Henry runs at the heart of the Madrid defence on his way to scoring Arsenal's winner.*

MAN OF THE MATCH

FRANCESC FABREGAS

Mins on pitch	90
Tackles won	2
Passes completed	36 (81%)
Shots on target	1
Shots off target	0

ARSENAL 0
Real Madrid 0

DATE **WEDNESDAY 8 MARCH 2006**
VENUE **HIGHBURY**
ATTENDANCE **35,487**
REFEREE **MICHEL LUBOS (SLOVAKIA)**

FORM		
W 2–0	(A)	Prem
D 1–1	(H)	Prem
L 0–1	(A)	Prem
W 1–0	(A)	CL
L 0–1	(A)	Prem
W 4–0	(A)	Prem

PIRES (REYES 68) — BERGKAMP (HLEB 86)

LEHMANN

EBOUE — TOURE — SENDEROS — FLAMINI

GILBERTO — REYES

HLEB — FABREGAS — LJUNGBERG

HENRY

RONALDO — RAÚL

ZIDANE — GUTI — BECKHAM

GRAVESEN

CARLOS — BRAVO — RAMOS — SALGADO

CASILLAS

BAPTISTA (GRAVESEN 68) — CASSANO (RAÚL 73) — ROBINHO (SALGADO 84)

Other Results:

AC Milan 4–1 Bayern Munich	(AC Milan win 5–2 on aggregate)
Liverpool 0–2 Benfica	(Benfica win 3–0 on aggregate)
Lyon 4–0 PSV Eindhoven	(Lyon win 5–0 on aggregate)
Barcelona 1–1 Chelsea	(Barcelona win 3–2 on aggregate)
Juventus 2–1 Werder Bremen	(4–4 on agg., Juventus win on away goals rule)
Villarreal 1–1 Rangers	(3–3 on agg., Villarreal win on away goals rule)
Inter Milan 1–0 Ajax	(Inter Milan win 3–2 on aggregate)

NIL-NIL TO THE ARSENAL! The old stadium has seen some thrilling matches in its 93-year history, but few could match this humdinger of a game, despite the absence of goals, and Arsenal's sixth consecutive clean sheet in the Champions League against Madrid's Galacticos set up a quarter-final clash with Patrick Vieira's Juventus.

If ever a game deserved a goal, though, it was this one. José Antonio Reyes struck the woodwork for Arsenal in the first half and Thierry Henry almost scored after the break. Real legend Raúl hit a post and keeper Jens Lehmann saved well from Robinho in the dying seconds.

Ronaldo had the first chance of the game after just two minutes, but his downward header was scrambled to safety by Lehmann. Cesc Fabregas was then denied by a brave clearance from Michel Salgado after 18 minutes and Reyes hit the bar from point-blank range with only Iker Casillas to beat just before the break.

Real piled on the pressure in the second half and Raúl was only denied by a fantastic save from Lehmann, who was scrambling back towards his goal. It was end-to-end stuff and the Highbury crowd were on the edge of their seats, admiring the quality of football on show.

Real were the side obligated to attack, desperately needing to cancel out Henry's goal from the Bernabeu, but, as the game wore

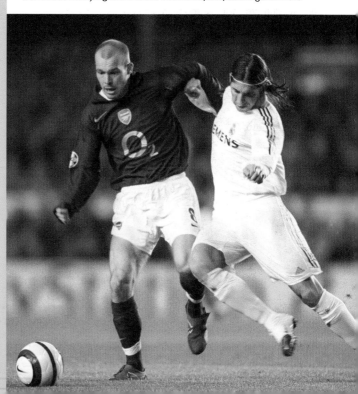

FINAL THOUGHTS

"Breathtaking. I have never seen a 0–0 draw like it. In fact, I can't think of a better game at Highbury for years. The whole team was brilliant and it was toss up between Jens and Kolo for the man of the match award."

MAL BRISSETT, HIGHGATE, LONDON

"To play two games against Real and not concede a goal shows remarkable spirit. Something is happening with this team. They are gelling together. They have shown character and that is very good. I feel we have grown as a team during these last two months." ARSÈNE WENGER

"End of an era for Real but just the start for Arsenal." DAILY EXPRESS

MAN OF THE MATCH

KOLO TOURE

Mins on pitch	90
Tackles won	4
Tackle success	100%
Passes completed	20 (87%)
Successful clearances	6

GAME STATISTICS

ARSENAL		REAL MADRID
0	GOALS	0
0	1ST HALF GOALS	0
2	SHOTS ON TARGET	4
6	SHOTS OFF TARGET	6
6	BLOCKED SHOTS	5
5	CORNERS	4
22	FOULS	18
2	OFFSIDES	1
1	YELLOW CARDS	4
0	RED CARDS	0
78.4	PASSING SUCCESS	77.0
27	TACKLES	37
77.8	TACKLES SUCCESS	70.3
44.5	POSSESSION	55.5
56.6	TERRITORIAL ADVANTAGE	43.4

on, the side's ageing limbs appeared to feel the strain more than Arsenal's young guns.

It was the home side who nearly broke the deadlock in injury time – Robert Pires' audacious 60-yard effort rolled towards goal, only for Roberto Carlos to sprint back and halt its progress – but the night belonged to Arsenal and seconds later the final whistle was blown.

DID YOU KNOW?

Real Madrid failed to score in a two-legged Champions League fixture for the first time ever.

Left *The heroic Jens Lehmann salutes the North Bank at the final whistle.*
Opposite *Fredrik Ljungberg battles for possession with Sergio Ramos.*

ARSENAL 2
FABREGAS 40,
HENRY 69

Juventus 0

DATE **TUESDAY 28 MARCH 2006**
VENUE **HIGHBURY**
ATTENDANCE **35,472**
REFEREE **PETER FROJDFELDT (SWEDEN)**

FORM		
W 1–0	(A)	CL
L 0–1	(A)	Prem
W 4–0	(A)	Prem
D 0–0	(H)	CL
W 2–1	(H)	Prem
W 3–0	(H)	Prem

ARSENAL TOOK FULL CONTROL of this Champions League quarter-final tie as Juve finished the game with just nine players on the pitch. It was billed as the return of Patrick Vieira, but the former Arsenal skipper was completely overshadowed in midfield by his teenage replacement Cesc Fabregas.

José Antonio Reyes gets the better of former Arsenal skipper Patrick Vieira.

DID YOU KNOW?
Arsenal tied with AC Milan's record of going seven Champions League matches without conceding.

The Spanish rookie produced a man of the match display – and a goal – as the runaway Serie A leaders had no answer to Arsenal's pressing game. Arsenal went ahead five minutes before the break after Robert Pires dispossessed Vieira in midfield and fed Thierry Henry, who in turn played in Fabregas whose cleverly disguised low drive wrong-footed Gianluigi Buffon.

A minute after Fabregas' goal, Henry went close with a shot from a very tight angle and the home team were firmly in the ascendancy at the break.

Juve were failing to cope with Arsenal's lightning breaks and quick passing and they soon fell further behind when Fabregas found space on the right side of the area and passed to Henry. The ball was played just behind the France striker, but he managed to scoop it into the net all the same with Buffon out of position.

Other Results:		
Benfica	0–0	Barcelona
Inter Milan	2–1	Villarreal
Lyon	0–0	AC Milan

Thierry Henry prepares to double Arsenal's lead.

MAN OF THE MATCH

FRANCESC FABREGAS

Mins on pitch	**90**
Tackles won	**0**
Passes completed	**43 (80%)**
Shots on target	**2**
Shots off target	**1**
Goals	**1**

GAME STATISTICS

ARSENAL		JUVENTUS
2	GOALS	0
1	1ST HALF GOALS	0
8	SHOTS ON TARGET	0
5	SHOTS OFF TARGET	2
1	BLOCKED SHOTS	4
4	CORNERS	2
12	FOULS	28
3	OFFSIDES	1
0	YELLOW CARDS	2
0	RED CARDS	2
76.2	PASSING SUCCESS	72.1
31	TACKLES	41
87.1	TACKLES SUCCESS	78.0
49.4	POSSESSION	50.6
50.6	TERRITORIAL ADVANTAGE	49.4

Vieira was then booked for a tackle on José Antonio Reyes – thus missing the return in Turin eight days later – as Arsenal stroked the ball about with ease. In the final minutes Mauro Camoranesi and Jonathan Zebina both received second yellow cards as Juve lost their heads.

Arsenal had produced one of their finest European displays and left the pitch knowing that a draw or even a narrow defeat in Turin would put them through to the semi-finals.

FINAL THOUGHTS

"What a night. We were brilliant and Fabregas is now becoming one of the best players in Europe. We have one foot in the semi-finals and Juve must be in a state of shock, because it could have been four or five. The Highbury fans were the twelfth man." ROHAN PATEL, SUDBURY

"I believe we will finish the job in the second leg in Italy, but there is still a lot to come. We have to keep our feet on the ground and keep our football simple. That is what the boys do and they can do better. They are not inhibited. There is quality in this team and they are good to watch." ARSÈNE WENGER

"Absolutely Fabregas!" DAILY EXPRESS

Juventus 0
ARSENAL 0

DATE WEDNESDAY 5 APRIL 2006
VENUE STADIO DELLE ALPI
ATTENDANCE 50,000
REFEREE HERBERT FANDEL (GERMANY)

PERFORMANCE IN THE PREMIERSHIP YEARS		FORM	
Stadio Delle Alpi		W 4–0 (A) Prem	
		D 0–0 (H) CL	
PLAYED	1	W 2–1 (H) Prem	
WON	0	W 3–0 (H) Prem	
DRAWN	0	W 2–0 (H) CL	
LOST	1	W 5–0 (H) Prem	
FOR	0		
AGAINST	1		

ZALAYETA (MUTU 61) BALZARETTI (CHIELLINI 66)

BUFFON

ZAMBROTTA KOVAC CANNAVARO CHIELLINI

MUTU EMERSON GIANNICHEDDA NEDVED

TREZEGUET IBRAHIMOVIC

HENRY

FABREGAS LJUNGBERG
REYES GILBERTO HLEB

FLAMINI SENDEROS TOURE EBOUE

LEHMANN

PIRES (REYES 62) DIABY (HLEB 87)

"THE SIMPLE EQUATION IS THAT THEY SCORED TWO AGAINST US and we scored none – they were better than us," said Fabio Capello, who was typically gracious after the Old Lady took a tumble in her own backyard in the last Champions League game at the Stadio Delle Alpi before the bulldozers moved in to renovate the huge, soulless arena.

Arsenal were superb on the night, defending the two-goal advantage picked up on that glorious evening at Highbury eight days earlier. In fact, on a night of tension in Turin, the visitors were never in any real danger and had little problem

Above *Thierry Henry shields the ball from Juve's defenders.*
Above, top *Mathieu Flamini manages to retain possession despite the close attentions of Gianluca Zambrotta.*

Other Results:
Barcelona 2–0 Benfica
(Barcelona win 2–0 on aggregate)
Villarreal 1–0 Inter Milan
(2–2 on agg., Villarreal win on away goals rule)
AC Milan 3–1 Lyon
(AC Milan win 3–1 on aggregate)

"It was easier than expected, to be honest. Juve looked terrified of us. They didn't really open up against us until it was too late, while Buffon kept them in the game. If we'd won 2–0 again they couldn't have complained. I can't believe we are in the last four... who'd have thought it a few weeks ago?" ALEX LANGHAM, GRAVESEND, KENT

"We are very proud. Two months ago no-one expected that from our players. It went according to plan in many ways, because they did not create a lot. We didn't suffer much in the first 20 minutes or the first 15 minutes of the second half. Pavel Nedved's sending-off was the end of the game. I felt he could have got them back to 2–1 and then it would have been difficult." ARSÈNE WENGER

"Arsenal maintain their dream of opening the Emirates Stadium as European champions." SUN

MAN OF THE MATCH

KOLO TOURE

Mins on pitch	90
Tackles won	1
Tackle success	100%
Passes completed	11 (64.7%)
Successful clearances	9

GAME STATISTICS

JUVENTUS		ARSENAL
0	GOALS	0
0	1ST HALF GOALS	0
2	SHOTS ON TARGET	5
3	SHOTS OFF TARGET	3
0	BLOCKED SHOTS	1
1	CORNERS	8
21	FOULS	14
13	OFFSIDES	0
1	YELLOW CARDS	2
1	RED CARDS	0
69.8	PASSING SUCCESS	66.6
36	TACKLES	18
75.0	TACKLES SUCCESS	83.3
55.7	POSSESSION	44.3
52.3	TERRITORIAL ADVANTAGE	47.7

keeping a competition record eight successive clean sheet to make history and progress to the semi-finals for the first time in the Club's history.

If anything, Arsenal could have extended their lead. Gilberto went close and Cesc Fabregas then raced through on goal, only to be denied by the magnificent Gianluigi Buffon. The Italy keeper then twice denied Henry on the Frenchman's return to his former employers, before Juve, missing former Gunner Patrick Vieira through suspension, slowly stirred.

A Pavel Nedved effort was well gathered by Jens Lehmann, but frustration got the better of him shortly after when he was sent off for a second yellow card – and Juve's chances were all but gone.

Arsenal famously earned a 1–0 win at Juve's old Stadio Communale in 1980 and they nearly repeated that scoreline when Fredrik Ljungberg went close with time almost up. Arsenal, however, had done enough to make history.

DID YOU KNOW?

This was a record for consecutive clean sheets in the Champions League (8).

ARSENAL 1 TOURE 41
Villarreal CF 0

DATE WEDNESDAY 19 APRIL 2006
VENUE HIGHBURY
ATTENDANCE 35,438
REFEREE KONRAD PLAUTZ (AUSTRIA)

FORM

W 2–0	(H)	CL
W 5–0	(H)	Prem
D 0–0	(A)	CL
L 2–0	(A)	Prem
D 1–1	(A)	Prem
W 3–1	(H)	Prem

BERGKAMP (HLEB 80)
VAN PERSIE (LJUNGBERG 80)

LEHMANN

EBOUE TOURE SENDEROS FLAMINI

GILBERTO

HLEB LJUNGBERG FABREGAS PIRES

HENRY

FORLAN MARI

RIQUELME

SORIN TACCHINARDI SENNA

ARRUABARRENA ARZO ALVAREZ VENTA

BARBOSA

FRANCO (MARI 55) JOSICO (SORIN 73) CALLEJA (FORLAN 90)

KOLO TOURE'S FIRST-HALF GOAL gave Arsenal a slender advantage to take to Spain for the second leg, but the question many fans were asking after the last ever European tie at Highbury was would one goal be enough?

Thierry Henry had 'scored' after just 12 minutes, sliding the ball home from Robert Pires' pass, only to be incorrectly ruled offside. Villarreal dangerman Riquelme, tipped to be the outstanding Argentinian performer at the forthcoming World Cup in Germany, was superbly shackled by Gilberto in midfield and the home side slowly took charge.

They made the vital breakthrough four minutes before half-time when Henry played a delightful disguised pass to Alexander Hleb, who slid in a cross for Toure to turn home.

Relief enveloped Highbury, but there were a few hearts in mouths just after when Gilberto scythed down Villarreal striker Jose Mari just inside the edge of the area, only for the Austrian referee Konrad Plautz to wave play on. Arsenal had been lucky.

The intervention of a squirrel on the pitch briefly lightened the mood, but Arsenal stayed focused and almost doubled their advantage after 55 minutes when Emmanuel Eboue's cross was met by Henry, but Arzo recovered to clear off the line.

DID YOU KNOW?
This was the last ever European fixture at Highbury.

Robert Pires struggles to maintain possession against a tenacious Villarreal side.

Other Results:

AC Milan	0–1	Barcelona

Kolo Toure (right) prepares to celebrate his first-half winner in front of the Clock End.

Jens Lehmann had been relatively untroubled, but he was forced to scramble to make a low save from Senna's 20-yard drive. However, it was Arsenal who came closest to scoring again when substitute Dennis Bergkamp almost snatched the crucial second in injury-time, until Javi Venta just beat him to the ball and cleared to safety.

FINAL THOUGHTS

"Before the game I feel some fans were being naïve. People were saying Arsenal would win 3–0 or 4–1, but I could never see it. Villarreal are in the semis on merit and are a tough team. However, we could have got another goal and now the tie is delicately in the balance. Gilberto was outstanding tonight – Riquelme didn't get a kick. Wenger said we would not man-mark Riquelme, but Gilberto never let him out of his sight."

JOHN DUNNE, DOLLIS HILL, LONDON

"It was a tense game and I think we could have got one more goal. Now we need a good defensive performance and to be very sharp on the counter-attack. I am confident we will do well... I believe in my team and our defensive record speaks for itself." ARSÈNE WENGER

"Toure gives Arsenal a foot in the final."
THE GUARDIAN

GAME STATISTICS		
ARSENAL		**VILLARREAL**
1	GOALS	0
1	1ST HALF GOALS	0
5	SHOTS ON TARGET	3
7	SHOTS OFF TARGET	4
4	BLOCKED SHOTS	1
5	CORNERS	2
17	FOULS	17
8	OFFSIDES	7
0	YELLOW CARDS	5
0	RED CARDS	0
76.8	PASSING SUCCESS	73.0
25	TACKLES	30
76.0	TACKLES SUCCESS	80.0
54.4	POSSESSION	45.6
51.5	TERRITORIAL ADVANTAGE	48.5

MAN OF THE MATCH

GILBERTO

Mins on pitch	90
Tackles won	7
Passes completed	50 (85%)
Shots on target	1
Shots off target	3

Villarreal CF 0
ARSENAL 0

DATE   TUESDAY 25 APRIL 2006
VENUE   EL MADRIGAL
ATTENDANCE   23,000
REFEREE   VALENTIN IVANOV (RUSSIA)

PERFORMANCE IN THE PREMIERSHIP YEARS	FORM	
El Madrigal	D 0–0 (A) CL	
This was Arsenal's first visit to this ground in the Champions League	L 2–0 (A) Prem	
	D 1–1 (A) Prem	
	W 3–1 (H) Prem	
	W 1–0 (H) CL	
	D 1–1 (H) Prem	

ARSENAL REACHED THEIR FIRST CHAMPIONS LEAGUE FINAL after shutting out Villarreal in Spain, with Jens Lehmann the hero after he saved a last-gasp penalty.

The team's 1–0 first-leg win, coupled with a record tenth successive European clean sheet, ensured the Gunners' place in Paris, but the tie looked to be heading for extra-time when Gael Clichy – on as an eighth-minute substitute for Mathieu Flamini – was harshly adjudged to have bundled over Jose Mari in the box.

Villarreal's Argentinian playmaker Riquelme stepped up to take the spot-kick, but Lehmann flung himself to his left to deny him and Arsenal were in the final.

The hosts had enjoyed most of the possession as Arsenal soaked up incessant pressure. Gilberto was outstanding, as he had been in the first leg, and the returning Sol Campbell showed immense spirit with a super display alongside Kolo Toure, at the heart of the defence.

DID YOU KNOW?
This is the first time Arsenal had played at this ground in the Champions League.

Above *Jens Lehmann dives to his left to keep out Juan Riquelme's last-minute penalty.*
Opposite *Kolo Toure, Robert Pires and Sol Campbell at the final whistle.*

Other Result:
Barcelona 0–0 Benfica
(Barcelona win 1–0 on aggregate)

VILLARREAL		ARSENAL
0	GOALS	0
0	1ST HALF GOALS	0
5	SHOTS ON TARGET	1
6	SHOTS OFF TARGET	3
2	BLOCKED SHOTS	1
3	CORNERS	3
16	FOULS	15
4	OFFSIDES	3
0	YELLOW CARDS	0
0	RED CARDS	0
81.3	PASSING SUCCESS	73.6
21	TACKLES	28
81.0	TACKLES SUCCESS	75.0
61.9	POSSESSION	38.1
53.0	TERRITORIAL ADVANTAGE	47.0

However, Arsenal barely mustered a shot at goal and rode their luck at times, with the big German excellent again, as he had been all season. He saved from Juan Pablo Sorin and then blocked a cross-shot from Javi Venta, which Franco dummied with a missed header at the near post.

In the 65th minute it began to look like Arsenal's night when Forlan rifled over from 15 yards while Lehmann was out of position. Villarreal started to gamble by pushing men forward and Franco found the net, but it was rightly ruled out for offside. Then Riquelme saw his spot-kick saved by Lehmann and the Yellow Submarine was finally sunk.

FINAL THOUGHTS

"When you are in football you can be close to being in hell – but you can rise to heaven just like that." JENS LEHMANN

"Jens The Saviour!" THE GUARDIAN

MAN OF THE MATCH

JENS LEHMANN

Mins on pitch	90
Saves	5
Catches	3
Passes completed	5 (29.4%)
Clearances	1

ARSENAL 1 CAMPBELL 37

FC Barcelona 2 ETO'O 77, BELLETTI 81

DATE **WEDNESDAY 17 MAY 2006**
VENUE **STADE DE FRANCE**
ATTENDANCE **79,500**
REFEREE **TERJE HAUGE (NORWAY)**

FORM		
W 1–0	(H)	CL
D 1–1	(H)	Prem
D 0–0	(A)	CL
W 3–0	(A)	Prem
W 3–1	(A)	Prem
W 4–2	(H)	Prem

AT A RAIN-SOAKED Stade de France, Arsenal came within a quarter of an hour of winning their first Champions League title, before two late goals sent the trophy to Catalonia.

The game hinged on Norwegian referee Terje Hauge's decision to send off the hero of Villarreal, Jens Lehmann, after 18 minutes. The German keeper hauled down Samuel Eto'o as he raced through, but, despite Ludovic Giuly rolling the loose ball into the Arsenal net, Hauge hauled the play back, showed Lehmann red and awarded a free-kick to Barca.

It was billed as Europe's dream final, but the entire complexion of the game changed in a crazy 60 seconds. Robert Pires was sacrificed as reserve keeper Manuel Almunia stepped into the fray.

Already Thierry Henry had twice gone close to opening the scoring and Arsenal, despite their numerical disadvantage, continued to push forward. They then shocked the La Liga leaders by taking a 37th minute lead through Sol Campbell. Henry flighted over a free-kick from the right and Campbell leapt high to head the ball past Victor Valdes. "1–0 To The Arsenal" chanted the travelling Gooners.

In the second half Barca set the pace, but Almunia managed to deny Eto'o when he turned the Cameroon star's shot against a post. However, just as the Spanish team seemed to be running out of ideas, and only a few minutes after Henry blew a super chance to add a second for Arsenal, Barca levelled, as sub Henrik Larsson touched the ball through to Eto'o – who looked a shade offside – and he finished at the near post.

DID YOU KNOW?
Arsenal lost their last European final in Paris – against Real Zaragoza in the Cup-Winners' Cup in 1995.

BARCELONA		ARSENAL
2	GOALS	1
0	1ST HALF GOALS	1
9	SHOTS ON TARGET	5
7	SHOTS OFF TARGET	3
5	BLOCKED SHOTS	1
3	CORNERS	4
20	FOULS	16
1	OFFSIDES	1
2	YELLOW CARDS	2
0	RED CARDS	1
85.8	PASSING SUCCESS	73.0
33	TACKLES	35
81.8	TACKLES SUCCESS	85.7
71.3	POSSESSION	28.7
61.2	TERRITORIAL ADVANTAGE	38.8

Ten-man Arsenal were finally broken and the Spaniards turned the game around less than three minutes later when another substitute, Juliano Belletti, fired through Almunia's legs for a heart-breaking winner.

Opposite Thierry Henry prepares to take the free-kick from which Campbell scores.
Left Sol Campbell leaps high to meet the flighted free-kick perfectly and head past Victor Valdés.

FINAL THOUGHTS

"The Arsenal lost possibly the most important game that I've attended in my 20 years of supporting them, but I left the stadium feeling almost victorious. It didn't hurt like it should have. Reason? That performance was what the Arsenal are all about and I know we'll be back." DAVID HAM, SOUTHEAST LONDON

"My biggest regret was that their first goal was offside. When you are playing 10 against 11, and you are still on top, to concede an offside goal and then nothing happens is difficult to accept." ARSÈNE WENGER

"We can be proud. We can be more proud, but I'm sorry, some of the refereeing today was horrendous. We will take this on the chin and come back even stronger. Hopefully we will be back [in the final]." THIERRY HENRY

"Nightmare end to Arsenal's dream final." DAILY TELEGRAPH

"No reward for Wenger's heroes." EVENING STANDARD

"Deux rois: une courounne." [Two kings, One crown] L'EQUIPE

MAN OF THE MATCH

KOLO TOURE

Mins on pitch	90
Tackles won	3
Tackes success	100%
Passes completed	15 (71%)
Successful clearances	7

Centre of attention:
José Antonio Reyes and
Thierry Henry prepare to kick-off the
second half against Wigan in the
last ever competitive game at Highbury.

THE PREMIERSHIP

Fourth place is the lowest any Arsène Wenger side has finished in the Premiership during his ten-year tenure, but that only tells half of the story. True, the Gunners struggled on the road for most of the campaign, losing nine times, but at Fortress Highbury it was business as usual, with 14 wins and 48 goals scored in 19 matches.

Wenger's young team slowly knitted together, with teenager Cesc Fabregas outstanding in midfield alongside Gilberto, and Thierry Henry plundering another 30-plus goal haul.

The team rallied as the season wore on and two away wins in the final week of the season, followed by a thrilling 4–2 win over Wigan in the last ever game at Highbury, snatched the coveted fourth place away from arch rivals Tottenham.

Arsenal had been out of the top four since early December, but finished with a flurry to earn a place in the third qualifying round of the Champions League next season.

PREMIERSHIP SEASON RECORD

BIGGEST WIN 7–0 v Middlesbrough (h) 14/1/06
Senderos, Gilberto, Pires, Henry 3, Hleb

BIGGEST DEFEAT 2–0 v Bolton (a) 3/12/05; v Chelsea (h) 18/12/05; v Manchester United (a) 9/4/06

LONGEST WINNING SEQUENCE Four games
4/3/06 Fulham (a) 4–0 to 1/4/06 Aston Villa (h) 5–0

LONGEST UNBEATEN SEQUENCE Six games
12/4/06 Portsmouth (a) to 7/5/06 Wigan Athletic (h)

QUICKEST GOAL Fabregas – Four minutes
v Blackburn Rovers (h) 26/11/05 (3–0)

MATCHES

MATCHES PLAYED	38
PLAYERS USED	27

GOALS

SCORED	68
Per game	1.79
CONCEDED	31
Per game	0.82

ATTENDANCE

AT HOME	725,499
Average home gate	38,184

Memorable moments

- Thrashing Middlesbrough 7–0 in January, an awesome display that included an Henry hat-trick
- An almost perfect performance at home to Villa on April Fools' Day with over 67% possession and a 5–0 victory
- Dennis' goal against West Bromwich Albion on 15 April 2006 – Dennis Bergkamp Day
- The emerging talent of Fabregas, Senderos, Eboue, Diaby, Adebayor and Hleb
- Thierry kissing the hallowed turf after his penalty – the last ever goal at Highbury – sealing a memorable win, a place in Europe and the end of an era

ARSENAL 2
HENRY 81 (PEN), VAN PERSIE 87

Newcastle United 0

DATE SUNDAY 14 AUGUST 2005
VENUE HIGHBURY
ATTENDANCE 38,072
REFEREE STEVE BENNETT

FORM		
W 2–0	(A)	Prem
W 3–1	(H)	Prem
W 7–0	(H)	Prem
L 1–2	(A)	Prem
D 0–0	(N)	FA Cup
(won 5–4 on pens)		
D 3–3	(A)	Friendly

HLEB (FABREGAS 72) · VAN PERSIE (BERGKAMP 72) · FLAMINI (PIRES 82)

LEHMANN

LAUREN · TOURE · SENDEROS · COLE

LJUNGBERG · GILBERTO · FABREGAS · PIRES

BERGKAMP · HENRY

SHEARER

EMRE · JENAS

BOWYER · PARKER · DYER

BABAYARO · TAYLOR · BOUMSONG · CARR

GIVEN

N'ZOGBIA (DYER 69) · MILNER (SHEARER 72) · FAYE (PARKER 82)

Other Results: Saturday

Aston Villa	2–2	Bolton Wanderers
Everton	0–2	Manchester United
Fulham	0–0	Birmingham City
Manchester City	0–0	West Bromwich Alb.
Middlesbrough	0–0	Liverpool
Portsmouth	0–2	Tottenham Hotspur
Sunderland	1–3	Charlton Athletic
West Ham United	3–1	Blackburn Rovers
*Wigan Athletic	0–1	Chelsea

Table position	P	W	D	L	F	A	Pts
3	1	1	0	0	2	0	3

* Played on Sunday

LATE GOALS FROM Thierry Henry and Robin van Persie helped Arsenal overcome a dogged ten-man Newcastle in the season opener at Highbury.

Henry finally broke the deadlock with a penalty on 81 minutes after Charles N'Zogbia upended Freddie Ljungberg, and van Persie put the icing on the cake when he produced a sharp finish at the near post from Ljungberg's cut-back six minutes later after a lightning Arsenal break.

The Gunners were playing the first match of their final season at Highbury and kicked off on a perfect surface with the words 'Highbury 1913–2006' marked on the grass. However, it was a slow start to the Highbury campaign, with Shay Given comfortably dealing with a Dennis Bergkamp effort.

Fabregas, playing in midfield alongside Gilberto, blocked a powerful drive from Newcastle debutant Emre as the visitors looked to respond, but the match swung Arsenal's way after 32 minutes when Jermaine Jenas was sent off. The England midfielder was shown a straight red by referee Steve Bennett after a reckless lunge on Brazilian Gilberto, who was left writhing in agony.

DID YOU KNOW?
This was the 5th consecutive opening day win.

United still managed to hold on until Arsène Wenger introduced new signing Alexander Hleb and Robin van Persie from the bench. The visitors then found themselves on the backfoot even more and the tide turned. Henry finally edged the Gunners ahead from the spot, before van Persie showed his class with a super second to earn the first three points of the season.

GAME STATISTICS

ARSENAL		NEWCASTLE UNITED
2	GOALS	0
0	1ST HALF GOALS	0
8	SHOTS ON TARGET	0
4	SHOTS OFF TARGET	1
6	BLOCKED SHOTS	1
8	CORNERS	3
16	FOULS	17
5	OFFSIDES	8
0	YELLOW CARDS	1
0	RED CARDS	1
84.1	PASSING SUCCESS	72.0
23	TACKLES	44
78.3	TACKLES SUCCESS	68.2
67.7	POSSESSION	32.3
56.7	TERRITORIAL ADVANTAGE	43.3

FINAL THOUGHTS

"Newcastle were a little unlucky. They worked hard and made it very difficult for us, but we were patient and it paid off. Hleb looked good when he came on and could have added a third. He seems to drift past players effortlessly."

SHARON GUIVER, WALTHAMSTOW, LONDON

"It is never easy to play against ten men, but I like the fact that we knew how to win because we kept patient."

ARSÈNE WENGER

"Statistics suggest a routine win. Yet it was anything but, with the Gunners emerging victorious after referee Steve Bennett's controversial decision to dismiss Jermaine Jenas with almost an hour left." THE SUN

MAN OF THE MATCH

ASHLEY COLE

Mins on pitch	90
Tackles won	3
Tackle success	100%
Passes completed	45 (88%)
Successful clearances	0

Opposite *The words 'Highbury 1913–2006' marked on the grass as the first match of the final season in Arsenal's 93-year history at Avenell Road.*
Above *Robin van Persie's instinctive strike flies inside Shay Given's near post.*

Chelsea 1 DROGBA 73
ARSENAL 0

DATE **SUNDAY 21 AUGUST 2005**
VENUE **STAMFORD BRIDGE**
ATTENDANCE **42,136**
REFEREE **GRAHAM POLL**

PERFORMANCE IN THE PREMIERSHIP YEARS			FORM	
Stamford Bridge			W 3–1 (H) Prem	
			W 7–0 (H) Prem	
PLAYED	16		L 1–2 (A) Prem	
WON	6		D 0–0 (N) FA Cup	
DRAWN	6		(won 5–4 on pens)	
LOST	4		D 3–3 (A) Friendly	
FOR	22		W 2–0 (H) Prem	
AGAINST	17			

Other Results: Saturday		
Birmingham City	1–2	Manchester City
Blackburn Rovers	2–1	Fulham
Charlton Athletic	1–0	Wigan Athletic
Liverpool	1–0	Sunderland
Manchester United	1–0	Aston Villa
Newcastle United	0–0	West Ham United
Tottenham Hotspur	2–0	Middlesbrough
West Bromwich Alb.	2–1	Portsmouth
*Bolton	0–1	Everton

Table position	P	W	D	L	F	A	Pts
9	2	1	0	1	2	1	3

* Played on Sunday

A LUCKY GOAL off substitute Didier Drogba's shin separated the two sides in an even game in west London. The goal that decided the contest came with just 17 minutes remaining, when the Ivory Coast hitman attempted to control Frank Lampard's free-kick, but instead the ball skewed off his shin and past a wrong-footed Jens Lehmann.

Drogba knew little about the goal, but it secured Chelsea's first Premiership win over the Gunners since September 1995, when Mark Hughes was the matchwinner for the Blues.

It was not the way Arsène Wenger would have wanted to end his 500th game in charge and his side were unlucky not to take at least a point back to Highbury after looking more than comfortable for much of the game.

The champions had few chances while Arsenal also rarely threatened in a largely uninspiring contest. Fredrik Ljungberg was alert to clear Asier Del Horno's header off the line early on and then the Swede moved up the other end, but blazed his shot high over the bar. However, he soon had to depart through injury and his absence took much of Arsenal's attacking sting out of the game.

The game finally opened up in the second half before Drogba's moment of fortune gave Chelsea the lead. It was his third goal against the Gunners in two weeks. The result also meant that Chelsea extended their unbeaten league run to 31 games having last lost at Manchester City the previous October.

Above *Alexander Hleb (right) closes down Chelsea's Paulo Ferreira.*
Opposite, top *Gilberto (right) battles for possession with John Terry.*

FINAL THOUGHTS

"I don't often listen to José Mourinho, but he said afterwards that Arsenal shouldn't panic after that and I agree. We didn't really go for the win, but we seemed to be able to cope with everything they threw at us. It's early days..." RYAN WHITE, CHERTSEY, SURREY

"I am disappointed, because we gave a cheap goal away. The overall level was not satisfying for me. I expected a much better game. We need to realise we can do much better." ARSÈNE WENGER

"Fortunate it may have been, but this was Chelsea's first league win over Arsenal for ten years." THE TIMES

MAN OF THE MATCH

FRANCESC FABREGAS

Mins on pitch	85
Tackles won	1
Passes completed	45 (88%)
Shots on target	0
Shots off target	1

GAME STATISTICS

CHELSEA		ARSENAL
1	GOALS	0
0	1ST HALF GOALS	0
5	SHOTS ON TARGET	3
3	SHOTS OFF TARGET	6
2	BLOCKED SHOTS	0
3	CORNERS	7
18	FOULS	22
4	OFFSIDES	0
1	YELLOW CARDS	3
0	RED CARDS	0
78.7	PASSING SUCCESS	81.2
32	TACKLES	26
75.0	TACKLES SUCCESS	73.1
44.2	POSSESSION	55.8
44.2	TERRITORIAL ADVANTAGE	55.8

DID YOU KNOW?

This was Chelsea's first league victory over the Gunners for ten years.

ARSENAL 4
CYGAN 32, 90,
HENRY 53, 82

Fulham 1
C JENSEN 22

DATE WEDNESDAY 24 AUGUST 2005
VENUE HIGHBURY
ATTENDANCE 37,867
REFEREE MARK CLATTENBURG

FORM		
W 7–0	(H)	Prem
L 1–2	(A)	Prem
D 0–0	(N)	FA Cup
(won 5–4 on pens)		
D 3–3	(A)	Friendly
W 2–0	(H)	Prem
L 0–1	(A)	Prem

THIERRY HENRY closed in on Ian Wright's Club record with a classy double, but it was defender Pascal Cygan who took the plaudits with a man of the match display, including two goals, as Fulham were swept away at Fortress Highbury.

The Cottagers must have felt slightly aggrieved at the size of the defeat after saving an early Arsenal penalty and then taking a 22nd-minute lead against the run of play.

Zat Knight brought down Henry in the box, but Tony Warner saved Lauren's spot-kick in the eighth minute. It was the first time the Cameroon international had ever missed a penalty for club or country. Claus Jensen then took advantage of a rare Kolo Toure error to curl a brilliant effort into the top corner.

However, Cygan sent the teams in level with an equaliser just after the half-hour mark, when he headed home Dennis Bergkamp's inviting free-kick. Henry then gave Arsenal the

DID YOU KNOW?
Fulham have never won at Highbury.

Pascal Cygan stoops to head home from Dennis Bergkamp's free-kick. The French defender would score again in the last minute.

Other Results: Tuesday		
Birmingham City	0–3	Middlesbrough
Portsmouth	1–1	Aston Villa
Sunderland	1–2	Manchester City
*Blackburn Rovers	0–0	Tottenham Hotspur
*Bolton Wanderers	2–0	Newcastle United
*Chelsea	4–0	West Bromwich Alb.

Table position	P	W	D	L	F	A	Pts
4	3	2	0	1	6	2	6

* Played on Wednesday

Arsenal take the lead as Thierry Henry slides the ball past Tony Warner in the 53rd minute, making the score 2–1.

GAME STATISTICS

ARSENAL		FULHAM
4	GOALS	1
1	1ST HALF GOALS	1
15	SHOTS ON TARGET	3
8	SHOTS OFF TARGET	7
1	BLOCKED SHOTS	1
6	CORNERS	7
18	FOULS	12
3	OFFSIDES	4
5	YELLOW CARDS	2
0	RED CARDS	0
80.7	PASSING SUCCESS	62.1
36	TACKLES	37
69.4	TACKLES SUCCESS	73.0
62.1	POSSESSION	37.9
43.5	TERRITORIAL ADVANTAGE	56.5

lead after the break when he controlled José Antonio Reyes' pass before firing past Warner.

Arsenal dominated play and Henry sealed the win in the 82nd minute when he raced on to Cesc Fabregas' cute pass and lofted the ball over Warner to take his tally to within one goal of Wright's record. That wasn't the end of the goals, though. With time almost up, Cygan reacted quickly as Bergkamp's free-kick ricocheted off Toure to smash the ball into the back of the net.

MAN OF THE MATCH

PASCAL CYGAN

Mins on pitch	90
Tackles won	0
Passes completed	56 (88)
Shots on target	2 (1 off)
Successful clearances	13
Goals	2

FINAL THOUGHTS

"Fulham always give us a good game, but we always seem to give them a good beating. Henry was excellent today, but I was pleased for Cygan with his goals. The man gets a lot of stick from the crowd, but he always works hard and does his best. This was Pascal's day!" GERAINT WEBB, OSWESTRY, SHROPSHIRE

"We wanted to transform the frustration, and the belief that we could get from the Chelsea game, the desire to win, and I think we got that. I felt that the concentration of the team was very high, because I was not completely happy with the fact that on Sunday we did not create enough, and the players as well. I feel tonight we had a good game." ARSÈNE WENGER

"The Gunners are rolling out the big guns in readiness for an all-out title assault – with the Blues in their sights!" THE SUN

Middlesbrough 2 YAKUBU 40, MACCARONE 58
ARSENAL 1 REYES 90

DATE **SATURDAY 10 SEPTEMBER 2005**
VENUE **THE RIVERSIDE**
ATTENDANCE **28,075**
REFEREE **MIKE RILEY**

PERFORMANCE IN THE PREMIERSHIP YEARS		FORM	
The Riverside		L 1–2 (A) Prem	
PLAYED	13	D 0–0 (N) FA Cup (won 5–4 on pens)	
WON	9	D 3–3 (A) Friendly	
DRAWN	1	W 2–0 (H) Prem	
LOST	3	L 0–1 (A) Prem	
FOR	22	W 4–1 (H) Prem	
AGAINST	17		

MIDDLESBROUGH CONDEMNED ARSENAL to their second league defeat of the season, with goals from Yakubu and Maccarone either side of half time.

The Gunners had an immaculate record against Steve McClaren's side, having beaten them in their previous eight meetings, but spirited Middlesbrough sensed an upset against an Arsenal side without talismanic skipper Thierry Henry, who had picked up a groin strain while on international duty for France in midweek.

His replacement, José Antonio Reyes, spurned two early opportunities to score, but Boro were also inspired by summer signing Yakubu and the Nigerian gave them the lead five minutes

[Team formation]

POGATETZ (JOHNSON 65)   DORIVA (MACCARONE 79)   GRAHAM (YAKUBU 90)

SCHWARZER

XAVIER   EHIOGU   SOUTHGATE   QUEUDRUE

PARLOUR   ROCHEMBACK

MACCARONE   BOATENG   JOHNSON

YAKUBU

REYES   BERGKAMP

HLEB   GILBERTO   FLAMINI   PIRES

COLE   CYGAN   TOURE   LAUREN

LEHMANN

FABREGAS (FLAMINI 60)   VAN PERSIE (PIRES 72)

Other Results: Saturday

Birmingham City	0–1	Charlton Athletic
Chelsea	2–0	Sunderland
Everton	0–1	Portsmouth
Manchester United	1–1	Manchester City
Newcastle United	1–1	Fulham
Tottenham Hotspur	0–0	Liverpool
West Bromwich Alb.	1–2	Wigan Athletic
*Bolton Wanderers	0–0	Blackburn Rovers
†West Ham United	4–0	Aston Villa

Table position	P	W	D	L	F	A	Pts
8	4	2	0	2	7	4	6

*Played on Sunday   †Played on Monday

Above *Alexander Hleb shows George Boateng of Middlesbrough a clean pair of heels.*
Opposite, top *Pat Rice and Arsène Wenger contemplate a second defeat of the season.*

DID YOU KNOW?
This was Kolo Touré's 150th appearance for the Club.

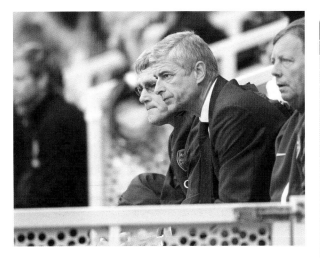

GAME STATISTICS

MIDDLESBROUGH		ARSENAL
2	GOALS	1
1	1ST HALF GOALS	0
4	SHOTS ON TARGET	4
1	SHOTS OFF TARGET	5
2	BLOCKED SHOTS	4
6	CORNERS	7
18	FOULS	17
4	OFFSIDES	2
3	YELLOW CARDS	4
0	RED CARDS	0
79.9	PASSING SUCCESS	83.2
43	TACKLES	40
67.4	TACKLES SUCCESS	75.0
43.7	POSSESSION	56.3
46.5	TERRITORIAL ADVANTAGE	53.5

before the break – the ball broke into his path and he turned smartly to curl a shot into the bottom corner.

Jens Lehmann denied Yakubu a second, when he turned his effort round the post early after the break, and Arsenal then claimed a penalty, when Alexander Hleb was stopped in the Boro box, but referee Mike Riley waved play on.

In the ensuing confusion, Boro made a lightning quick break and Maccarone picked up the ball after Toure tackled Yakubu, before finishing easily to double the lead.

There was still half an hour to play, but Arsenal could only score once – three minutes into injury time – when Reyes, who had prompted and probed the Boro backline for most of the game, finally got a reward for all his hard work and shot past Mark Schwarzer for a late consolation.

FINAL THOUGHTS

"We never should have lost. We should have shown more determination. I feel that we had very good patches in the game. We could have won this game in the first 20 minutes with three clear chances, but we did not take them. We missed our chances and we gave them presents for their two goals. We were good enough to win this game." ARSÈNE WENGER

"Arsenal's hoodoo over Middlesbrough finally ends." BBC ONLINE

"It would be too easy to say we lost because Thierry wasn't playing – we lost because Boro were really up for it. They were first to most balls and threw themselves into tackles. Our run against them had to end one day." DAMIEN MACKAY, WALTHAM CROSS, HERTS

MAN OF THE MATCH

JOSÉ ANTONIO REYES

Mins on pitch	90
Tackles won	5
Passes completed	31 (76%)
Shots on target	4
Shots off target	2
Goals	1

ARSENAL 2
CAMPBELL 11, 30

Everton 0

DATE **MONDAY 19 SEPTEMBER 2005**
VENUE **HIGHBURY**
ATTENDANCE **38,121**
REFEREE **ALAN WILEY**

FORM		
D	3–3 (A)	Friendly
W	2–0 (H)	Prem
L	0–1 (A)	Prem
W	4–1 (H)	Prem
L	1–2 (A)	Prem
W	2–1 (H)	CL

HLEB (PIRES 29) • BERGKAMP (VAN PERSIE 66) • SONG (REYES 85)

LEHMANN

LAUREN • TOURE • CAMPBELL • COLE

LJUNGBERG • FABREGAS • GILBERTO • PIRES

REYES • VAN PERSIE

BENT

McFADDEN • ARTETA • CAHILL • OSMAN

NEVILLE

FERRARI • WEIR • YOBO • HIBBERT

MARTYN

FERGUSON (CAHILL 67) • KILBANE (BENT 80) • DAVIES (ARTETA 85)

THE PREVIOUS PREMIERSHIP GAME at Highbury had seen his centre-back partner Pascal Cygan net twice. Now, in the absence of Thierry Henry, Sol Campbell took on his share of goalscoring responsibilities and two headers from him saw off Everton and pushed Arsenal up to seventh in the table.

The first came just after 11 minutes, when José Antonio Reyes was fouled on the edge of the Toffees' penalty area. The Spaniard took the free-kick himself and planted a pinpoint ball on the head of Campbell, who did the rest, with Everton goalkeeper Nigel Martyn stranded in no-man's land.

> ## DID YOU KNOW?
> *This was Ashley Cole's 150th appearance for Arsenal and fellow defender Sol Campbell's brace came the day after his 31st birthday.*

Sol Campbell rises highest to steer the ball past a stranded Nigel Martyn for the opening goal of the game.

With Arsenal sweeping forward, Robin van Persie then hit the post, but with half an hour of the game played Campbell did it again – and it was Reyes who was, again, the architect. The former Sevilla star sent over a free-kick from the left and Campbell found his goal touch once more with a powerful header at the far post.

Other Results: Saturday		
Aston Villa	1–1	Tottenham Hotspur
Charlton Athletic	0–2	Chelsea
Fulham	1–2	West Ham United
Portsmouth	1–1	Birmingham City
Sunderland	1–1	West Bromwich Alb.
*Blackburn Rovers	0–3	Newcastle United
*Liverpool	0–0	Manchester United
*Wigan Athletic	1–1	Middlesbrough

Table position	P	W	D	L	F	A	Pts
7	5	3	0	2	9	4	9

Played on Sunday

Everton headed to Highbury on the back of a demoralising 5–1 defeat at Dinamo Bucharest in a first-leg UEFA Cup tie and their confidence was clearly low.

Arsenal, on the other hand, smelt more goals and substitute Alexander Hleb – on the pitch for the injured Robert Pires – set up Fredrik Ljungberg, who just failed to add a deserved third.

However, as the game wore on and with the Merseysiders barely troubling Jens Lehmann, who was back in goal after missing the midweek win against FC Thun through suspension, Arsenal seemed content with just the two goals, although Alexandre Song, 17, made a late appearance from the bench for his first-team debut.

FINAL THOUGHTS

"I think we're slowly getting into gear and it was great to see Sol score. He should get more – people forget he started at Spurs as a striker. I want another 18 goals from him this season!!"

MARLON BENNETT, KENTISH TOWN, LONDON

"It was important to win and I feel we did it well and in a controlled way. We scored two unusual goals from set-pieces and I hoped in the second half we would find some more space, but Everton never came out. Without the third goal you have to play a bit in a controlled way – less sharp, but tactically controlled." ARSÈNE WENGER

"There is still some way to go before Arsenal make Chelsea sweat again. But at least they are moving in the right direction." THE SUN

GAME STATISTICS

ARSENAL		EVERTON
2	GOALS	0
2	1ST HALF GOALS	0
5	SHOTS ON TARGET	2
12	SHOTS OFF TARGET	3
3	BLOCKED SHOTS	0
5	CORNERS	0
14	FOULS	20
1	OFFSIDES	2
2	YELLOW CARDS	2
0	RED CARDS	0
82.2	PASSING SUCCESS	73.0
34	TACKLES	47
67.6	TACKLES SUCCESS	66.0
63.3	POSSESSION	36.7
51.4	TERRITORIAL ADVANTAGE	48.6

MAN OF THE MATCH

SOL CAMPBELL

Mins on pitch	90
Tackles	4
Tackle success	25%
Passes completed	71.1%
Successful clearances	8
Goals	2

Robin van Persie twists Toffees defender Tony Hibbert inside out.

West Ham 0
ARSENAL 0

DATE **SATURDAY 24 SEPTEMBER 2005**

VENUE **UPTON PARK**

ATTENDANCE **34,742**

REFEREE **MIKE DEAN**

PERFORMANCE IN THE PREMIERSHIP YEARS		FORM		
Upton Park		W 2–0	(H)	Prem
PLAYED	9	L 0–1	(A)	Prem
WON	4	W 4–1	(H)	Prem
DRAWN	4	L 1–2	(A)	Prem
LOST	1	W 2–1	(H)	CL
FOR	13	W 2–0	(H)	Prem
AGAINST	6			

ZAMORA (SHERINGHAM 81)　　NEWTON (ETHERINGTON 84)

CARROLL

REPKA　FERDINAND　GABBIDON　KONCHESKY

REO-COKER　BENAYOUN　MULLINS　ETHERINGTON

SHERINGHAM　HAREWOOD

REYES　VAN PERSIE

HLEB　FABREGAS　GILBERTO　LJUNGBERG

COLE　CAMPBELL　TOURE　LAUREN

LEHMANN

FLAMINI (GILBERTO 71)　OWUSU-ABEYIE (REYES 73)　CLICHY (VAN PERSIE 82)

Other Results: Saturday

Birmingham City	2–2	Liverpool
Bolton Wanderers	1–0	Portsmouth
Chelsea	2–1	Aston Villa
Everton	0–1	Wigan Athletic
Manchester United	1–2	Blackburn Rovers
Newcastle United	1–0	Manchester City
West Bromwich Alb.	1–2	Charlton Athletic
*Middlesbrough	0–2	Sunderland
†Tottenham Hotspur	1–0	Fulham

Table position	P	W	D	L	F	A	Pts
7	6	3	1	2	9	4	10

*Played on Sunday　†Played on Monday

A CLEAN SHEET and a first away point of the season meant Arsenal should have been the happier of the two sides after this short trip to the East End ended all square.

Arsenal were missing the experienced trio of Thierry Henry, Robert Pires and Dennis Bergkamp, but there was no lack of effort from young double-act Robin van Persie and José Antonio Reyes. However, it was the oldest player on the pitch who nearly broke the deadlock when Teddy Sheringham, 39, curled a free-kick just past the Gunners post.

West Ham's Israeli schemer Yossi Benayoun was the other potent threat for the hosts and he displayed some inventive passing that bore more than a passing resemblance to another Israeli Hammer – Eyal Berkovic. Arsenal, though, despite enjoying some possession of their own, rarely threatened Roy Carroll's goal.

DID YOU KNOW?
The last time Arsenal played the Hammers in the League was in January 2003 when Arsenal won 3–1 thanks to an Henry hat-trick.

Above Dutch youngster Quincy Owusu-Abeyie chases after the ball.
Opposite Sol Campbell contests a corner with Anton Ferdinand and Matthew Etherington.

The second half began with West Ham forcing corner after corner and Benayoun should have done better when one clearance landed at his feet on the edge of the box, but his shot was poor. Next, Sol Campbell looked to have handled in the area, but referee Mike Dean waved play on and Arsenal survived again.

West Ham couldn't keep up their attacking passage and the game settled with Arsenal pushing for the winner. Van Persie had a shot deflected wide and then Fredrik Ljungberg, now in attack with sub Quincy, could have snatched it with five minutes to go, only to miscontrol at the vital moment.

FINAL THOUGHTS

"I'm disappointed. We were just toothless. There was no cutting edge at all. Yes, we've got injuries, but I don't know what the answer is. I still feel we lack that, dare I say it, a 'fox in the box' on some occasions." DARRYL CHANDLER, BUSHEY, HERTS

"If West Ham can maintain that physical presence, then it will certainly be a good point." ARSÈNE WENGER

"Nervous Arsenal lose more ground." THE TIMES

GAME STATISTICS

WEST HAM UNITED		ARSENAL
0	GOALS	0
0	1ST HALF GOALS	0
0	SHOTS ON TARGET	1
6	SHOTS OFF TARGET	7
2	BLOCKED SHOTS	4
4	CORNERS	3
13	FOULS	8
4	OFFSIDES	1
2	YELLOW CARDS	0
0	RED CARDS	0
66.9	PASSING SUCCESS	73.2
41	TACKLES	34
78.0	TACKLES SUCCESS	82.4
45.8	POSSESSION	54.2
51.2	TERRITORIAL ADVANTAGE	48.8

ARSENAL 1 CLEMENCE 81 (OG)
Birmingham City 0

DATE **SUNDAY 2 OCTOBER 2005**
VENUE **HIGHBURY**
ATTENDANCE **37,891**
REFEREE **CHRIS FOY**

FORM		
W	4–1 (H)	Prem
L	1–2 (A)	Prem
W	2–1 (H)	CL
W	2–0 (H)	Prem
D	0–0 (A)	Prem
W	2–1 (A)	CL

Other Results: Saturday		
Blackburn Rovers	2–0	West Bromich Alb.
Charlton Athletic	2–3	Tottenham Hotspur
Fulham	2–3	Manchester United
Portsmouth	0–0	Newcastle United
Sunderland	1–1	West Ham United
*Aston Villa	2–3	Middlesbrough
*Liverpool	1–4	Chelsea
*Manchester City	2–0	Everton
*Wigan Athletic	2–1	Bolton Wanderers

Table position	P	W	D	L	F	A	Pts
7	7	4	1	2	10	4	13

Played on Sunday

A DEFLECTED ROBIN VAN PERSIE EFFORT nine minutes from time sealed maximum points for Arsenal on an afternoon that nearly ended in frustration.

The substitute, who had only come on moments before for Robert Pires, let fly with a speculative drive and was relieved to see the ball bobble over Blues goalkeeper Maik Taylor after taking a huge deflection off Stephen Clemence's leg.

Taylor had kept City in the game with several saves that his boss Steve Bruce described as world class. He had even blocked a Pires penalty after Fredrik Ljungberg had been felled in the penalty area.

After only 24 minutes Ireland defender Kenny Cunningham tripped Ljungberg as he was clear on goal and was shown a straight red. Then, in the 36th minute, Arsenal were handed a chance to edge in front, when Ljungberg was felled by Dominic Johnson and a penalty was awarded. Taylor dived full length to his right to beat out Pires' penalty and the Frenchman stuck the rebound into the netting.

As the interval beckoned, Reyes then had several attempts at goal, but couldn't make the breakthrough with Taylor in majestic form, clearly buoyed by his penalty save.

Birmingham's attacking threat dimmed in the second half, with

DID YOU KNOW?
Arsenal extended their unbeaten home record to 13 games.

Above *Fredrik Ljungberg tussles with Blues defender Olivier Tebily.*
Opposite, top *Robin van Persie's effort is on its way into the net, via Stephen Clemence.*

Arsenal continuing the onslaught, and Taylor pulled off the save of the match to claw away Ljungberg's first-time effort.

He then deflected Pires' neat flick against the foot of the post, but with each spurned chance it looked as if Birmingham would head up the M1 with a valuable point. That was until the introduction of van Persie, whose effort ricocheted off Clemence and into the goal for a fortunate winner.

FINAL THOUGHTS

"Taylor was outstanding and if it wasn't for him we'd have won by three or four. We dominated Birmingham and Reyes showed flashes of the talent he has today – he played well and looked sharp. We easily deserved it and the Blues can have no complaints."

MO IQBAL, DUNSTABLE, BEDS

"Maik Taylor was superb. The goal looked small when he was in it. Give him ten out of ten." ARSÈNE WENGER

"Arsenal indebted to Clemence's slice of bad luck." THE GUARDIAN

GAME STATISTICS

ARSENAL		BIRMINGHAM CITY
1	GOALS	0
0	1ST HALF GOALS	0
11	SHOTS ON TARGET	2
7	SHOTS OFF TARGET	3
4	BLOCKED SHOTS	3
11	CORNERS	4
13	FOULS	17
3	OFFSIDES	2
0	YELLOW CARDS	1
0	RED CARDS	1
81.4	PASSING SUCCESS	66.4
27	TACKLES	38
77.8	TACKLES SUCCESS	78.9
61.6	POSSESSION	38.4
51.2	TERRITORIAL ADVANTAGE	48.8

MAN OF THE MATCH

JOSÉ ANTONIO REYES

Mins on pitch	90
Tackles won	3
Passes completed	23 (52%)
Shots on target	6
Shots off target	1

West Bromwich Albion 2
KANU 38, CARTER 77

ARSENAL 1
SENDEROS 18

DATE **SATURDAY 15 OCTOBER 2005**
VENUE **THE HAWTHORNS**
ATTENDANCE **26,604**
REFEREE **BARRY KNIGHT**

PERFORMANCE IN THE PREMIERSHIP YEARS		FORM	
The Hawthorns		L 1–2 (A) Prem	
PLAYED	3	W 2–1 (H) CL	
WON	3	W 2–0 (H) Prem	
DRAWN	0	D 0–0 (A) Prem	
LOST	0	W 2–1 (A) CL	
FOR	6	W 1–0 (H) Prem	
AGAINST	1		

CARTER (WALLWORK 68) **MOORE** (KANU 70) **ELLINGTON** (HORSFIELD 78)

KIRKLAND

ALBRECHTSON DAVIES CLEMENT ROBINSON

WATSON WALLWORK GREENING

KAMARA KANU HORSFIELD

BERGKAMP REYES

LJUNGBERG FABREGAS FLAMINI PIRES

LAUREN TOURE SENDEROS CLICHY

LEHMANN

EBOUE (LJUNGBERG 36) **OWUSU-ABEYIE** (FLAMINI 77)

Other Results: Saturday

Chelsea	5–1	Bolton Wanderers
Liverpool	1–0	Blackburn Rovers
Middlesbrough	1–1	Portsmouth
Sunderland	1–3	Manchester United
Tottenham Hotspur	2–0	Everton
Wigan Athletic	1–0	Newcastle United
*Birmingham City	0–1	Aston Villa
*Manchester City	2–1	West Ham United
†Charlton Athletic	1–1	Fulham

Table position	P	W	D	L	F	A	Pts
8	8	4	1	3	11	6	13

Played on Sunday †Played on Monday

FORMER GUNNER NWANKWO KANU helped West Brom to an unlikely win as Arsenal slipped to a third defeat in eight league games. The stats, though, tell the real story.

Arsenal peppered the Baggies' goal with 15 shots – compared to the hosts' six attempts – and enjoyed 65% possession, but a combination of poor finishing and inspired goalkeeping by on-loan Chris Kirkland in the West Brom goal meant the eventual scoreline didn't reflect this.

It was not the result Dennis Bergkamp would have expected on his 400th appearance for the Club, especially after he had two early chances. Cesc Fabregas' pass put Bergkamp clear – via a ricochet off Curtis Davis – and the Dutch striker bore down on goal, only to be denied by a great recovering tackle by Paul Robinson. Kirkland then rushed out off his line to foil him again, just as he was about to pull the trigger.

Arsenal went in front on 18 minutes when Philippe Senderos volleyed his first goal for the club, but the contest was turned on its head when Kanu popped up to level the scores, driving the ball past Jens Lehmann after he collected Senderos' poor clearance.

DID YOU KNOW?
This was Bergkamp's 400th appearance for Arsenal and Senderos' first goal.

Above *Star performer Dennis Bergkamp in the thick of the action at the Hawthorns.*
Opposite *Philippe Senderos (right) celebrates his goal with Mathieu Flamini.*

MAN OF THE MATCH

DENNIS BERGKAMP

Mins on pitch	90
Tackles won	0
Passes completed	24 (62%)
Shots on target	2
Shots off target	1

GAME STATISTICS		
WEST BROMWICH ALBION		**ARSENAL**
2	GOALS	1
1	1ST HALF GOALS	1
4	SHOTS ON TARGET	9
2	SHOTS OFF TARGET	6
0	BLOCKED SHOTS	2
3	CORNERS	6
22	FOULS	10
4	OFFSIDES	2
1	YELLOW CARDS	1
0	RED CARDS	0
62.8	PASSING SUCCESS	81.0
30	TACKLES	19
76.7	TACKLES SUCCESS	68.4
34.9	POSSESSION	65.1
51.3	TERRITORIAL ADVANTAGE	48.7

Arsenal turned up the heat with Bergkamp going close for the umpteenth time with a dipping drive, but there was one goal left in the game and it was a stunner. Darren Carter controlled the ball on the edge of the box and sent an unstoppable shot past Lehmann for the Baggies' first home win over the Gunners since 1972.

FINAL THOUGHTS

"We hammered them – pure and simple. We had chance after chance and should have wrapped it up long before Kanu equalised. I am astonished. West Brom worked hard, but they must be pinching themselves." MARK SOWERSBY, WANDSWORTH, LONDON

"We lacked maturity – with a bit more experience we'd have won easily." ARSÈNE WENGER

"Arsenal artists fall to artisans." THE TIMES

ARSENAL 1 PIRES 61 (PEN)
Manchester City 0

DATE **SATURDAY 22 OCTOBER 2005**
VENUE **HIGHBURY**
ATTENDANCE **38,189**
REFEREE **MIKE RILEY**

FORM		
W 2–0 (H)	Prem
D 0–0 (A)	Prem
W 2–1 (A)	CL
W 1–0 (H)	Prem
L 1–2 (A)	Prem
W 2–0 (A)	CL

THREE POINTS, a clean sheet and Thierry Henry honoured for breaking Ian Wright's goalscoring record, but that was all eclipsed by a tale of two penalties – one scored, the other farcically missed.

Stuart Pearce's side had, for the most part, matched Arsenal and there were a lot of anxious faces in the home crowd before the goal came, but on the hour mark Thierry Henry's passage was halted by the outstretched hand of City goalkeeper David James as he chased a Kolo Toure pass and referee Mike Riley had no hesitation in awarding a penalty.

Pires showed nerves of steel to score the 500th Premiership goal Arsenal have scored at Highbury, so when, 11 minutes later, Riley awarded Arsenal a second penalty after Stephen Jordan fouled Dennis Bergkamp, Pires purposefully strolled forward.

However, instead of shooting, he bizarrely tried to roll the ball forward for the incoming Henry to strike, but he barely made any contact with the ball, Henry stopped in bemusement and the City players cleared.

It was a poorly executed attempt to recreate a great Johan Cruyff goal in December 1982 for Ajax against Helmond Sport, when he exchanged passes with Jesper Olsen before scoring.

Other Results: Saturday

Aston Villa	0–2	Wigan Athletic
Blackburn Rovers	2–0	Birmingham City
Fulham	2–0	Liverpool
Manchester United	1–1	Tottenham Hotspur
Portsmouth	1–2	Charlton Athletic
*Bolton Wanderers	2–0	West Bromwich Alb.
*Everton	1–1	Chelsea
*Newcastle United	3–2	Sunderland
*West Ham United	2–1	Middlesbrough

Table position	P	W	D	L	F	A	Pts
7	9	5	1	3	12	6	16

Played on Sunday

MAN OF THE MATCH

ROBERT PIRES

Mins on pitch	**90**
Tackles won	**3**
Passes completed	**33 (75%)**
Shots on target	**1**
Shots off target	**1**
Goals	**1**

DID YOU KNOW?

This was Dennis Bergkamp's 250th League start for Arsenal in a game that saw their sixth penalty this season.

Pires and Henry's move – straight off the training ground – was inventive, but looked like a disastrous mistake when Darius Vassell tucked away a neat header from Kiki Musampa's cross. A raised flag from the referee's assistant saved the day for Arsenal.

What did Wrighty, sitting in the stands after presenting Henry with a solid silver cannon before kick-off to commemorate his magnificent achievement, make of it all?

GAME STATISTICS

ARSENAL		MANCHESTER CITY
1	GOALS	0
0	1ST HALF GOALS	0
2	SHOTS ON TARGET	3
2	SHOTS OFF TARGET	4
1	BLOCKED SHOTS	1
4	CORNERS	3
25	FOULS	20
2	OFFSIDES	4
3	YELLOW CARDS	5
0	RED CARDS	0
78.0	PASSING SUCCESS	67.2
27	TACKLES	37
70.4	TACKLES SUCCESS	78.4
59.4	POSSESSION	40.6
43.5	TERRITORIAL ADVANTAGE	56.5

FINAL THOUGHTS

"Should Pires have tried that penalty? Yes, if we were 3–0 up. I couldn't understand why he did at 1–0 against a side who always play well at Highbury. However, for people to say he was being disrespectful to City is rubbish. There's nothing wrong with trying different things, but there's a time and a place."

NICHOLAS ATHANASIOU, HARINGEY, LONDON

"What was strange was that Pires had smashed the previous penalty and he must have been confident, but he was not trying to be disrespectful." ARSÈNE WENGER

"Football thrives on invention, but when the operatives get it wrong, creativity turns into farce, as witnessed at Highbury."

DAILY TELEGRAPH

Opposite Thierry Henry tries an outrageous overhead kick with Sylvain Distin in close attendance.
***Above, left** Ian Wright hands over a special award to the Club's new record scorer Henry.*

Tottenham Hotspur 1 KING 17

ARSENAL 1 PIRES 77

DATE **SATURDAY 29 OCTOBER 2005**
VENUE **WHITE HART LANE**
ATTENDANCE **36,154**
REFEREE **STEVE BENNETT**

THE NUMBER 13 PROVED LUCKY for Arsenal as Robert Pires' strike 13 minutes from time saw Arsenal stretch their unbeaten run in north London derbies to, you've guessed it, 13 matches.

Tottenham deservedly took a 17th-minute lead when England defender Ledley King rose magnificently to meet Michael Carrick's cross and sent a thumping header beyond Jens Lehmann.

PERFORMANCE IN THE PREMIERSHIP YEARS	FORM		
White Hart Lane	W 2–1	(A)	CL
	W 1–0	(H)	Prem
PLAYED 13	L 1–2	(A)	Prem
WON 3	W 2–0	(A)	CL
DRAWN 6	W 1–0	(H)	Prem
LOST 4	W 3–0	(A)	C Cup
FOR 17			
AGAINST 17			

REID (LENNON 73)   MENDES (TAINIO 79)   KEANE (DEFOE 82)

ROBINSON

STALTERI   DAWSON   KING   LEE

LENNON   JENAS   CARRICK   TAINIO

DEFOE   MIDO

BERGKAMP   REYES

FABREGAS   FLAMINI   GILBERTO   LJUNGBERG

LAUREN   TOURE   CAMPBELL   CLICHY

LEHMANN

PIRES (FLAMINI 45)   VAN PERSIE (LJUNGBERG 65)   CYGAN (REYES 90)

Other Results: Saturday

Birmingham City	0–1	Everton
Charlton Athletic	0–1	Bolton Wanderers
Chelsea	4–2	Blackburn Rovers
Liverpool	2–0	West Ham United
Middlesbrough	4–1	Manchester United
Sunderland	1–4	Portsmouth
Wigan Athletic	1–0	Fulham
*West Bromwich Alb.	0–3	Newcastle United

Table position	P	W	D	L	F	A	Pts
7	10	5	2	3	13	7	17

Played on Sunday

FINAL THOUGHTS

"We were dreadful in the first half, far too tentative and Spurs took advantage, but we were a different side after the break and Pires showed just how important he is for us, not just with goal but with the way he helped us retain possession. Spurs had their best chance in years to beat us – and they still couldn't do it."
CHRISTOPHER SMITH, MILTON KEYNES, BUCKS

"We got caught up in the hype about Tottenham and their so-called superiority. At half-time we realised we were the better team." ARSÈNE WENGER

"Pires' artistry helps Arsenal resist the flowering of Spurs' young talent." THE INDEPENDENT

DID YOU KNOW?
This was the 150th North London Derby in which Arsenal's record is P150 W63 D38 L49.

Further inroads were made into the visitors' backline as the Gunners, still missing Thierry Henry, looked a shell of the side that had won 5–4 at the same ground the previous season.

Spurs had gone into the game as favourites, the first time that had happened for more than ten years, and they had justified the bookies' confidence in them with a stirring opening 45 minutes.

Jermain Defoe and Carrick could both have doubled Spurs' advantage and perhaps put the game beyond Arsenal's reach, while Jermaine Jenas' fierce drive was brilliantly tipped over by Lehmann.

But Arsenal fought back. Pires was introduced after the break and by the time his eighth goal in ten derbies arrived it had an air of inevitability about it – England goalkeeper Paul Robinson could only parry Bergkamp's free-kick and Pires steered the loose ball over the line.

It was his fifth goal in as many games at the Lane and Arsenal could have won it, when substitute Robin van Persie saw his drive blocked and cleared to safety.

Tottenham's Dutch head coach Martin Jol said: "Arsenal were very happy at the end – they were shouting and yelling. It must have been a very long time since they last settled for a draw."

MAN OF THE MATCH

ROBERT PIRES

Mins on pitch	**45**
Tackles won	**2**
Passes completed	**23 (85%)**
Shots on target	**1**
Shots off target	**1**
Goals	**1**

GAME STATISTICS

TOTTENHAM HOTSPUR		ARSENAL
1	GOALS	1
1	1ST HALF GOALS	0
4	SHOTS ON TARGET	3
7	SHOTS OFF TARGET	4
1	BLOCKED SHOTS	3
6	CORNERS	1
17	FOULS	14
4	OFFSIDES	6
4	YELLOW CARDS	2
0	RED CARDS	0
69.8	PASSING SUCCESS	80.8
43	TACKLES	31
76.7	TACKLES SUCCESS	74.2
41.5	POSSESSION	58.5
53.6	TERRITORIAL ADVANTAGE	46.4

Opposite, top Jens Lehmann thwarts a rare second half Spurs attack.
Opposite, bottom Robert Pires (second right) is mobbed by teammates after his equaliser.

ARSENAL 3
VAN PERSIE 12,
HENRY 36, 82

Sunderland 1
STUBBS 75

DATE SATURDAY 5 NOVEMBER 2005
VENUE HIGHBURY
ATTENDANCE 38,210
REFEREE ALAN WILEY

FORM		
L	1–2 (A)	Prem
W	2–0 (A)	CL
W	1–0 (H)	Prem
W	3–0 (A)	C Cup
D	1–1 (A)	Prem
W	3–0 (H)	CL

THIERRY HENRY and Robin van Persie's fledgling partnership was looking the real deal after an eighth win in eight Highbury games put Arsenal in third place – their highest league position since May.

Sunderland put up a spirited display, but, languishing at the foot of the table, it was never going to be easy for Mick McCarthy's side, and their task was made more difficult with only 12 minutes gone when van Persie kept up his excellent scoring record.

Sol Campbell thumped the ball forward and van Persie nipped clear of Alan Stubbs and dispatched the ball past the advancing Ben Alnwick, who was making his Premiership debut.

The 18-year-old goalkeeper was beaten again nine minutes before the interval when Lauren sent a raking cross-field pass to Henry and he clinically finished.

It was becoming all so predictable, with the Gunners front pair clearly enjoying themselves against a defence that had a rabbit-caught-in-headlights look about it all afternoon.

Henry could even afford a smile when van Persie lobbed the ball to him and, with his back to goal, he gently teed the ball up before unleashing a bicycle kick that rebounded off the woodwork.

Bergkamp then replaced van Persie for his 300th Premiership appearance and rising youngster Emmanuel Eboue was also

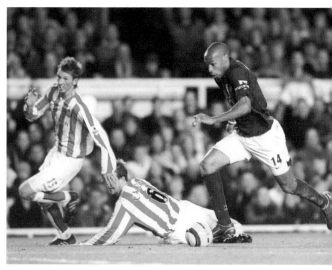

Above Thierry Henry cuts through Sunderland's backline to hit his second of the game.
Opposite Robin van Persie leaves Alan Stubbs in his wake to fire home the opening goal at Highbury.

Other Results: Saturday

Aston Villa	0–2	Liverpool
Blackburn Rovers	4–1	Charlton Athletic
Fulham	2–1	Manchester City
Newcastle United	1–0	Birmingham City
Portsmouth	0–2	Wigan Athletic
West Ham United	1–0	West Bromwich Alb.
*Everton	1–0	Middlesbrough
*Manchester United	1–0	Chelsea
†Bolton Wanderers	1–0	Tottenham Hotspur

Table position	P	W	D	L	F	A	Pts
3	11	6	2	3	16	8	20

*Played on Sunday   †Played on Monday

MAN OF THE MATCH

THIERRY HENRY

Mins on pitch	**90**
Tackles won	**0**
Passes completed	**38 (73%)**
Shots on target	**2**
Shots off target	**1**
Goals	**2**

GAME STATISTICS

ARSENAL		SUNDERLAND
3	GOALS	1
2	1ST HALF GOALS	0
5	SHOTS ON TARGET	1
5	SHOTS OFF TARGET	3
2	BLOCKED SHOTS	0
4	CORNERS	6
12	FOULS	16
12	OFFSIDES	5
0	YELLOW CARDS	1
0	RED CARDS	0
84.4	PASSING SUCCESS	71.5
23	TACKLES	21
69.6	TACKLES SUCCESS	71.4
64.8	POSSESSION	35.2
48.2	TERRITORIAL ADVANTAGE	51.8

given 25 minutes to make an impression, but the Black Cats set up a grandstand finish when Stubbs stabbed the ball in.

That was until Henry killed off the game with a sublime third to end the Wearside fans' hopes of a rare Highbury point. Cesc Fabregas played Henry in on goal with a magnificent pass and he buried the ball past the teenage keeper.

FINAL THOUGHTS

"We seem to be building up a head of steam and some of the lads coming through, I feel, are making a difference. Eboue looks strong and direct – much like Kolo Toure when he goes forward – and Fabregas just gets better and better." MELISSA JACOBS, DUBLIN

"The confidence is back. We played with style and combinations." ARSÈNE WENGER

"The cliché is that there are no easy games. This one certainly was." SUNDAY TIMES

DID YOU KNOW?
Alan Stubbs' goal was the first Arsenal had conceded in 414 minutes of football at Highbury.

Wigan Athletic 2
CAMARA 28,
BULLARD 45

ARSENAL 3
VAN PERSIE 11,
HENRY 21, 41

DATE **SATURDAY 19 NOVEMBER 2005**
VENUE **JJB STADIUM**
ATTENDANCE **25,004**
REFEREE **GRAHAM POLL**

PERFORMANCE IN THE PREMIERSHIP YEARS	FORM	
JJB Stadium	W 2–0 (A)	CL
This was Arsenal's first visit to this ground in Premiership history	W 1–0 (H)	Prem
	W 3–0 (A)	C Cup
	D 1–1 (A)	Prem
	W 3–0 (H)	CL
	W 3–1 (H)	Prem

IN A THRILLER AT THE JJB, Arsenal claimed their first away victory in the Premiership since May. It took them just 11 minutes to pierce Wigan's defence, which had not conceded a goal for six matches, and by the 41st minute they had scored twice more. Three goals away from home by half-time should have guaranteed an easy victory, but second-placed Wigan also scored two of their own in a thundering first half.

Robin van Persie hit the first of the game in front of a new JJB record crowd of 25,004 when he rounded Arjan de Zeeuw and beat John Filan with a 25-yard drive. Ten minutes elapsed before Thierry Henry then got his trademark goal to put the Gunners firmly in the driving seat – Cesc Fabregas sliced open the Latics' defence with a diagonal pass and the France striker sidefooted past Filan without breaking stride.

In-form Robin van Persie scores after 11 minutes in front of a record crowd at the JJB Stadium.

Wigan hit back quickly through Henri Camara, but just as the home side were growing in confidence, Henry hit a third, as he flighted a quickly-taken free-kick over the wall and into the corner, with Filan a mere spectator. The strike pushed Henry's goal tally into double figures for the season.

Other Results: Saturday

Charlton Athletic	1–3	Manchester United
Chelsea	3–0	Newcastle United
Liverpool	3–0	Portsmouth
Manchester City	0–0	Blackburn Rovers
Sunderland	1–3	Aston Villa
West Bromwich Alb.	4–0	Everton
*Middlesbrough	3–2	Fulham
*Tottenham Hotspur	1–1	West Ham United

Table position	P	W	D	L	F	A	Pts
3	12	7	2	3	19	10	23

* Played on Sunday

MAN OF THE MATCH

THIERRY HENRY

Mins on pitch	90
Tackles won	1
Passes completed	34 (79%)
Shots on target	3
Shots off target	1
Goals	2

However, with Arsenal cruising at 3–1 it was energetic Eastender Jimmy Bullard who added another twist with the goal of the game on the stroke of half-time. The blonde midfielder stepped round Sol Campbell's challenge with ease and unleashed a shot into the far corner. It was the final goal of a super game.

Thierry Henry curls a glorious free-kick past a helpless John Filan.

FINAL THOUGHTS

"That was a hell of a result for so many reasons. It was a very tough pitch to play our usual game on, but we showed heart. They may be a small club, but few sides will come here and beat Wigan." DEREK TILSLEY, HOMERTON, LONDON

"We were mentally and physically tested by a determined, brave Wigan." ARSÈNE WENGER

"Jewell's men forced to bow to a gem of a display from Henry." THE OBSERVER

GAME STATISTICS

WIGAN ATHLETIC		ARSENAL
2	GOALS	3
2	1ST HALF GOALS	3
2	SHOTS ON TARGET	5
7	SHOTS OFF TARGET	5
3	BLOCKED SHOTS	3
2	CORNERS	2
18	FOULS	18
5	OFFSIDES	0
3	YELLOW CARDS	2
0	RED CARDS	0
66.7	PASSING SUCCESS	77.7
29	TACKLES	23
58.6	TACKLES SUCCESS	73.9
41.4	POSSESSION	58.6
47.8	TERRITORIAL ADVANTAGE	52.2

ARSENAL 3
FABREGAS 4, HENRY 45, VAN PERSIE 90

Blackburn Rovers 0

DATE   SATURDAY 26 NOVEMBER 2005
VENUE   HIGHBURY
ATTENDANCE   38,192
REFEREE   CHRIS FOY

FORM		
W 3–0	(A)	C Cup
D 1–1	(A)	Prem
W 3–0	(H)	CL
W 3–1	(H)	Prem
W 3–2	(A)	Prem
W 1–0	(A)	CL

Other Results: Saturday		
Aston Villa	3–0	Charlton Athletic
Manchester City	0–1	Liverpool
Portsmouth	0–2	Chelsea
Sunderland	0–1	Birmingham City
Wigan Athletic	1–2	Tottenham Hotspur
*Everton	1–0	Newcastle United
*Fulham	2–1	Bolton Wanderers
*Middlesbrough	2–2	West Bromwich Alb.
*West Ham United	1–2	Manchester United

Table position	P	W	D	L	F	A	Pts
2	13	8	2	3	22	10	26

* Played on Sunday

THIERRY HENRY LIT UP A ROUTINE HOME VICTORY over Blackburn with his 100th Premiership goal at Highbury and that goal, Arsenal's second of the game, provided the side with a much-needed cushion after an improving Blackburn side asked all the questions.

A minute's silence was impeccably observed by the crowd in memory of George Best, who had died the day before, but Spanish youngster Cesc Fabregas had the crowd roaring its approval just minutes later when he gave the hosts an early lead on a freezing cold north London afternoon. Andy Todd managed to halt José Antonio Reyes' wriggling run, but Fabregas picked up the loose ball and expertly curled it past Brad Friedel.

Morten Gamst Pedersen and Shefki Kuqi both went close to levelling, but, just as Rovers appeared to be in the ascendancy, Henry's special moment arrived. With half-time looming, Robert Pires played his Les Bleus team-mate in with a delightful diagonal pass and Henry adjusted his body beautifully to send a curling effort into the far corner.

Robin van Persie, who had been rested after two games in four days, replaced Dennis Bergkamp for the final eight minutes and made his mark with the final goal of the afternoon. Like Henry's, it was an absolute stunner as, seemingly marooned at the corner flag, he ghosted between Savage and Michael Gray and then fired a glorious effort from an impossible angle, the ball smacking against the inside of the far post as it made its way in. But even a goal like that couldn't steal King Henry's limelight.

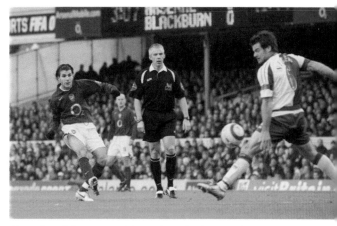

Above Cesc Fabregas started the scoring early when he curled home this fourth-minute opener.
Opposite, top Robin van Persie is a picture of concentration as he sends another cross into the Blackburn box.

MAN OF THE MATCH

THIERRY HENRY

Mins on pitch	90
Tackles won	3
Passes completed	24 (60%)
Shots on target	2
Shots off target	2
Goals	1

DID YOU KNOW?

Thierry Henry became the first player to score 100 Premier League goals at one venue.

GAME STATISTICS

ARSENAL		BLACKBURN ROVERS
3	GOALS	0
2	1ST HALF GOALS	0
9	SHOTS ON TARGET	4
4	SHOTS OFF TARGET	8
2	BLOCKED SHOTS	6
9	CORNERS	10
10	FOULS	14
2	OFFSIDES	2
1	YELLOW CARDS	2
0	RED CARDS	0
76.1	PASSING SUCCESS	71.4
20	TACKLES	27
65.0	TACKLES SUCCESS	66.7
52.1	POSSESSION	47.9
42.9	TERRITORIAL ADVANTAGE	57.1

FINAL THOUGHTS

"It seems Thierry breaks a new record, or reaches a new landmark, every time he plays. The man is a phenomenon, but there is another hero on the horizon in van Persie. He is very special. That goal at the end was just stunning. On days like today the future just seems rosier than ever." GREG ALLISON, WATFORD, HERTS

"The finishing quality between the two teams made the difference today." ARSÈNE WENGER

"Thierry adds to his record collection." INDEPENDENT ON SUNDAY

Bolton Wanderers 2
DIAGNE-FAYE 20, GIANNAKOPOULOS 32

ARSENAL 0

DATE	SATURDAY 3 DECEMBER 2005
VENUE	REEBOK STADIUM
ATTENDANCE	26,792
REFEREE	HOWARD WEBB

PERFORMANCE IN THE PREMIERSHIP YEARS		FORM	
		W 3–0 (H) CL	
Reebok Stadium		W 3–1 (H) Prem	
PLAYED	7	W 3–2 (A) Prem	
WON	2	W 1–0 (A) CL	
DRAWN	3	W 3–0 (H) Prem	
LOST	2	W 3–0 (H) C Cup	
FOR	8		
AGAINST	7		

VAZ TE (GIANNAKOPOULOS 81) — JAIDI (DIAGNE-FAYE 86)

JAASKELAINEN

O'BRIEN — N'GOTTY — BEN HAIM — GARDNER

NOLAN — SPEED

DIAGNE-FAYE — GIANNAKOPOULOS — DIOUF

DAVIES

VAN PERSIE — HENRY

LJUNGBERG — GILBERTO — FABREGAS — PIRES

CYGAN — TOURE — CAMPBELL — LAUREN

LEHMANN

BERGKAMP (VAN PERSIE 69) — REYES (FABREGAS 69) — EBOUE (LAUREN 74)

Other Results: Saturday

Blackburn Rovers	0–2	Everton
Chelsea	1–0	Middlesbrough
Liverpool	3–0	Wigan Athletic
Manchester United	3–0	Portsmouth
Newcastle United	1–1	Aston Villa
Tottenham Hotspur	3–2	Sunderland
West Bromwich Alb.	0–0	Fulham
*Charlton Athletic	2–5	Manchester City
†Birmingham City	1–2	West Ham United

Table position	P	W	D	L	F	A	Pts
5	14	8	2	4	22	12	26

* Played on Sunday   †Played on Monday

BEFORE THE GAME, a confident Arsène Wenger declared: "The season starts here!" By the end of it, the Arsenal manager was left scratching his head in bewilderment as Bolton took all three points at the Reebok.

Above *Arsène Wenger looks tense as Arsenal's poor run at Bolton continues.*
Opposite *Thierry Henry skips over the prostrate Bruno N'Gotty.*

DID YOU KNOW?
This was the first time Arsenal had lost by more than one goal all season.

The Gunners arrived in free-scoring form, having hit 20 goals in eight games, but found themselves up against a Bolton defence that had not conceded a goal at home since August.

Sam Allardyce's side imposed their physical style on the game early on and took a 20th-minute lead. Young Irish defender Joey O'Brien won possession and slung over yet another cross into the danger zone. Lauren failed to clear the ball adequately and Stelios Giannakopoulos clipped it back to Senegal midfielder Abdoulaye Diagne-Faye who rose easily above Cesc Fabregas to send a powerful header flying past Jens Lehmann.

Skipper Thierry Henry immediately tried to pull Arsenal level with an ambitious long-range effort, but things got worse with

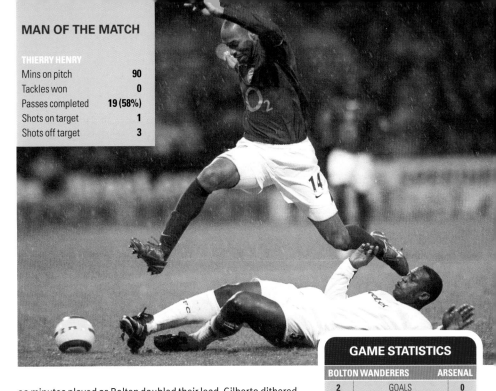

MAN OF THE MATCH

THIERRY HENRY

Mins on pitch	90
Tackles won	0
Passes completed	19 (58%)
Shots on target	1
Shots off target	3

GAME STATISTICS

BOLTON WANDERERS		ARSENAL
2	GOALS	0
2	1ST HALF GOALS	0
6	SHOTS ON TARGET	3
3	SHOTS OFF TARGET	7
2	BLOCKED SHOTS	1
9	CORNERS	3
18	FOULS	17
5	OFFSIDES	0
1	YELLOW CARDS	2
0	RED CARDS	0
53.9	PASSING SUCCESS	74.1
35	TACKLES	24
65.7	TACKLES SUCCESS	66.7
36.9	POSSESSION	63.1
49.6	TERRITORIAL ADVANTAGE	50.4

32 minutes played as Bolton doubled their lead. Gilberto dithered too long and was dispossessed by the energetic Kevin Davies and the former Southampton striker crossed for Giannakopoulos to slide the ball into the unguarded net.

However, the visitors finally stirred and began to show their quality, and Henry was unlucky to see his magnificent shot hit the post, while Gilberto shot wide.

Again, Henry looked to have given Arsenal a lifeline, only to see his 25-yard shot hit the inside of the post and fly away to safety, and it was Bolton who finished the stronger of the two sides, even though Diagne-Faye had another goal disallowed for blatant handball.

FINAL THOUGHTS

"Had to feel sorry for Thierry – he was desperately unlucky not to have scored. Still, there's no two ways about it. Bolton once again proved a thorn in our side – they deserved the points." STEVEN PRESTWICH, ELSTREE, HERTS

"We were tentative and frail. The first quality you must show in this job is commitment and in the first half they were stronger in every challenge." ARSÈNE WENGER

"Wenger lost his cool as Arsenal slumped to their first defeat in 11." NEWS OF THE WORLD

Newcastle United 1 SOLANO 82
ARSENAL 0

DATE SATURDAY 10 DECEMBER 2005
VENUE ST JAMES' PARK
ATTENDANCE 52,297
REFEREE DERMOT GALLAGHER

PERFORMANCE IN THE PREMIERSHIP YEARS		FORM	
St James' Park		W 3–2 (A) Prem	
PLAYED	13	W 1–0 (A) CL	
WON	4	W 3–0 (H) Prem	
DRAWN	5	W 3–0 (H) C Cup	
LOST	4	L 0–2 (A) Prem	
FOR	11	D 0–0 (H) CL	
AGAINST	13		

NOLBERTO SOLANO'S THUMPING SHOT eight minutes from the end of a blood-and-thunder St James' Park affair condemned Arsenal to a fifth Premiership defeat of the campaign.

The Gunners also had Brazil midfielder Gilberto sent off for two questionable bookings, while others on the pitch – notably in black and white – appeared to get away with some more robust challenges.

The scoreline, in fairness, flattered the Toon as Arsenal appeared to have rediscovered their fluidity in a glorious first-half display. All that was missing was a goal.

Thierry Henry, in particular, was in the mood, with a series of delightful touches, including one magnificent piece of trickery, which was only foiled by a last-gasp tackle and then an outstanding save from Ireland goalkeeper Shay Given, who kept out his brilliant first-time volley after 27 minutes.

Then it all went wrong. Gilberto had already been booked for a trip when referee Dermot Gallagher decided to show him another yellow for an innocuous challenge on Jean Alain Boumsong.

The industrious Alexander Hleb stretches his legs and attempts to outrun Amdy Faye.

Other Results: Saturday

Birmingham City	1–0	Fulham
Blackburn Rovers	3–2	West Ham United
Bolton Wanderers	1–1	Aston Villa
Charlton Athletic	2–0	Sunderland
Chelsea	1–0	Wigan Athletic
Liverpool	2–0	Middlesbrough
West Bromwich Alb.	2–0	Manchester City
*Manchester United	1–1	Everton
†Tottenham Hotspur	3–1	Portsmouth

Table position	P	W	D	L	F	A	Pts
6	15	8	2	5	22	13	26

*Played on Sunday †Played on Monday

> "The papers will be harsh on the lads, but they were unlucky... the referee lost us the game, not the players."
>
> NIKKI PENDERGRAST, SOMERS TOWN, LONDON

> "If Gilberto deserved to be sent off, I need to re-adjust my eyes."
>
> ARSÈNE WENGER

> "For two consecutive weekends Arsenal have been out-fought, out-muscled and battered into submission." DAILY MIRROR

It was a decision that surprised even the home side and looked even more eccentric just minutes later when Alan Shearer scythed down Sol Campbell. Gallagher's verdict? Play on.

The numerical advantage meant United took control in the middle of the park and Solano took advantage. Shearer held off two tackles before rolling the ball into the path of the Peruvian, who came racing in on the right flank to flash in a superb first-time drive under Jens Lehmann and into the far corner.

DID YOU KNOW?

This was the first time the Gunners had failed to score in back-to-back games since November 2000.

MAN OF THE MATCH

THIERRY HENRY

Mins on pitch	**90**
Tackles won	**0**
Passes completed	**32 (67%)**
Shots on target	**1**
Shots off target	**2**

GAME STATISTICS

NEWCASTLE UNITED		ARSENAL
1	GOALS	0
0	1ST HALF GOALS	0
2	SHOTS ON TARGET	2
4	SHOTS OFF TARGET	4
2	BLOCKED SHOTS	2
5	CORNERS	4
23	FOULS	15
6	OFFSIDES	2
1	YELLOW CARDS	0
0	RED CARDS	1
59.9	PASSING SUCCESS	72.2
49	TACKLES	40
77.6	TACKLES SUCCESS	67.5
46.1	POSSESSION	53.9
49.1	TERRITORIAL ADVANTAGE	50.9

The hard-working Kolo Toure shows characteristic willing as he forays forward in search of a goal.

ARSENAL 0

Chelsea 2

ROBBEN 39,
COLE 72

DATE SUNDAY 18 DECEMBER 2005
VENUE HIGHBURY
ATTENDANCE 38,347
REFEREE ROB STYLES

FORM		
W 1–0	(A)	CL
W 3–0	(H)	Prem
W 3–0	(H)	C Cup
L 0–2	(A)	Prem
D 0–0	(H)	CL
L 1–0	(A)	Prem

BERGKAMP
(LJUNGBERG 70)

PIRES
(HLEB 70)

OWUSU-ABEYIE
(VAN PERSIE 81)

LEHMANN

TOURE SENDEROS CAMPBELL LAUREN

LJUNGBERG FABREGAS FLAMINI HLEB

VAN PERSIE HENRY

DROGBA

ROBBEN J COLE LAMPARD ESSIEN

MAKELELE

GALLAS TERRY CARVALHO FERREIRA

CECH

GEREMI
(ROBBEN 77)

HUTH
(DROGBA 88)

Other Results: Saturday

Aston Villa	0–2	Manchester United
Everton	0–4	Bolton Wanderers
Fulham	2–1	Blackburn Rover
Manchester City	4–1	Birmingham City
Portsmouth	1–0	West Bromwich Alb.
West Ham United	2–4	Newcastle United
Wigan Athletic	3–0	Charlton Athletic
*Middlesbrough	3–3	Tottenham Hotspur

Table position	P	W	D	L	F	A	Pts
8	16	8	2	6	22	15	26

* Played on Sunday

CHELSEA'S FIRST LEAGUE VICTORY at Highbury since March 1990 gave the champions a 20-point advantage over Arsenal – effectively ending their title hopes before Christmas – and gave them a nine-point lead over second-placed Manchester United.

It ended Arsenal's 100% home record and another blank day meant the misfiring Gunners had gone four games without a goal for the first time in more than ten years.

It could have been so different, though, after Thierry Henry wove through and hit the woodwork after 20 minutes and less than 60 seconds had elapsed before a referee's assistant's flag wrongly ruled out Robin van Persie's tidy early strike for offside.

Arsenal were rightly cursing their bad luck – and a poor decision by the officials – for not giving them that precious, early

DID YOU KNOW?
This was the first loss at Highbury this season and the first victory for Chelsea at Highbury in the League since 1990.

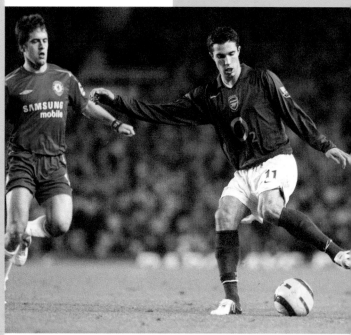

Above *Robin van Persie prepares to shield the ball from Chelsea goalscorer Joe Cole.*
Opposite, top *Lauren tries his luck as Ricardo Carvalho makes a desperate attempt to close him down.*

ARSENAL		CHELSEA
0	GOALS	2
0	1ST HALF GOALS	1
5	SHOTS ON TARGET	6
5	SHOTS OFF TARGET	4
2	BLOCKED SHOTS	4
5	CORNERS	5
14	FOULS	19
2	OFFSIDES	4
3	YELLOW CARDS	4
0	RED CARDS	0
69.4	PASSING SUCCESS	61.0
30	TACKLES	36
73.3	TACKLES SUCCESS	75.0
58.4	POSSESSION	41.6
55.4	TERRITORIAL ADVANTAGE	44.6

lead. And Michael Essien, who in the weeks before had hit the headlines for a horror tackle on Liverpool's Dietmar Hamann, was lucky not to be shown a straight red for swinging an arm at Lauren. Then Chelsea took the lead.

Six minutes before the break Arjen Robben raced on to Didier Drogba's through ball, his pace pulling him clear of Sol Campbell, and he squeezed a delicate finish past Jens Lehmann and in off the far post.

A quick response was needed by the home side. Instead, an ultra-confident Chelsea sat back and closed the door on Arsenal, conceding possession and opting to play on the break. The victory was clinched in the 73rd minute, when Lauren needlessly lost the ball to Joe Cole and he tucked a well-placed side-footed shot inside the far post.

FINAL THOUGHTS

"If van Persie's goal had been given, the whole complexion of the game would have been different. Once Chelsea take the lead they are very hard to score against, because they just sit back. It is a simple plan, but very effective."

TONY MAIDMENT, WALLASEY, MERSEYSIDE

"There were a few turning points on both sides and they went for them." ARSÈNE WENGER

"Ruthless Chelsea Conquer Highbury." THE INDEPENDENT

MAN OF THE MATCH

PHILIPPE SENDEROS

Mins on pitch	90
Tackles won	4
Tackle success	80%
Passes completed	28 (61%)
Successful clearances	9

Charlton Athletic 0
ARSENAL 1 REYES 58

DATE MONDAY 26 DECEMBER 2005
VENUE THE VALLEY
ATTENDANCE 27,111
REFEREE STEVE BENNETT

PERFORMANCE IN THE PREMIERSHIP YEARS		FORM
The Valley		W 3–0 (H) C Cup
		L 0–2 (A) Prem
PLAYED	6	D 0–0 (H) CL
WON	4	
DRAWN	1	L 0–1 (A) Prem
LOST	1	L 0–2 (H) Prem
FOR	11	D 2–2 (A) C Cup
AGAINST	3	(won 3–1 on pens)

ON BOXING DAY José Antonio Reyes returned to the starting line-up after injury and made a key contribution with the only goal of the game at the Valley.

His strike – the first in four league games for the Gunners – provided some much-needed Christmas cheer as well as ensuring the team's first Premiership victory for exactly a month.

Thierry Henry was passed fit to make his 200th Premiership appearance, but it was Gilberto who was first with an attempt on goal, except his 30-yard effort barely troubled Addicks 'keeper Thomas Myhre.

His Arsenal counterpart Jens Lehmann then had to react sharply after Danny Murphy's pass released the impressive Darren Bent, but the visitors were beginning to rediscover their famous passing game and Reyes was soon scuttling free after some wonderful interplay between Alexander Hleb and Henry. With Charlton carved open, the Spaniard fed Fredrik Ljungberg, but the Swede could only shoot straight at Myhre.

The second half continued with Arsenal looking the likelier to score and only a last-gasp block denied Henry, but Charlton had lost seven of their previous eight games and Arsenal smelt blood.

The winner, much to Arsenal's relief, finally came 13 minutes into the second half. Ljungberg cut inside to find Henry, who saw

Alexander Hleb tries a long-range effort at the Valley.

Other Results: Saturday

Aston Villa	4–0	Everton
Chelsea	3–2	Fulham
Liverpool	2–0	Newcastle United
Manchester United	3–0	West Bromwich Alb.
Middlesbrough	0–2	Blackburn Rover
Portsmouth	1–1	West Ham United
Sunderland	0–0	Bolton Wanderers
Tottenham Hotspur	2–0	Birmingham City
Wigan Athletic	4–3	Manchester City

Table position	P	W	D	L	F	A	Pts
7	17	9	2	6	23	15	29

José Antonio Reyes tucks the ball home from close range to seal three vital points for Arsenal.

his first shot blocked, but he reacted quickly to try again and the ball ballooned off Myhre and into the path of Reyes, who kept his head to push the ball over the line.

Charlton's cause was not helped when England midfielder Danny Murphy was shown a second yellow card with less than 20 minutes remaining.

FINAL THOUGHTS

"Relief – that is the only way I can describe it. It has been a rotten month, so to get three points, and away from home, and with José getting the winner… it's just great. Our passing was almost as good as last season – there was a real buzz about the boys today."

JONATHAN COLLINS, NEWINGTON GREEN, LONDON

"I like 4-4-2, but we have played some physical games away from home and needed to strengthen in the middle of the park."

ARSÈNE WENGER

"Rare goal makes life rosy for José." DAILY MAIL

GAME STATISTICS

CHARLTON ATHLETIC		ARSENAL
0	GOALS	1
0	1ST HALF GOALS	0
1	SHOTS ON TARGET	7
8	SHOTS OFF TARGET	8
0	BLOCKED SHOTS	6
4	CORNERS	10
17	FOULS	11
3	OFFSIDES	6
2	YELLOW CARDS	2
1	RED CARDS	0
53.5	PASSING SUCCESS	72.5
33	TACKLES	15
78.8	TACKLES SUCCESS	93.3
35.5	POSSESSION	64.5
47.5	TERRITORIAL ADVANTAGE	52.5

DID YOU KNOW?

This was Arsenal's eighth game without defeat against the Addicks.

ARSENAL 4
BERGKAMP 7, REYES 13,
HENRY 36, 42 (PEN)

Portsmouth 0

DATE **WEDNESDAY 28 DECEMBER 2005**
VENUE **HIGHBURY**
ATTENDANCE **38,223**
REFEREE **MARK CLATTENBURG**

ARSENAL CLICKED BACK INTO FORM with a red-hot display to warm up icy Highbury and secure the first home win for a month. They led 4–0 by the 42nd minute and could have doubled that tally by the end, as returning Pompey boss Harry Redknapp watched his side hopelessly outclassed.

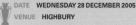

FORM			
L	0–2	(A)	Prem
D	0–0	(H)	CL
L	0–1	(A)	Prem
L	0–2	(H)	Prem
D	2–2	(A)	C Cup
	(won 3–1 on pens)		
W	1–0	(A)	Prem

EBOUE
(REYES 67)

FABREGAS
(GILBERTO 72)

LEHMANN

LAUREN   TOURE   CAMPBELL   CYGAN

PIRES   GILBERTO   FLAMINI   REYES

BERGKAMP   HENRY

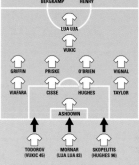

LUA LUA

VUKIC

GRIFFIN   PRISKE   O'BRIEN   VIGNAL

VIAFARA   CISSE   HUGHES   TAYLOR

ASHDOWN

TODOROV
(VUKIC 45)

MORNAR
(LUA LUA 83)

SKOPELITIS
(HUGHES 90)

Other Results: Wednesday		
Birmingham City	2–2	Manchester United
Everton	1–3	Liverpool
Fulham	3–3	Aston Villa
Manchester City	0–1	Chelsea
West Bromwich Alb.	2–0	Tottenham Hotspur
West Ham United	0–2	Wigan Athletic

Table position	P	W	D	L	F	A	Pts
6	18	10	2	6	27	15	32

Bergkamp scored the first after seven minutes, his 200th league strike since making his Ajax debut as a fresh-faced 17-year-old against Roda JC in December 1986.

Reyes showed Andy Griffin a clean pair of heels and placed a perfectly-weighted pass into the path of the Dutch veteran, returning to the side after injury, who expertly side-footed past Jamie Ashdown. Incredibly, it was his first Premiership goal of the season.

In the season to date, Arsenal had won all eight Premiership games in which they had scored first and by the 13th minute they had raced into a 2–0 lead.

Thierry Henry outpaced the Pompey backline to latch on to Kolo Toure's raking through ball and cut inside to feed Reyes who roofed the finish. Portsmouth's Gary O'Neil had claimed before the game that they could chalk up their first win at Highbury since September 1955. Not a chance.

Henry sealed victory with a fine double before the break; first collecting Mathieu Flamini's super pass and rounding Ashdown to score and then making it four with a coolly-taken spot-kick after Reyes – a thorn in Portsmouth's side for the 67 minutes he was on the pitch – was fouled by the tormented Andy Griffin.

Opposite, top Dennis Bergkamp opens the scoring with a smooth finish.
Opposite, bottom José Antonio Reyes, fresh from his confidence-boosting goal at Charlton, scores again to double Arsenal's lead.

FINAL THOUGHTS

"What a first-half performance! We needed that. I thought some of the football we played today was as good as anything we have produced in the last year. Henry was mesmerising at times and what a landmark for Bergy!" MARTIN SEGAL, HENDON, LONDON

"The desire and commitment is back. When we play our one- and two-touch football, it is another story." THIERRY HENRY

"Dennis is not only in the top ten Arsenal scorers of all time now but the top ten players." ARSÈNE WENGER

"Henry inspires carnage at Highbury." THE INDEPENDENT

GAME STATISTICS

ARSENAL		PORTSMOUTH
4	GOALS	0
4	1ST HALF GOALS	0
5	SHOTS ON TARGET	3
3	SHOTS OFF TARGET	2
1	BLOCKED SHOTS	1
3	CORNERS	1
12	FOULS	15
1	OFFSIDES	8
0	YELLOW CARDS	1
0	RED CARDS	0
85.9	PASSING SUCCESS	74.3
32	TACKLES	48
75.0	TACKLES SUCCESS	75.0
65.5	POSSESSION	34.5
41.0	TERRITORIAL ADVANTAGE	59.0

MAN OF THE MATCH

THIERRY HENRY

Mins on pitch	90
Tackles won	3
Passes completed	34 (77%)
Shots on target	2
Shots off target	1
Goals	2

DID YOU KNOW?

In the last six meetings between these clubs Arsenal have averaged 2.5 goals a game.

Aston Villa 0
ARSENAL 0

DATE **SATURDAY 31 DECEMBER 2005**
VENUE **VILLA PARK**
ATTENDANCE **37,114**
REFEREE **URIAH RENNIE**

PERFORMANCE IN THE PREMIERSHIP YEARS		FORM	
Villa Park		D 0–0 (H) CL	
		L 0–1 (A) Prem	
PLAYED	14	L 0–2 (H) Prem	
WON	5	D 2–2 (A) C Cup	
DRAWN	6	(won 3–1 on pens)	
LOST	3	W 1–0 (A) Prem	
FOR	20	W 4–0 (H) Prem	
AGAINST	13		

ARSENAL ENDED 2005 with a hard-earned draw at in-form Villa. The Gunners arrived in Birmingham brimming with confidence after two wins, five goals and two clean sheets from their holiday programme so far, but the Villans would prove to be a tough nut to crack, after just one defeat in seven games.

Mathieu Flamini had the first clear chance of the contest in the 27th minute and should have given Arsenal a precious lead. The young midfielder found himself all alone on the right-hand side of the six-yard box with the ball at his feet, but despite having time to steady himself he hurried his shot and the ball flew over the bar.

Villa, as expected, enjoyed most of the possession, although they found it hard to find gaps in Arsenal's yellow defensive wall. However, Luke Moore's clever pass gave Milan Baros space – in virtually the same spot as Flamini in the first half – but at the crucial moment he lost confidence and blazed over.

DID YOU KNOW?
This was the 14th consecutive game against Villa without defeat.

ANGEL
(MOORE 76)

SORENSEN

HUGHES   DELANEY   RIDGEWELL   BARRY

DAVIS   McCANN   BAKKE   MILNER

MOORE   ANGEL

VAN PERSIE   HENRY

LJUNGBERG   FABREGAS   FLAMINI   HLEB

CYGAN   TOURE   CAMPBELL   LAUREN

LEHMANN

BERGKAMP   REYES   PIRES
(VAN PERSIE 68)   (HLEB 76)   (LJUNGBERG)

Other Results: Saturday

Charlton Athletic	2–0	West Ham United
Chelsea	2–0	Birmingham City
Liverpool	1–0	West Bromwich Alb.
Manchester United	4–1	Bolton Wanderers
Middlesbrough	0–0	Manchester City
Portsmouth	1–0	Fulham
Sunderland	0–1	Everton
Tottenham Hotspur	2–0	Newcastle United
Wigan Athletic	0–3	Blackburn Rovers

Table position	P	W	D	L	F	A	Pts
6	19	10	3	6	27	15	33

Above *The grounded Gavin McCann fails to halt the progress of Cesc Fabregas.*
Opposite, top left *Robin van Persie keeps his eye on the ball despite the close attentions of Villa's Gareth Barry.*

MAN OF THE MATCH

Referee Uriah Rennie then waved away Villa appeals for a penalty after Moore fell easily under the challenge of Kolo Toure.

As the game wore on, Arsenal had the better chances; Fredrik Ljungberg hitting the bar and Robin van Persie firing straight at Sorensen. Toure might have snatched a second successive away victory from Arsenal's first corner of the game when, after 89 minutes, Sol Campbell rose brilliantly to head the ball into his path, but just six yards out he steered the ball wide of the post and Villa were let off the hook.

FINAL THOUGHTS

"A point is a point and Villa is always a tough place to go. Some of the lads looked tired, but that is three clean sheets on the spin and, to be fair, Villa have been superb recently and were up for this." HARRY LILLIE, RUISLIP

"We know we can play much better than this, but you also have to be realistic – even in super seasons we only got a draw here at Villa." ARSÈNE WENGER

"The ghost of Patrick Vieira continues to haunt the Marble Halls of Highbury." THE SUN

GAME STATISTICS

ASTON VILLA		ARSENAL
0	GOALS	0
0	1ST HALF GOALS	0
3	SHOTS ON TARGET	2
9	SHOTS OFF TARGET	7
4	BLOCKED SHOTS	1
10	CORNERS	1
21	FOULS	12
8	OFFSIDES	1
1	YELLOW CARDS	1
0	RED CARDS	0
59.9	PASSING SUCCESS	72.7
40	TACKLES	46
85.0	TACKLES SUCCESS	69.6
41.7	POSSESSION	58.3
59.6	TERRITORIAL ADVANTAGE	40.4

ARSENAL 0
Manchester United 0

DATE **TUESDAY 3 JANUARY 2006**
VENUE **HIGHBURY**
ATTENDANCE **38,313**
REFEREE **GRAHAM POLL**

FORM	
L 0–1 (A) Prem	
L 0–2 (H) Prem	
D 2–2 (A) C Cup (won 3–1 on pens)	
W 1–0 (A) Prem	
W 4–0 (H) Prem	
D 0–0 (A) Prem	

BERGKAMP (HLEB 73) FLAMINI (FABREGAS 80) EBOUE (REYES 90)

LEHMANN

LAUREN CAMPBELL TOURE CYGAN

HLEB GILBERTO

PIRES FABREGAS REYES

HENRY

VAN NISTELROOY ROONEY

GIGGS O'SHEA FLETCHER RONALDO

SILVESTRE FERDINAND BROWN NEVILLE

VAN DER SAR

PARK (GIGGS 73)

Other Results: Monday

Birmingham City	2–0	Wigan Athletic
Blackburn Rovers	2–1	Portsmouth
Bolton Wanderers	2–2	Liverpool
Everton	3–1	Charlton Athletic
Fulham	2–1	Sunderland
Newcastle United	2–2	Middlesbrough
West Bromwich Alb.	1–2	Aston Villa
West Ham United	1–3	Chelsea
*Manchester City	0–2	Tottenham Hotspur

Table position	P	W	D	L	F	A	Pts
5	20	10	4	6	27	15	34

*Played on Wednesday

THE TWO OLD FOES – the dominant forces in English football for the past decade – cancelled each other in their last ever Highbury clash before the Gunners' relocation to Emirates Stadium.

It didn't go unnoticed, either, that this was the first time in nearly ten years that the two captain fantastics were not involved. Both Patrick Vieira and Roy Keane, two men whose passion shone in this

Above Robert Pires advances towards international teammate Mikael Silvestre.
Opposite, top Wes Brown keeps close to Cesc Fabregas.

fixture in previous seasons, had moved on to pastures new and the 'midfield bite' they provided was clearly missing.

Ruud van Nistelrooy had the best chance of the game when Kolo Toure failed to clear his lines and the Dutchman burst through, only to fire into the side-netting. Arsenal, though, had the better of much of the game and Edwin van der Sar had to be alert to paw away Robert Pires' near-post effort, while Thierry Henry, strangely subdued, was a touch unfortunate in the 32nd minute when he bent his free-kick just a couple of yards wide of the top corner.

Ryan Giggs, so often a masterful performer at Highbury, almost broke the deadlock, but lashed his volley wide after Cristiano

Ronaldo had picked him out with a fine cross. And Arsenal could count themselves unlucky not have been awarded a penalty when Gary Neville appeared to foul Cesc Fabregas in the area, this coming shortly after Pires nearly tucked away a cute pass from Henry.

No goals, no incidents of note and both sides content with a share of the spoils – how times had changed!

FINAL THOUGHTS

"It was strange really, because although the passion was still there, this game didn't have that edge we come to expect. There was maybe a little lack of the killer touch. I think if we'd have gone for it we'd have won." FRANKLIN BRIGGS, LEIGHTON BUZZARD, BEDS

"We tried to win the game... you could feel, though, you couldn't find the spark to make the difference."
ARSÈNE WENGER

"It was like watching two ageing fighters going through the motions."
DAILY STAR

GAME STATISTICS

ARSENAL		MANCHESTER UNITED
0	GOALS	0
0	1ST HALF GOALS	0
2	SHOTS ON TARGET	2
3	SHOTS OFF TARGET	10
3	BLOCKED SHOTS	6
6	CORNERS	9
17	FOULS	14
1	OFFSIDES	2
2	YELLOW CARDS	3
0	RED CARDS	0
77.3	PASSING SUCCESS	71.3
39	TACKLES	45
56.4	TACKLES SUCCESS	73.3
53.4	POSSESSION	46.6
50.5	TERRITORIAL ADVANTAGE	49.5

MAN OF THE MATCH

KOLO TOURE

Mins on pitch	90
Tackles won	1
Tackle success	25%
Passes completed	82.9%
Successful clearances	12

ARSENAL 7

HENRY 20, 30, 68, SENDEROS 22,
PIRES 45, GILBERTO 59, HLEB 84

Middlesbrough 0

DATE **SATURDAY 14 JANUARY 2006**
VENUE **HIGHBURY**
ATTENDANCE **38,186**
REFEREE **ROB STYLES**

FORM

W	1–0 (A)	Prem
W	4–0 (H)	Prem
D	0–0 (A)	Prem
D	0–0 (H)	Prem
W	2–1 (H)	FA Cup
L	0–1 (A)	C Cup

THIERRY HENRY equalled Cliff Bastin's Club record of 150 league goals with a stunning hat-trick as miserable Middlesbrough were blown off the radar at Highbury.

Henry opened the goal-fest with a sensational volley past Brad Jones for his 14th of the season. Just two more minutes elapsed before rampant Arsenal made it two, when Senderos rose unchallenged in the six-yard box to head home.

On the half-hour mark Arsenal made it three, as José Antonio Reyes released Henry with an inch-perfect ball and the France striker did the rest. Poor Boro were reeling and, with the sanctuary of the dressing room still some minutes away, Arsenal put a fourth past them, Robert Pires producing a stupendous lob over Jones to cap a destructive 45 minutes of football.

Henry had a hand in the fifth when he whipped in an inviting free-kick and Gilberto headed home just before the hour mark. Then came the record-equalling moment when Reyes fed Henry and he accelerated away before clipping a delicious finish over Jones.

Boro were in disarray and their cause wasn't helped

DID YOU KNOW?
This was the second time Arsenal had beaten a side 7–0 at home in eight months, having put Everton to the sword at the end of the previous season.

Philippe Senderos rises unchallenged to double Arsenal's lead.

Other Results: Saturday

Aston Villa	1–2	West Ham United
Blackburn Rovers	0–0	Bolton Wanderers
Charlton Athletic	2–0	Birmingham City
Fulham	1–0	Newcastle United
Liverpool	1–0	Tottenham Hotspur
Manchester City	3–1	Manchester United
Portsmouth	0–1	Everton
*Sunderland	1–2	Chelsea
*Wigan Athletic	0–1	West Bromwich Alb.

Table position	P	W	D	L	F	A	Pts
5	21	11	4	6	34	15	37

*Played on Sunday

Alexander Hleb opens his Gunners account with the seventh.

when Brazilian Guidoni Junior Doriva was shown a second yellow for pulling back Henry as he bore down on goal.

Minutes later Arsenal equalled their seven-goal haul against Everton in the final home game of last season when Alexander Hleb blasted his first goal in English football from six yards out. It capped a magnificent team display on the day another Club record tumbled.

FINAL THOUGHTS

"It was obvious from the very first few minutes that there had been a total change in attitude and belief – the old Arsenal were back. Tackles were being won and the ball was being moved around with pace and accuracy. Senderos and Djorou , despite having the experienced duo of Yakubu and Viduka up against them, looked in a different class. What more can be said about Thierry? Its just a privilege to watch him." MARK BRINDLE, SOUTH WOODHAM FERRERS, ESSEX

"We could have scored more." ARSÈNE WENGER

"The air was thick with memories – so Henry decided to make a few more." THE INDEPENDENT

GAME STATISTICS

ARSENAL		MIDDLESBROUGH
7	GOALS	0
4	1ST HALF GOALS	0
12	SHOTS ON TARGET	4
9	SHOTS OFF TARGET	6
5	BLOCKED SHOTS	0
4	CORNERS	6
12	FOULS	15
1	OFFSIDES	7
1	YELLOW CARDS	0
0	RED CARDS	1
80.6	PASSING SUCCESS	71.3
20	TACKLES	25
75.0	TACKLES SUCCESS	76.0
60.4	POSSESSION	39.6
49.0	TERRITORIAL ADVANTAGE	51.0

MAN OF THE MATCH

THIERRY HENRY

Mins on pitch	90
Tackles won	1
Passes completed	34 (67%)
Shots on target	4
Shots off target	4
Goals	3

Everton 1 BEATTIE 13
ARSENAL 0

DATE SATURDAY 21 JANUARY 2006
VENUE GOODISON PARK
ATTENDANCE 36,920
REFEREE ALAN WILEY

PERFORMANCE IN THE PREMIERSHIP YEARS		FORM	
Goodison Park		W 4–0 (H) Prem	
		D 0–0 (A) Prem	
PLAYED	13	D 0–0 (H) Prem	
WON	6	W 2–1 (H) FA Cup	
DRAWN	5	L 0–1 (A) C Cup	
LOST	2	W 7–0 (H) Prem	
FOR	18		
AGAINST	10		

IN THIS 170TH LEAGUE MEETING between the two longest-serving top-flight clubs, Arsenal suffered their sixth away defeat of the campaign and had Cesc Fabregas sent off.

England striker James Beattie hit the winner after just 13 minutes when he raced on to Tim Cahill's long pass and squeezed between Philippe Senderos and Sol Campbell to fire home. However, Fredrik Ljungberg and Cesc Fabregas had both seen shots saved by Nigel Martyn prior to Beattie's strike, as Arsenal enjoyed most of the possession in the opening half-hour.

Hammersmith-born defender Kerrea Gilbert was also looking comfortable on his league debut for the club – and posing an unlikely attacking threat by setting off on a series of threatening runs from his full-back berth.

As the game wore on Arsenal began to dominate possession, but without threatening the Toffees' goal too often, although Beattie's muscular play was also causing problems at the other end.

DID YOU KNOW?
Diaby and Gilbert both made league debuts in the 170th league meeting between these sides.

Above Emmanuel Eboue athletically keeps possession.
Opposite, top Fredrik Ljungberg glides past Nuno Valente.

Other Results: Saturday	
Birmingham City 5–0	Portsmouth
Bolton Wanderers 2–0	Manchester City
Middlesbrough 2–3	Wigan Athletic
Newcastle United 0–1	Blackburn Rovers
Tottenham Hotspur 0–0	Aston Villa
West Bromwich Alb. 0–1	Sunderland
*Chelsea 1–1	Charlton Athletic
*Manchester United 1–0	Liverpool
†West Ham United 2–1	Fulham

Table position	P	W	D	L	F	A	Pts
5	22	11	4	7	34	16	37

Played on Sunday †Played on Monday

GAME STATISTICS

EVERTON		ARSENAL
1	GOALS	0
1	1ST HALF GOALS	0
2	SHOTS ON TARGET	2
6	SHOTS OFF TARGET	7
4	BLOCKED SHOTS	3
5	CORNERS	6
19	FOULS	19
4	OFFSIDES	3
4	YELLOW CARDS	2
0	RED CARDS	1
58.7	PASSING SUCCESS	68.6
33	TACKLES	31
57.6	TACKLES SUCCESS	77.4
41.5	POSSESSION	58.5
54.3	TERRITORIAL ADVANTAGE	45.7

With Arsenal leaving gaps at the back, Everton could have added a second, only for Tim Cahill to head Mikel Arteta's cross just wide of Jens Lehmann's post. Sol Campbell also had to be sharp to deny Beattie, as he closed in on Leon Osman's cross with the Goodison Park crowd roaring their side on.

Abou Diaby came on for Robert Pires, to make his debut for the Gunners, but as Arsenal's frustration grew, Fabregas barged Cahill to the ground and was sent off.

Everton's midfield man also picked up a yellow card, but Beattie's strike had earned resurgent Everton a fourth successive Premiership win and Arsène Wenger was left wondering why it was all going wrong away from the sanctuary of north London.

FINAL THOUGHTS

"Today was bad. We barely had a decent shot at goal. Everton, no doubt about it, raised their game, but there is clearly a problem away from home." PETER JACKSON, BARNES, LONDON

"Away from home we have a problem. We always lose 1–0 and we need to find a response by the end of the season to finish in the top four." ARSÈNE WENGER

"Wenger hit by travel sickness." THE TIMES

MAN OF THE MATCH

SOL CAMPBELL

Mins on pitch	90
Tackles won	1
Tackle success	100%
Passes completed	29 (83%)
Successful clearances	13

ARSENAL 2
HENRY 45,
PIRES 89

West Ham United 3
REO-COKER 25, ZAMORA 32,
ETHERINGTON 80

DATE **WEDNESDAY 1 FEBRUARY 2006**
VENUE **HIGHBURY**
ATTENDANCE **38,216**
REFEREE **MARK HALSEY**

ARSENAL'S 2000TH MATCH at Highbury was an eventful affair. Sol Campbell's half-time departure would dominate the following day's back pages and that was a shame, as it overshadowed a magnificent match in which Arsenal were unlucky to lose against their East End rivals and Thierry Henry finally edged past Cliff Bastin's League goals record.

FORM		
W 2–1	(H)	FA Cup
L 0–1	(A)	C Cup
W 7–0	(H)	Prem
L 0–1	(A)	Prem
W 2–1	(H)	C Cup
L 0–1	(A)	FA Cup

FLAMINI (GILBERT 27) LARSSON (CAMPBELL 45) BERGKAMP (DIABY 71)

LEHMANN

GILBERT SENDEROS CAMPBELL DJOUROU

LJUNGBERG DIABY GILBERTO PIRES

VAN PERSIE HENRY

ZAMORA HAREWOOD

ETHERINGTON MULLINS REO-COKER BENAYOUN

KONCHESKY FERDINAND GABBIDON CLARKE

HISLOP

NEWTON (BENAYOUN 66) ASHTON (ZAMORA 73) FLETCHER (CLARKE 76)

Above, top *Fredrik Ljungberg gets in a tangle with only Shaka Hislop to beat.*
Above *New boy Abou Diaby impressed in midfield.*

Other Results: Tuesday

Charlton Athletic	0–0	West Bromwich Alb.
Fulham	1–0	Tottenham Hotspur
Sunderland	0–3	Middlesbrough
Wigan Athletic	1–1	Everton
*Aston Villa	1–1	Chelsea
*Blackburn Rovers	4–3	Manchester United
*Liverpool	1–1	Birmingham City
*Manchester City	3–0	Newcastle United
*Portsmouth	1–1	Bolton Wanderers

Table position	P	W	D	L	F	A	Pts
6	23	11	4	8	36	19	37

* Played on Wednesday

THIERRY HENRY

Mins on pitch	90
Tackles won	1
Passes completed	27 (71%)
Shots on target	1
Shots off target	3
Goals	1

GAME STATISTICS

ARSENAL		WEST HAM UNITED
2	GOALS	3
1	1ST HALF GOALS	2
9	SHOTS ON TARGET	4
7	SHOTS OFF TARGET	1
10	BLOCKED SHOTS	0
12	CORNERS	2
7	FOULS	16
3	OFFSIDES	5
1	YELLOW CARDS	1
0	RED CARDS	0
79.4	PASSING SUCCESS	67.8
17	TACKLES	38
88.2	TACKLES SUCCESS	84.2
66.5	POSSESSION	33.5
58.2	TERRITORIAL ADVANTAGE	41.8

Arsenal started with the look of a side wanting to wrap up the game early on. Thierry Henry's effort hit team-mate Fredrik Ljungberg with the goal at his mercy and then Robin van Persie struck a post in a frantic opening that put the Hammers on the back foot.

Then it all went wrong. First Campbell failed to control the ball and the impressive Nigel Reo-Coker ran through to beat Jens Lehmann. And it got worse as, first, young full-back Kerrea Gilbert hobbled off injured, and then Bobby Zamora held off Campbell to steer a second past Lehmann.

Arsenal were stunned, but pulled a goal back on the stroke of half-time when Henry touched in Robert Pires' shot to finally overtake the great 'Boy' Bastin's long-standing record.

Campbell failed to reappear for the second half as the Gunners fielded a backline of young guns – average age 21. Arsenal controlled most of the second 45 minutes, but the fourth goal of a pulsating game came from the men in claret and blue, Matthew Etherington drilling home with ten minutes left.

Pires set up a thrilling finale in the final minute of normal time after Shaka Hislop spilled Dennis Bergkamp's effort, but the Hammers held on to win on their last visit to Highbury.

DID YOU KNOW?

Henry breaks Bastin's League scoring record in Highbury's 2000th match.
Arsenal's record: P2,000 W1,188 D473 L339 F4,016 A1,949.

FINAL THOUGHTS

"Brilliant game, but the luck didn't go our way. If we'd won 6–3 West Ham couldn't have complained. We have lost too often due to lack of heart this season, but not today. And well done, Thierry."
THOMAS EDGAR, DOLLIS HILL, LONDON

"We wanted to fight for Sol in the second half. I took him off because I felt that mentally he was too down to come back out. He did not mean to be disrespectful to the Club or the team, but he is very down. His confidence is not at the highest at the moment." ARSÉNE WENGER

"Arsenal, at times, played sublimely. And despite their faults, came close to saving the draw." THE INDEPENDENT

Birmingham City 0
ARSENAL 2   ADEBAYOR 21, HENRY 63

DATE   SATURDAY 4 FEBRUARY 2006
VENUE   ST ANDREWS
ATTENDANCE   27,075
REFEREE   MIKE RILEY

PERFORMANCE IN THE PREMIERSHIP YEARS	FORM	
St Andrews	L 0–1 (A) C Cup	
	W 7–0 (H) Prem	
PLAYED 3	L 0–1 (A) Prem	
WON 2	W 2–1 (H) C Cup	
DRAWN 0	L 0–1 (A) FA Cup	
LOST 1	L 2–3 (H) Prem	
FOR 8		
AGAINST 2		

Other Results: Saturday

Bolton Wanderers	1–1	Wigan Athletic
Everton	1–0	Manchester City
Manchester United	4–2	Fulham
Middlesbrough	0–4	Aston Villa
Newcastle United	2–0	Portsmouth
West Bromwich Alb.	2–0	Blackburn Rovers
West Ham United	2–0	Sunderland
*Chelsea	2–0	Liverpool
*Tottenham Hotspur	3–1	Charlton Athletic

Table position	P	W	D	L	F	A	Pts
5	24	12	4	8	38	19	40

*Played on Sunday

ANOTHER GAME, ANOTHER RECORD for Thierry Henry, as the Gallic genius became the first Arsenal player to score 200 goals for the Club. Coupled with new boy Emmanuel Adebayor scoring on his debut and the first away win since Boxing Day, it was a good day all round.

The Togo international barely had time to recover from his side's African Cup of Nations campaign before being thrown into the

Togo international striker Emmanuel Adebayor made a dream debut with a 21st-minute goal at St Andrew's.

Premiership fray, but from the off he showed he can give his new club an alternative attacking dimension. Comparisons to another African star who excelled for the club – Nwankwo Kanu – were inevitable.

Adebayor, the former AS Monaco man, needed only 21 minutes to get off the mark when he nodded into the net after fellow new

"Adebayor has only been in England for three days, but he looked fresh and, so importantly, he offers us an aerial threat. We haven't had that since Alan Smith retired over ten years ago!"

LEWIS CREALY, BILLERICAY, ESSEX

"We can be proud. They showed great spirit considering we had so many players out. It was the kind of performance we needed."

ARSÈNE WENGER

"Some world-class finishing from Henry proved the difference."

THE TIMES

DID YOU KNOW?

This was Henry's 200th goal for the Gunners in his 322nd appearance.

boy Abou Diaby's cross deflected into his path off Birmingham goalkeeper Maik Taylor. It wasn't a pretty goal, but with such a poor run of form outside N5, Arsenal were grateful for anything.

Struggling Birmingham pushed Arsenal back, but the visitors broke to double their advantage shortly after the hour mark, when Cesc Fabregas played in Henry and, as ever, the net bulged, with Taylor helpless.

Recently arrived from Celtic, Chris Sutton – once a Gunners target for George Graham – showed some invention for the Blues, while ex-Arsenal winger Jermaine Pennant was keen to impress his former employers, but the game was over as a contest when Emile Heskey was sent off for a second yellow card in the 83rd minute.

MAN OF THE MATCH

THIERRY HENRY

Mins on pitch	**90**
Tackles won	**0**
Passes completed	**21 (57%)**
Shots on target	**1**
Shots off target	**0**
Goals	**1**

GAME STATISTICS

BIRMINGHAM CITY		ARSENAL
0	GOALS	2
0	1ST HALF GOALS	1
4	SHOTS ON TARGET	4
10	SHOTS OFF TARGET	3
5	BLOCKED SHOTS	1
6	CORNERS	5
18	FOULS	25
5	OFFSIDES	2
1	YELLOW CARDS	3
1	RED CARDS	0
55.1	PASSING SUCCESS	66.5
17	TACKLES	17
94.1	TACKLES SUCCESS	88.2
44.0	POSSESSION	56.0
50.0	TERRITORIAL ADVANTAGE	50.0

Abou Diaby crosses with Nicky Butt in close attendance.

ARSENAL 1 GILBERTO 90

Bolton Wanderers 1 NOLAN 12

DATE **SATURDAY 11 FEBRUARY 2006**
VENUE **HIGHBURY**
ATTENDANCE **38,193**
REFEREE **HOWARD WEBB**

FORM		
W 7–0 (H)	Prem
L 0–1 (A)	Prem
W 2–1 (H)	C Cup
L 0–1 (A)	FA Cup
L 2–3 (H)	Prem
W 2–0 (A)	Prem

BOLTON HAVE BECOME ARSENAL'S NEMESIS in recent years and could already boast two victories over the Gunners this season at their futuristic Reebok Stadium. However, Gilberto snatched an injury-time equaliser to earn Arsenal a deserved point after a spirited second-half display, volleying home just as it looked as if Sam Allardyce had masterminded a famous Highbury victory.

An unprecedented third win over Arsène Wenger's injury-hit side had been on the cards after Trotters' captain Kevin Nolan gave them the lead with a delightful goal. Only 12 minutes had been played when he showed great technique to cheekily flick the ball over a stranded Jens Lehmann and inside the far post.

In fact, Arsenal could have trailed twice inside the opening 90 seconds when Lehmann acrobatically denied Nolan and then, from the resulting corner, Bruno N'Gotty headed against the crossbar.

It was an out-of-sorts Arsenal who left the field at half-time, but the transformation was astonishing after Arsène Wenger found a few well chosen words back in the dressing room. Bolton custodian Jussi Jaaskelainen denied Robert Pires and Thierry Henry in quick succession and was tested further by Johan Djourou, Cesc Fabregas and Gilberto.

Other Results: Saturday

Aston Villa	1–2	Newcastle United
Everton	1–0	Blackburn Rovers
Fulham	6–1	West Bromwich Alb.
Middlesbrough	3–0	Chelsea
Portsmouth	1–3	Manchester United
Wigan Athletic	0–1	Liverpool
*Manchester City	3–2	Charlton Athletic
*Sunderland	1–1	Tottenham Hotspur
†West Ham United	3–0	Birmingham City

Table position	P	W	D	L	F	A	Pts
5	25	12	5	8	39	20	41

*Played on Sunday   †Played on Monday

Above *Thierry Henry gets airborne against the Trotters.*
Opposite *Bolton striker Kevin Davies' sliding challenge fails to stop José Antonio Reyes from keeping possession.*

DID YOU KNOW?

Jens Lehmann is Arsenal's only ever-present in the Premiership.

MAN OF THE MATCH

ABOU DIABY	
Mins on pitch	**45**
Tackles won	**0**
Passes completed	**23 (77%)**
Shots on target	**0**
Shots off target	**1**

Dennis Bergkamp was also called up from the bench and with two minutes of time added on, and Arsenal heading for a second successive home defeat, Fabregas crossed from the right and Gilberto steered the ball home to break Bolton's resistance.

FINAL THOUGHTS

"Bolton seem to know how to play against us, but, credit to our lads, they fought for every ball after the break and matched Bolton physically. We left it late, but we fully deserved that. If only Thierry had scored at the end too..." NILS LINGAARD, PORTISHEAD, AVON

"It was one-way traffic – we should have won this game comfortably." ARSÈNE WENGER

"It would take a rabid Lancastrian to argue that Arsenal were less than full value for a point." SUNDAY TELEGRAPH

GAME STATISTICS

ARSENAL		BOLTON WANDERERS
1	GOALS	1
0	1ST HALF GOALS	1
8	SHOTS ON TARGET	3
8	SHOTS OFF TARGET	2
7	BLOCKED SHOTS	1
8	CORNERS	6
15	FOULS	13
2	OFFSIDES	6
2	YELLOW CARDS	1
0	RED CARDS	0
75.2	PASSING SUCCESS	59.0
29	TACKLES	44
72.4	TACKLES SUCCESS	68.2
63.4	POSSESSION	36.6
54.7	TERRITORIAL ADVANTAGE	45.3

Liverpool 1 LUIS GARCIA 87
ARSENAL 0

DATE TUESDAY 14 FEBRUARY 2006
VENUE ANFIELD
ATTENDANCE 44,065
REFEREE GRAHAM POLL

PERFORMANCE IN THE PREMIERSHIP YEARS	
Anfield	
PLAYED	13
WON	3
DRAWN	3
LOST	7
FOR	10
AGAINST	24

FORM		
L	0–1 (A)	Prem
W	2–1 (H)	C Cup
L	0–1 (A)	FA Cup
L	2–3 (H)	Prem
W	2–0 (A)	Prem
D	1–1 (H)	Prem

IT WAS VALENTINE'S DAY and Luis Garcia broke Arsenal hearts with a late winner. Jens Lehmann had repelled everything Liverpool had thrown at him – including a first-half penalty from Steven Gerrard – but in the 87th minute his resistance was finally broken.

His Germany team-mate Didi Hamann unleashed a speculative drive, which skidded across the greasy Anfield surface. Lehmann palmed it out and the Spain international reacted first to drill the ball back into the far corner.

Arsenal may have showed little ambition, but it was harsh on Lehmann who had been magnificent, giving the watching crowd and those viewing at home a masterclass in the art of goalkeeping. He showed his athleticism to beat out a looping header from his own defender, Philippe Senderos, and then

Above, top Mathieu Flamini gets the better of Steven Gerrard.
Above Emmanuel Adebayor attempts to round Jerzy Dudek.
Opposite Jens Lehmann saves Steven Gerrard's penalty.

Other Result: Wednesday							
Blackburn Rovers 2–0 Sunderland							

Table position	P	W	D	L	F	A	Pts
5	26	12	5	9	39	21	41

FINAL THOUGHTS

"Jens Lehmann has been one of our players of the season and tonight he showed why. He was so unlucky, but the team kept losing the ball and when that happens it gets dangerous. Our passing was poor too... I expected more from some of the players." STEVE GOODWIN, WOKING, SURREY

"We conceded a goal at a time where we could not respond and we lost three points. That hurt us very much. We had the ball, we had possession. It was a throw-in for us." ARSÈNE WENGER

"Garcia arrival undoes Lehmann's heroics – and Arsenal's hopes."
THE GUARDIAN

GAME STATISTICS

LIVERPOOL		ARSENAL
1	GOALS	0
0	1ST HALF GOALS	0
9	SHOTS ON TARGET	2
13	SHOTS OFF TARGET	4
2	BLOCKED SHOTS	0
13	CORNERS	1
11	FOULS	16
1	OFFSIDES	6
0	YELLOW CARDS	1
0	RED CARDS	0
70.2	PASSING SUCCESS	75.4
48	TACKLES	39
62.5	TACKLES SUCCESS	61.5
54.3	POSSESSION	45.7
52.8	TERRITORIAL ADVANTAGE	47.2

stretched to save Gerrard's penalty, given when Fernando Morientes went down under minimal contact from Emmanuel Eboue.

The Gunners were strangely subdued in attack, with Thierry Henry and Emmanuel Adebayor offering little, but, even so, Adebayor was denied the chance to give the visitors the lead when he was wrongly waved offside after rounding Jerzy Dudek in the Liverpool goal.

Liverpool dominated huge swathes of this game and, urged on by a lively Kop, searched for the winner. Harry Kewell's spectacular overhead kick nearly broke the deadlock, while Lehmann saved well from returning Reds hero Robbie Fowler.

The Arsenal fans constantly reminded their hosts of Michael Thomas' late goal back in May 1989, which secured Arsenal's first title in 18 years, but this time Arsenal were on the receiving end of a last-gasp strike when Hamann's shot created the chance for Garcia, who gratefully took it.

DID YOU KNOW?

This was Arsenal's seventh away defeat of the season.

MAN OF THE MATCH

JENS LEHMANN

Mins on pitch	90
Saves	9
Catches	1
Passes completed	4 (44%)
Successful clearances	1

Blackburn Rovers 1   PEDERSEN 18
ARSENAL 0

DATE   SATURDAY 25 FEBRUARY 2006
VENUE   EWOOD PARK
ATTENDANCE   22,504
REFEREE   URIAH RENNIE

AFTER THE GLORY OF MADRID, Ewood Park would prove a match too far as an improving Blackburn side inflicted Arsenal's eighth away defeat of the Premiership season. However, although the Gunners had been accused of giving up the fight in previous away fixtures, that was not the case on a cold afternoon in Lancashire.

They went behind to an 18th-minute Morten Pedersen goal, but, on another day, would certainly have earned a point and maybe all three. On this particular afternoon, though, Lehmann was beaten after Craig Bellamy bamboozled Philippe Senderos with some magnificent footwork and a burst of pace, hit the byline and sent a super cross into the path of Pedersen, who netted from close range.

The visitors were denied a penalty after Michael Gray appeared to trip Cesc Fabregas in the area, but referee Uriah Rennie waved play on. Robert Pires then found himself clean through but, with only goalkeeper Brad Friedel to beat, he failed to pull the trigger and the chance was lost.

Next, Swiss defender Senderos steamed forward and met Fabregas' perfect cross, only for his header to fly inches over the Rovers crossbar. Arsenal could not find the goal their attacking play deserved and Blackburn seemed more than happy to sit on what they had.

Italian teenager Arturo Lupoli was given eight minutes to make himself a hero, but he failed to make an impact in his short time on the field and Rovers held on comfortably in the final stages.

PERFORMANCE IN THE PREMIERSHIP YEARS		FORM	
Ewood Park		L 0–1 (A) FA Cup	
PLAYED	11	L 2–3 (H) Prem	
WON	6	W 2–0 (A) Prem	
DRAWN	2	D 1–1 (H) Prem	
LOST	3	L 0–1 (A) Prem	
FOR	17	W 1–0 (A) CL	
AGAINST	12		

Other Results: Saturday	
Birmingham City 1–0 Sunderland	
Charlton Athletic 0–0 Aston Villa	
Chelsea 2–0 Portsmouth	
Newcastle United 2–0 Everton	
*Bolton Wanderers 2–1 Fulham	
*Liverpool 1–0 Manchester City	
*West Bromwich Alb. 0–2 Middlesbrough	

Table position	P	W	D	L	F	A	Pts
6	27	12	5	10	39	22	41

*Played on Sunday

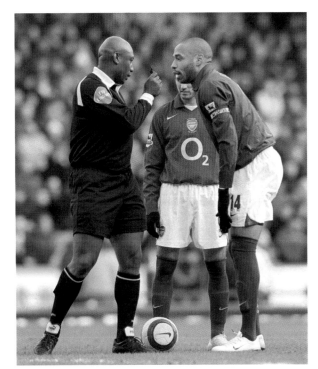

Above Referee Uriah Rennie has a few words to say to a disbelieving Thierry Henry.
Opposite Cesc Fabregas holds off Rovers' Ryan Nelson.

GAME STATISTICS

BLACKBURN ROVERS		ARSENAL
1	GOALS	0
1	1ST HALF GOALS	0
2	SHOTS ON TARGET	3
5	SHOTS OFF TARGET	5
2	BLOCKED SHOTS	3
3	CORNERS	5
24	FOULS	12
10	OFFSIDES	5
3	YELLOW CARDS	2
0	RED CARDS	0
62.5	PASSING SUCCESS	74.0
37	TACKLES	24
78.4	TACKLES SUCCESS	79.2
39.9	POSSESSION	60.1
47.9	TERRITORIAL ADVANTAGE	52.1

MAN OF THE MATCH

FRANCESC FABREGAS

Mins on pitch	90
Tackles won	5
Passes completed	59 (77%)
Shots on target	1
Shots off target	0

FINAL THOUGHTS

"When will our luck change away from home? I really thought the Madrid result would push us on in the Premiership, but it was more of the same. We were unlucky, but the bottom line is that was our eighth defeat away in the league."
ELIZABETH CHANNING, AMERSHAM, BUCKS

"In the second half we went up a gear. I am sad for the players, because they gave everything and did not deserve to lose. We were really unlucky, because we were on top."
ARSÈNE WENGER

"Wenger's Madrid hangover." MAIL ON SUNDAY

DID YOU KNOW?

This was Arturo Lupoli's Premiership debut in front of the lowest attendance at an Arsenal match this season.

Fulham 0
ARSENAL 4

HENRY 31, 77, ADEBAYOR 35, FABREGAS 86

DATE   SATURDAY 4 MARCH 2006
VENUE   CRAVEN COTTAGE
ATTENDANCE 22,397
REFEREE   ROB STYLES

PERFORMANCE IN THE PREMIERSHIP YEARS		FORM	
Craven Cottage		L 2–3 (H) Prem	
PLAYED	4	W 2–0 (A) Prem	
WON	4	D 1–1 (H) Prem	
DRAWN	0	L 0–1 (A) Prem	
LOST	0	W 1–0 (A) CL	
FOR	8	L 0–1 (A) Prem	
AGAINST	1		

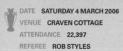

ARSENAL WARMED UP for their crunch Champions League clash against Real Madrid with an impressive destruction of Fulham on the banks of the Thames. However, the Gunners missed a host of chances before, on 31 minutes, Thierry Henry set them on the way when he picked up Abou Diaby's pass and finished with a powerful shot at the near post.

From that moment Arsenal took complete control of the match and added a second just four minutes later when Freddie Ljungberg played a perfect ball through to Emmanuel Adebayor, who slipped it past Warner.

Fulham lost their composure and, as the teams went to the changing rooms at half-time, Cottagers team-mates Zat Knight and Moritz Volz did some pushing and shoving, but Henry stepped in as the surprise peacemaker. It was the nearest they got to the magical Frenchman all afternoon.

Arsenal continued to provide an attacking masterclass after the break and Henry netted his second and Arsenal's third when Ljungberg played him in and he steered the ball across Warner and into the far corner.

Above, top *Emmanuel Adebayor celebrates his goal at Craven Cottage.*
Above *Gilberto and former Gunner Luis Boa Morte stretch for the ball.*

Other Results: Saturday	
Aston Villa	1–0 Portsmouth
Liverpool	0–0 Charlton Athletic
Middlesbrough	1–0 Birmingham City
Newcastle United	3–1 Bolton Wanderers
West Bromwich Alb.	1–2 Chelsea
West Ham United	2–2 Everton
*Manchester City	2–1 Sunderland
*Tottenham Hotspur	3–2 Blackburn Rovers
†Wigan Athletic	1–2 Manchester United

Table position	P	W	D	L	F	A	Pts
5	28	13	5	10	43	22	44

* Played on Sunday   †Played on Monday

FINAL THOUGHTS

"This was superb and as good as anything we've shown in the past couple of years... pace, power and lethal up front. I honestly feel we are back to our very best."
GRAHAM CREAGH, PALMERS GREEN, LONDON

"I feel the team is developing well and we will gain some confidence, but we need to be consistent. We have shown a lot of mental strength recently and that is very encouraging. Thierry was immense, but I think the whole team played very well."
ARSÈNE WENGER

"Henry sparkles in preparation for Real." THE OBSERVER

Fulham had been in sparkling form all season at their Craven Cottage home and had thrashed West Bromwich Albion 6–1 in their previous home game, but they were no match for Arsenal, who finished them off with an easy fourth goal four minutes from the end. Mathieu Flamini crossed and Cesc Fabregas produced a simple finish to sweep the ball past Warner and seal the Gunners' best away win of the season.

GAME STATISTICS

FULHAM		ARSENAL
0	GOALS	4
0	1ST HALF GOALS	2
3	SHOTS ON TARGET	10
4	SHOTS OFF TARGET	10
2	BLOCKED SHOTS	3
0	CORNERS	7
12	FOULS	14
4	OFFSIDES	5
0	YELLOW CARDS	1
0	RED CARDS	0
64.5	PASSING SUCCESS	77.3
34	TACKLES	34
76.5	TACKLES SUCCESS	76.5
39.6	POSSESSION	60.4
52.3	TERRITORIAL ADVANTAGE	47.7

DID YOU KNOW?

Arsenal have won 28 out of 39 meetings with Fulham in all competitions.

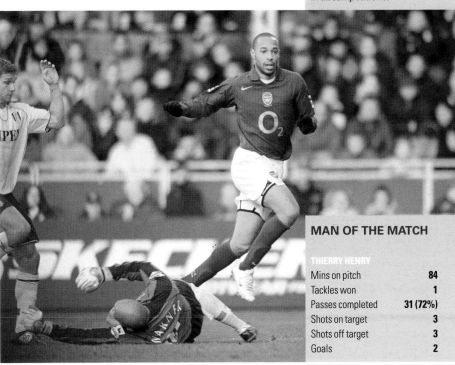

MAN OF THE MATCH

THIERRY HENRY

Mins on pitch	84
Tackles won	1
Passes completed	31 (72%)
Shots on target	3
Shots off target	3
Goals	2

ARSENAL 2 HENRY 21, 84

Liverpool 1 LUIS GARCIA 75

DATE SUNDAY 12 MARCH 2006
VENUE HIGHBURY
ATTENDANCE 38,221
REFEREE STEVE BENNETT

FORM		
D	1–1 (H)	Prem
L	0–1 (A)	Prem
W	1–0 (A)	CL
L	0–1 (A)	Prem
W	4–0 (A)	Prem
D	0–0 (H)	CL

A MOMENT OF MADNESS from Steven Gerrard condemned Liverpool to defeat – and gained revenge for Arsenal's Valentine's Day defeat at Anfield.

The England midfielder blindly played a backpass to his goalkeeper Jose Reina, but Thierry Henry nipped in to intercept the ball and coolly rounded the Spaniard before rolling the ball into an empty net to give Arsenal a deserved victory. It capped an awful couple of minutes for the European champions, who had seen Xabi Alonso sent off for a second bookable offence just moments earlier.

Arsenal's pursuit of fourth-placed Spurs had not let up despite Champions League distractions and they took a 21st-minute lead through Henry when he latched on to a magnificent pass from Cesc Fabregas and produced an exquisite finish to score his seventh goal against Liverpool.

In contrast, England forward Peter Crouch had missed a gilt-edged opportunity for the visitors when he headed wide from an inch-perfect Steve Finnan centre, but his side hauled themselves level with 15 minutes remaining when Steven Gerrard's powerful shot was only parried by Jens Lehmann and Luis Garcia followed up to head the ball into an unguarded net.

DID YOU KNOW?
Thierry Henry moves past Robbie Fowler into third place in the Premiership all-time scoring charts with 156 goals – only Alan Shearer and Andy Cole have scored more.

Other Results: Saturday

Birmingham City	1–1	West Bromwich Alb.
Blackburn Rovers	2–0	Aston Villa
Bolton Wanderers	4–0	West Ham United
Chelsea	2–0	Tottenham Hotspur
Everton	3–0	Fulham
Portsmouth	2–1	Manchester City
Sunderland	0–1	Wigan Athletic
*Charlton Athletic	2–1	Middlesbrough
*Manchester United	2–0	Newcastle United

Table position	P	W	D	L	F	A	Pts
5	29	14	5	10	45	23	47

Played on Sunday

MAN OF THE MATCH

THIERRY HENRY

Mins on pitch	90
Tackles won	2
Passes completed	25 (60%)
Shots on target	5
Shots off target	2
Goals	2

Liverpool looked the likelier winners at that stage, until Alonso was shown red and then Gerrard's sloppy play handed Henry his second goal of the game. It was also his 156th Premiership strike and, overtaking Reds legend Robbie Fowler, he moved into third place in the league's all-time scoring charts, with only Alan Shearer and Andy Cole ahead of him. As Arsenal finished strongly, Pires nearly added a third in the final minute, but his effort cannoned off a post.

Opposite Emmanuel Eboue is determined to keep the ball in his and Arsenal's possession and away from Sami Hyypia.
Below Robert Pires bamboozles the Liverpool backline.

FINAL THOUGHTS

"We're on a roll and deserved it today. I was surprised just how hard the lads worked after all the efforts against Madrid. Liverpool improved, but, as ever, Henry was the difference. What Gerrard was doing with that backpass I'll never know. I hope he doesn't do it in Germany in the summer!"
STEVE DAWSELL, SANDY, BEDS

"We gave a lot on Wednesday night, but I feel it was a third great performance from the team in the week. This team is slowly discovering its potential I feel, as well improving its belief and its confidence. You could see that today."
ARSÈNE WENGER

"Arsenal's season of transition has looked more like a transformation in the past week" THE GUARDIAN

ARSENAL 3
PIRES 13, ADEBAYOR 32, HLEB 49

Charlton Athletic 0

DATE SATURDAY 18 MARCH 2006
VENUE HIGHBURY
ATTENDANCE 38,223
REFEREE DERMOT GALLAGHER

FORM		
L	0–1 (A)	Prem
W	1–0 (A)	CL
L	0–1 (A)	Prem
W	4–0 (A)	Prem
D	0–0 (H)	CL
W	2–1 (H)	Prem

BERGKAMP (ADEBAYOR 68) VAN PERSIE (HLEB 68) SONG (FABREGAS 78)

LEHMANN

EBOUE   TOURE   SENDEROS   FLAMINI

HLEB   FABREGAS   GILBERTO   PIRES

HENRY   ADEBAYOR

D BENT

KISHISHEV   EUELL

THOMAS   HUGHES   ROMMEDAHL

SPECTOR   PERRY   HREIDARSSON   YOUNG

MYHRE

BARTLETT (HUGHES 45)   HOLLAND (THOMAS 65)   POWELL (YOUNG 73)

Other Results: Saturday

Birmingham City	0–2	Tottenham Hotspur
Blackburn Rovers	3–2	Middlesbrough
Bolton Wanderers	2–0	Sunderland
Everton	4–1	Aston Villa
Manchester City	0–1	Wigan Athletic
West Bromwich Alb.	1–2	Manchester United
West Ham United	2–4	Portsmouth
*Fulham	1–0	Chelsea
*Newcastle United	1–3	Liverpool

Table position	P	W	D	L	F	A	Pts
4	30	15	5	10	48	23	50

* Played on Sunday

ARSENAL SWAGGERED THEIR WAY to a crushing win at Highbury, even though Thierry Henry failed to get on the scoresheet, but he did set up the opener when he finished off a four-man move and cut the ball back for Robert Pires to slide home the opening goal after 13 minutes.

Arsenal dominated against the Addicks from start to finish, January signing Emmanuel Adebayor nodding wide after a pin-point cross from Henry before he finally scored after a Charlton defensive error. The big striker got off the mark at Highbury in the 32nd minute, when he took advantage of Hermann Hreidarsson's stumble to poke home the second.

Jens Lehmann was making his 30th appearance of the season – more than any other Gunner – but was a virtual spectator, watching his teammates rip the south Londoners apart at will with slick move after slick move.

Shortly after the interval Arsenal struck a third when Alexander Hleb volleyed in after a surging run, while Pires was only denied his

DID YOU KNOW?
Jens Lehmann made his 30th League appearance of the season.

Emmanuel Adebayor bursts through to score his first Highbury goal. The powerful Togo striker slowly endeared himself to the fans with his goals as the season wore on.

Cesc Fabregas moves menacingly forward with the ball.

GAME STATISTICS

ARSENAL		CHARLTON ATHLETIC
3	GOALS	0
2	1ST HALF GOALS	0
5	SHOTS ON TARGET	1
7	SHOTS OFF TARGET	1
5	BLOCKED SHOTS	0
8	CORNERS	1
6	FOULS	13
1	OFFSIDES	5
0	YELLOW CARDS	1
0	RED CARDS	0
82.1	PASSING SUCCESS	68.0
41	TACKLES	35
78.0	TACKLES SUCCESS	54.3
63.8	POSSESSION	36.2
59.3	TERRITORIAL ADVANTAGE	40.7

second of the game by an upright. Cesc Fabregas continued to boss the midfield and enhanced his growing reputation still further, before Alex Song replaced him for the final 12 minutes.

The victory gave Arsenal the double over Charlton after a 1–0 win at the Valley in December, courtesy of a José Antonio Reyes strike. It also kept the ever-improving Gunners within touching distance of north London rivals Spurs in the battle for that precious fourth place.

FINAL THOUGHTS

"It was too easy today... Charlton didn't make a game of it, but then they seemed shellshocked after the opening 20 minutes. Our speed in attack was outstanding – and Cesc was amazing in the middle." CHRIS BURGESS, MALAGA, SPAIN

"We dominated the game. We scored early on and sometimes it became too easy for us, but the confidence is back in the team and we have found the way we want to play the game. It is enjoyable to see how quickly the young players have improved and how strong they look. I am very, very happy for them and for the Club." ARSÈNE WENGER

"Arsenal's football flowed even if the goals did not."
DAILY TELEGRAPH

MAN OF THE MATCH

FRANCESC FABREGAS

Mins on pitch	78
Tackles won	6
Passes completed	73 (79%)
Shots on target	1
Shots off target	0

ARSENAL 5
ADEBAYOR 18, HENRY 25, 46, VAN PERSIE 72, DIABY 81

Aston Villa 0

DATE SATURDAY 1 APRIL 2006
VENUE HIGHBURY
ATTENDANCE 38,183
REFEREE MARTIN ATKINSON

FORM

L	0–1	(A)	Prem
W	4–0	(A)	Prem
D	0–0	(H)	CL
W	2–1	(H)	Prem
W	3–0	(H)	Prem
W	2–0	(H)	CL

DIABY (FABREGAS 16) **VAN PERSIE** (HENRY 64) **DJOUROU** (EBOUE 67)

LEHMANN

EBOUE **TOURE** **SENDEROS** **FLAMINI**

PIRES **FABREGAS** **GILBERTO** **REYES**

ADEBAYOR **HENRY**

MOORE **PHILLIPS**

BARRY **DAVIS** **McCANN** **HENDRIE**

BOUMA **RIDGEWELL** **HUGHES** **DE LA CRUZ**

SORENSEN

ANGEL (PHILLIPS 45) **AGBONLAHOR** (BARRY 53) **CAHILL** (DE LA CRUZ 53)

Other Results: Saturday		
Birmingham City	0–0	Chelsea
Bolton Wanderers	1–2	Manchester United
Everton	2–2	Sunderland
Fulham	1–3	Portsmouth
Newcastle United	3–1	Tottenham Hotspur
West Bromwich Alb.	0–2	Liverpool
*Manchester City	0–1	Middlesbrough
*West Ham United	0–0	Charlton Athletic

Table position	P	W	D	L	F	A	Pts
5	31	16	5	10	53	23	53

*Played on Sunday

IT MIGHT HAVE BEEN APRIL FOOLS DAY, but it was the visitors who were the fall guys as Arsenal produced a five-star display to thrash Aston Villa and stay in the hunt for a place in next season's Champions League.

Cesc Fabregas hobbled off with a foot injury after a quarter of an hour, but it didn't affect Arsenal's rhythm and they took the lead minutes later when Emmanuel Adebayor headed home his fourth Premiership goal from under the bar. Thierry Henry's sublime lob from José Antonio Reyes' superb through ball made it two six minutes later as Arsenal dominated the first half.

In fact, the Gunners' overall mastery was such that by the end of the game they had enjoyed a massive 67.5% of the possession, and Villa were further put in their place a minute after the change of ends, when Henry hit a brilliant third with a 25-yard curler past Thomas Sorensen, after he was superbly teed up by Adebayor.

The match had been designated a day to pay tribute to former great David Rocastle, who had died five years previously, and he would have approved of Henry's magical feet and finish.

DID YOU KNOW?
This was Arsenal's highest percentage of possession against any team this season.

MAN OF THE MATCH

THIERRY HENRY

Mins on pitch	64
Tackles won	5
Passes completed	34 (81%)
Shots on target	4
Shots off target	1
Goals	2

GAME STATISTICS

ARSENAL		ASTON VILLA
5	GOALS	0
2	1ST HALF GOALS	0
14	SHOTS ON TARGET	5
4	SHOTS OFF TARGET	5
4	BLOCKED SHOTS	1
8	CORNERS	8
9	FOULS	11
0	OFFSIDES	3
0	YELLOW CARDS	1
0	RED CARDS	0
87.9	PASSING SUCCESS	73.5
26	TACKLES	40
80.8	TACKLES SUCCESS	65
67.5	POSSESSION	32.5
43	TERRITORIAL ADVANTAGE	57

Above The popular Abou Diaby scores his first goal in redcurrant.
Opposite Robin van Persie shows lightning feet to score a magnificent fourth.

With one eye on the following Wednesday's Champions League trip to Juventus, Henry made way for Robin van Persie just after the hour mark – and the Dutchman soon made his mark when he showed brilliant skills to bamboozle the Villa defence and fire home from an acute angle. With nine minutes left, Abou Diaby – a sub for Fabregas – rounded things off with his first goal for the club, leaving David O'Leary's Villa well and truly deflated.

FINAL THOUGHTS

"Arsenal were as brilliant as Villa were awful. Rocky will hopefully have been looking down and be proud of such a great performance on such a special day for his family. Special mention to Emmanuel Eboue, who didn't stop working for the 67 minutes he was on the pitch – he's been a revelation." JEM MAIDMENT, WEST KENSINGTON, LONDON

"Scoring the third goal so early in the second half allowed us to control the game and it was a very positive performance. The team is continuing to develop well." ARSÈNE WENGER

"Highbury revels in a perfect day." DAILY TELEGRAPH

Manchester United 2

ROONEY 54,
PARK 78

ARSENAL 0

DATE **SUNDAY 9 APRIL 2006**

VENUE **OLD TRAFFORD**

ATTENDANCE **70,908**

REFEREE **GRAHAM POLL**

PERFORMANCE IN THE PREMIERSHIP YEARS	FORM
Old Trafford	D 0–0 (H) CL
	W 2–1 (H) Prem
PLAYED 15	W 3–0 (H) Prem
WON 3	W 2–0 (H) CL
DRAWN 4	W 5–0 (H) Prem
LOST 8	D 0–0 (A) CL
FOR 7	
AGAINST 19	

WAYNE ROONEY once again proved Arsenal's nemesis with a match-winning display that brought the Gunners down to earth with a bump after the highs of Turin. The defeat at Old Trafford also meant the Gunners had now lost 11 games this season, as many as they lost in the previous three campaigns put together.

DID YOU KNOW?

This was the 11th League game of the season Arsenal had lost – the same as the last three seasons combined.

Nonetheless, a new record Premiership crowd of more than 70,000 saw Arsenal – without Thierry Henry, who was rested on the bench – make the early running and Robin van Persie produce the first shot of note, although it was saved well by Edwin van der Sar.

Jens Lehmann then dealt with Rooney's low drive and was alert to deny the England striker again from an acute angle. Lehmann then punched Cristiano Ronaldo's free-kick away to safety, but United were denied the opener just before the break when Rooney's powerful shot struck Kolo Toure's arm and deflected on to the post.

Referee Graham Poll failed to spot Toure's illegal intervention and the Arsenal man was lucky to stay on the pitch, but Rooney, in magnificent form, did finally break the deadlock nine minutes after

Other Results: Saturday	
Charlton Athletic 0–0	Everton
Portsmouth 2–2	Blackburn Rovers
Tottenham Hotspur 2–1	Manchester City
Wigan Athletic 1–1	Birmingham City
*Aston Villa 0–0	West Bromwich Alb.
*Chelsea 4–1	West Ham United
*Liverpool 1–0	Bolton Wanderers
*Middlesbrough 1–2	Newcastle United

Table position	P	W	D	L	F	A	Pts
6	32	16	5	11	53	25	53

Played on Sunday

Above *Robin van Persie shows fine balance as he probes the United defence.*
Opposite *Emmanuel Adebayor under pressure from United defender Mikael Silvestre.*

half-time, when he brilliantly controlled Mikael Silvestre's cross and crashed the ball past Lehmann for his fourth goal against the Gunners.

Arsenal went in search of an equaliser, with Adebayor shooting narrowly over and van Persie failing to convert Emmanuel Eboue's cross, but Rooney helped finish the game off when he proved too strong for Philippe Senderos and delivered a simple chance to Ji-Sung Park, who tapped home the second.

FINAL THOUGHTS

"United didn't play midweek and Wenger was right that they were physically better for it. Arsenal could have taken an early lead, but in the second half I felt a few of the players looked tired. Rooney, however, was magnificent."

GREG SHEWARD, TOWCESTER, NORTHANTS

"We had chances early in the first half and after that I believe United were sharper than us physically."

ARSÈNE WENGER

"Perhaps yesterday was a result Wenger was willing to sacrifice for longer-term gains." DAILY MIRROR

GAME STATISTICS

MANCHESTER UNITED		ARSENAL
2	GOALS	0
0	1ST HALF GOALS	0
8	SHOTS ON TARGET	3
6	SHOTS OFF TARGET	7
2	BLOCKED SHOTS	0
5	CORNERS	3
17	FOULS	16
3	OFFSIDES	1
3	YELLOW CARDS	1
0	RED CARDS	0
75.2	PASSING SUCCESS	80.8
48	TACKLES	40
75.0	TACKLES SUCCESS	77.5
47.1	POSSESSION	52.9
52.2	TERRITORIAL ADVANTAGE	47.8

MAN OF THE MATCH

EMMANUEL EBOUE

Mins on pitch	90
Tackles won	2
Tackle success	67%
Passes completed	49 (85%)
Clearances	2

Portsmouth 1 LUA LUA 66

ARSENAL 1 HENRY 37

DATE WEDNESDAY 12 APRIL 2006
VENUE FRATTON PARK
ATTENDANCE 20,230
REFEREE URIAH RENNIE

PERFORMANCE IN THE PREMIERSHIP YEARS			FORM
Fratton Park			W 2–1 (H) Prem
PLAYED		3	W 3–0 (H) Prem
WON		2	W 2–0 (H) CL
DRAWN		1	W 5–0 (H) Prem
LOST		0	D 0–0 (A) CL
FOR		7	L 2–0 (A) Prem
AGAINST		2	

THE GUNNERS welcomed back Sol Campbell, while Alex Song made his first Premiership start in the centre of midfield, but Arsenal were dealt a huge blow in their bid for Champions League football next season when Lua Lua struck a second-half leveller for in-form Pompey.

Not so long ago, Fratton Park had been the scene when the entire home crowd stood as one to chant Thierry Henry's name… and he had more reason to enjoy his return to the South Coast when he broke the deadlock on 37 minutes. The France striker shoved former Fulham midfielder Sean Davis off the ball and exchanged passes with Emmanuel Adebayor before firing past Dean Kiely.

Adebayor then missed the first of two gilt-edged opportunities to add a second for the Gunners. The Togo international was brilliantly set up by Henry and José Antonio Reyes, but with the goal at his mercy he scooped the ball over the bar.

DID YOU KNOW?
Thierry Henry takes the lead in the race for the Golden Boot ahead of Ruud van Nistelrooy.

Above *On one of his favourite grounds outside Highbury, Thierry Henry put in another great performance, scoring once and almost setting up Adebayor for another.*
Opposite *Johan Djourou finds his path blocked by Dejan Stefanovic.*

Table position	P	W	D	L	F	A	Pts
5	33	16	6	11	54	26	54

MAN OF THE MATCH

KOLO TOURE

Mins on pitch	90
Tackles won	3
Tackle success	100%
Passes completed	35 (83%)
Clearances	22

GAME STATISTICS

PORTSMOUTH		ARSENAL
1	GOALS	1
0	1ST HALF GOALS	1
3	SHOTS ON TARGET	2
6	SHOTS OFF TARGET	9
1	BLOCKED SHOTS	0
3	CORNERS	10
11	FOULS	9
4	OFFSIDES	0
1	YELLOW CARDS	1
0	RED CARDS	0
59.5	PASSING SUCCESS	74.8
43	TACKLES	37
72.1	TACKLES SUCCESS	62.2
39.4	POSSESSION	60.6
54.6	TERRITORIAL ADVANTAGE	45.4

Shortly after the break Adebayor then came up with a miss to rival his first one, when he headed a Reyes cross well wide while completely unmarked. And those misses proved costly when the resurgent home side, stuck in another relegation battle, won a free-kick when Campbell fouled Lua Lua on the right.

Argentinian Andres D'Alessandro swung over the free-kick and the ex-Newcastle United striker leapt in front of Abou Diaby to divert a header into the far corner. Arsenal could have won it in the final minute, when Johan Djourou found space in the box, but with only Kiely to beat he headed wide of the far post.

ARSENAL 3
HLEB 44, PIRES 76, BERGKAMP 89

West Bromich Albion 1
QUASHIE 72

DATE **SATURDAY 15 APRIL 2006**
VENUE **HIGHBURY**
ATTENDANCE **38,167**
REFEREE **MIKE DEAN**

FORM	
W 3–0 (H)	Prem
W 2–0 (H)	CL
W 5–0 (H)	Prem
D 0–0 (A)	CL
L 2–0 (A)	Prem
D 1–1 (A)	Prem

IT WAS DENNIS BERGKAMP DAY at Highbury and the Dutch maestro came off the bench to provide a masterclass in forward play, scoring one and creating another in a brilliant late cameo.

Thousands of fans wore the famous orange of the Netherlands in honour of the Gunners legend, who leaves Highbury this summer after 11 seasons, but while their hero was left on the bench, they watched as Thierry Henry missed Arsenal's best chance of the first half when he pushed his shot wide of the post when clean through on goal.

Above *Robert Pires keeps his composure in a crowded area to tap home and restore Arsenal's lead.*
Opposite *The great Dennis Bergkamp scored a stunner on a special day for the Dutchman.*

Relegation-haunted West Brom looked to be heading into the break level, until Alexander Hleb powered Arsenal ahead just before the interval. The Belarus international charged into the box, exchanged a neat one-two with Henry and blasted a vicious left-foot strike into the roof of the net.

Bergkamp's introduction midway through the second half, at the expense of fellow Dutchman Robin van Persie, brought a huge roar from the crowd, but they were soon deflated when Nigel Quashie took advantage of Emmanuel Eboue's slip to drill home.

Bergkamp, however, was in superb form and immediately linked up with Frenchman Robert Pires who poked home past two defenders. And then came the coup de grace.

ADEBAYOR (HENRY 62) **BERGKAMP** (VAN PERSIE 71) **PIRES** (HLEB 71)

LEHMANN

EBOUE **TOURE** **SENDEROS** **FLAMINI**

HLEB **GILBERTO** **DIABY** **REYES**

HENRY **VAN PERSIE**

KANU **KAMARA**

GERA **QUASHIE** **WALLWORK** **GREENING**

ROBINSON **CLEMENT** **DAVIES** **ALBRECHTSEN**

KUSZCZAK

CAMPBELL (KANU 59) **INAMOTO** (GERA 63) **CARTER** (WALLWORK 80)

Other Results: Saturday	
Bolton Wanderers 0–2	Chelsea
Everton 0–1	Tottenham Hotspur
Fulham 2–1	Charlton Athletic
Newcastle United 3–1	Wigan Athletic
Portsmouth 1–0	Middlesbrough
West Ham United 1–0	Manchester City
*Aston Villa 3–1	Birmingham City
*Blackburn Rovers 0–1	Liverpool

Table position	P	W	D	L	F	A	Pts
5	34	17	6	11	57	27	57

* Played on Sunday

FINAL THOUGHTS

"I was here when Bergkamp scored his first goals for the Club against Southampton back in 1995. I can't believe he has been here for 11 years – the time has flown by. He has been outstanding and was the catalyst for the Club becoming a European superpower. For me, he is the greatest player we've ever had. He is pure class and will always be remembered as a legend along with James, George, Adams and Henry." TIM DOBSON, BEDFORD, BEDS

"He never loses the class and after ten fantastic years he proves that he can still play. It would have been sad not to have brought him on and I felt we were looking for his quality to create the opportunities we needed at the end. We showed a great reaction at 1–1 and I'm pleased with the chances we made." ARSÈNE WENGER

"Juicy finish to Orange Day." SUNDAY TELEGRAPH

GAME STATISTICS

ARSENAL		WEST BROMWICH ALBION
3	GOALS	1
1	1ST HALF GOALS	0
8	SHOTS ON TARGET	1
5	SHOTS OFF TARGET	8
4	BLOCKED SHOTS	1
5	CORNERS	1
10	FOULS	7
7	OFFSIDES	6
0	YELLOW CARDS	1
0	RED CARDS	0
76.0	PASSING SUCCESS	62.7
18	TACKLES	43
66.7	TACKLES SUCCESS	79.1
61.2	POSSESSION	38.8
48.6	TERRITORIAL ADVANTAGE	51.4

Bergkamp gained possession 30 yards out, adjusted his feet and sent a trademark 25-yard curler into the far corner to seal the win on a special day for the Bergkamp family, watching in an executive box behind the Clock End goal. As one banner in the North Bank read: "Bergkamp doesn't fly – he walks on water."

MAN OF THE MATCH

DENNIS BERGKAMP

Mins on pitch	18
Tackles won	0
Passes completed	8 (89%)
Shots on target	2
Shots off target	0
Goals	1

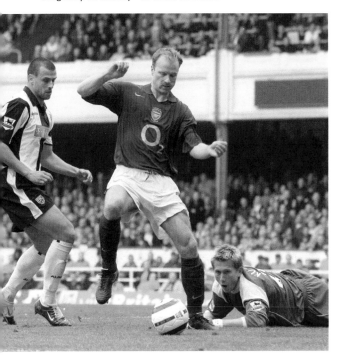

DID YOU KNOW?

This game saw Bergkamp's 120th goal and Jens Lehmann's 100th League appearance.

ARSENAL 1 HENRY 84

Tottenham Hotspur 1 KEANE 66

DATE SATURDAY 22 APRIL 2006
VENUE HIGHBURY
ATTENDANCE 38,326
REFEREE STEVE BENNETT

FORM

W 5–0	(H)	Prem
D 0–0	(A)	CL
L 2–0	(A)	Prem
D 1–1	(A)	Prem
W 3–1	(H)	Prem
W 1–0	(H)	CL

EBOUE (SENDEROS 54)   DIABY (FABREGAS 62)   HENRY (VAN PERSIE 62)

LEHMANN

DJOUROU   TOURE   SENDEROS   FLAMINI

PIRES   GILBERTO   DIABY   REYES

VAN PERSIE   ADEBAYOR

KEANE   DEFOE

TAINIO   DAVIDS   CARRICK   LENNON

LEE   GARDNER   DAWSON   STALTERI

ROBINSON

MURPHY (LENNON 76)

Other Results: Saturday

Bolton Wanderers	4–1	Charlton Athletic
Everton	0–0	Birmingham City
Newcastle United	3–0	West Bromwich Alb.
Portsmouth	2–1	Sunderland
*Fulham	1–0	Wigan Athletic

Table position	P	W	D	L	F	A	Pts
5	35	17	7	11	58	28	58

* Played on Monday

ARSENAL'S HOPES OF QUALIFYING for the Champions League were at stake when they faced arch rivals Tottenham in this end-of-season meeting – and Thierry Henry kept those hopes alive with a late equaliser.

The French star came off the bench to brilliantly beat Paul Robinson just six minutes from the end of a pulsating battle, but until then Spurs had looked set for their first Premiership win at Highbury since May 1993 and, despite only drawing, they left as favourites to finish fourth and book their place in the Champions League for the first time.

Above *Spurs' England goalkeeper Paul Robinson keeps the hold of the ball despite Emmanuel Adebayor's considerable presence.*
Opposite *Thierry Henry steers the ball into the net for a vital equaliser.*

Tottenham were given a boost when Arsène Wenger opted to start with Emmanuel Adebayor and Robin van Persie in attack, leaving Henry on the bench. And Spurs dominated with Michael Carrick masterful in midfield and Aaron Lennon outstanding on the right wing. In fact, Carrick almost broke the deadlock when he danced through the Gunners' backline, but shot into the side netting with Lehmann beaten.

The misfiring Gunners were lucky to start the second half on level terms and Henry was finally thrown on after 62 minutes, provoking a huge roar of approval from the Highbury faithful. They were silenced four minutes later, though, when Robbie Keane gave Spurs the lead in controversial circumstances.

Carrick picked up the loose ball after Gilberto and Emmanuel Eboue ran into each other. Arsenal screamed for play to stop, but

FINAL THOUGHTS

"Spurs may have been the better side and dominated for most of the game, but they could still only draw. They're in the driving seat for fourth place, but we still have a chance and they will know they should have all but sealed a Champions League berth today." KEV PILLEY, NORTHANTS

"Tottenham played well, but when someone stays down you kick the ball away. I don't know why they couldn't do that."
ARSÈNE WENGER

"Wenger loses shirt gambling without Henry." THE GUARDIAN

GAME STATISTICS

ARSENAL		TOTTENHAM HOTSPUR
1	GOALS	1
0	1ST HALF GOALS	0
5	SHOTS ON TARGET	6
6	SHOTS OFF TARGET	3
7	BLOCKED SHOTS	0
5	CORNERS	4
9	FOULS	9
2	OFFSIDES	5
1	YELLOW CARDS	0
0	RED CARDS	1
74.9	PASSING SUCCESS	79.0
42	TACKLES	36
73.8	TACKLES SUCCESS	55.6
47.3	POSSESSION	52.7
57.2	TERRITORIAL ADVANTAGE	42.8

Carrick found Teemu Tainio and he crossed for Keane to convert, sparking bitter exchanges between the two benches.

However, with the game seemingly lost, Henry showed his worth once again by picking up Adebayor's cute pass and producing a deft finish. Edgar Davids was shown a second yellow card a minute later, but Spurs held on for a point, when they could have had all three...

MAN OF THE MATCH

THIERRY HENRY

Mins on pitch	28
Tackles won	0
Passes completed	6 (55%)
Shots on target	1
Shots off target	0
Goals	1

DID YOU KNOW?

Tottenham haven't beaten Arsenal this Millennium in any competition.

Sunderland 0

ARSENAL 3
COLLINS 28 (OG), FABREGAS 40, HENRY 43

DATE **MONDAY 1 MAY 2006**
VENUE **STADIUM OF LIGHT**
ATTENDANCE **44,003**
REFEREE **DERMOT GALLAGHER**

ARSENAL'S COMFORTABLE 3–0 WIN was tainted by Abou Diaby's ankle injury, ruling out the 20-year-old Frenchman for the rest of the season. Dan Smith's wild, late lunge on Diaby was quickly condemned by Arsène Wenger on a day when Thierry Henry shone again for the Gunners.

Arsenal coasted to victory with three goals inside the opening 43 minutes against a dispirited Sunderland side already condemned to Championship football next season.

A bumper crowd of 44,000 packed the Stadium of Light to greet former Black Cats and Arsenal striker Niall Quinn, who was heading a consortium keen to take over the beleaguered club, but any optimism the Mackems may have had soon disappeared as the Londoners' clear superiority shone from the first whistle.

Three goals in 14 minutes put paid to the hosts. Arsenal went ahead on 28 minutes when Danny Collins deflected past his own keeper from a deadly Henry free-kick. The second goal was more of Arsenal's design and Henry was again the instigator. His perfect pass to Cesc Fabregas was arrogantly dinked over Sunderland's Kelvin Davis to double Arsenal's lead.

PERFORMANCE IN THE PREMIERSHIP YEARS		FORM	
Stadium of Light		L 2–0 (A) Prem	
		D 1–1 (A) Prem	
PLAYED	7	W 3–1 (H) Prem	
WON	3	W 1–0 (H) CL	
DRAWN	2	D 1–1 (H) Prem	
LOST	2	D 0–0 (A) CL	
FOR	10		
AGAINST	3		

LE TALLEC (STEAD 32) **SMITH** (MURPHY 62) **LEADBITTER** (MILLER 81)

DAVIS

NOSWORTHY **BREEN** **COLLINS** **McCARTNEY**

STEAD **WHITEHEAD** **MILLER** **MURPHY**

BROWN **KYLE**

ADEBAYOR **HENRY**

PIRES **SONG** **DIABY** **FABREGAS**

CLICHY **CAMPBELL** **TOURE** **EBOUE**

LEHMANN

COLE (PIRES 64) **VAN PERSIE** (ADEBAYOR 64) **BERGKAMP** (HENRY 71)

Above *Sunderland's Danny Collins (left) heads the ball past his own goalkeeper to give Arsenal the lead at a packed Stadium of Light.*
Opposite, top left *Cesc Fabregas lifts the ball into the net.*

Other Results:

*Tottenham Hotspur	1–0	Bolton Wanderers
†Manchester United	0–0	Middlesbrough
†West Bromwich Alb.	0–1	West Ham United

Table position	P	W	D	L	F	A	Pts
5	36	18	7	11	61	28	61

* Played on Saturday   †Played on Monday

DID YOU KNOW?
This was Fabregas' fifth goal of the season.

MAN OF THE MATCH

THIERRY HENRY

Mins on pitch	**71**
Tackles won	**0**
Passes completed	**24 (62%)**
Shots on target	**2**
Shots off target	**0**
Goals	**1**

And two minutes before the break, Arsenal made it three when out-of-position Davis was exposed by Henry's curling effort into the bottom left-hand corner of the goal. It was Henry's 24th league goal of the season, Sunderland's 28th league defeat and the game was well and truly finished with a half left to play.

Henry left proceedings after 71 minutes to a standing ovation from the Sunderland crowd, but he was not a happy man. "Sunderland were not interested in kicking the ball. All they wanted to do was kick our players," he said.

FINAL THOUGHTS

"We always looked like we were playing within ourselves, which was perhaps not surprising given the team's busy schedule. But when Thierry Henry is on the pitch you always feel confident. He made two, scored another, and it was game over by half-time. The win was overshadowed somewhat by Abou Diaby's nasty injury near the end, but the three away points were very welcome." JOSH JAMES, ST ALBANS, HERTS

"We know that Thierry can do these things; he does it so often for us. He took his goal well and set up the other two. That's the thing about him – he can score and provide. We want to make the maximum points and see how far it takes us now." ARSÈNE WENGER

"Diaby injury mars Arsenal victory." BBC ONLINE

GAME STATISTICS

SUNDERLAND		ARSENAL
0	GOALS	3
0	1ST HALF GOALS	3
2	SHOTS ON TARGET	3
6	SHOTS OFF TARGET	4
0	BLOCKED SHOTS	1
5	CORNERS	3
18	FOULS	8
6	OFFSIDES	2
2	YELLOW CARDS	0
0	RED CARDS	0
73.2	PASSING SUCCESS	81.6
44	TACKLES	28
65.9	TACKLES SUCCESS	82.1
42.1	POSSESSION	57.9
56.2	TERRITORIAL ADVANTAGE	43.8

Manchester City 1 SOMMEIL 39

ARSENAL 3 LJUNGBERG 30, REYES 78,84

DATE THURSDAY 4 MAY 2006
VENUE CITY OF MANCHESTER STADIUM
ATTENDANCE 41,875
REFEREE GRAHAM POLL

PERFORMANCE IN THE PREMIERSHIP YEARS		FORM		
City of Manchester Stadium		D 1–1 (A)	Prem	
		W 3–1 (H)	Prem	
PLAYED	8	W 1–0 (H)	CL	
WON	7	D 1–1 (H)	Prem	
DRAWN	1	D 0–0 (A)	CL	
LOST	0	W 3–0 (A)	Prem	
FOR	16			
AGAINST	3			

CROFT (SINCLAIR 76)
FLOOD (RIERA 82)
JAMES
SOMMEIL RICHARDS DUNNE JIHAI
SINCLAIR REYNA BARTON RIERA
VASSELL SAMARAS
HENRY VAN PERSIE
HLEB SONG GILBERTO LJUNGBERG
COLE CAMPBELL TOURE EBOUE
LEHMANN
FABREGAS (SONG 58)
PIRES (HLEB 71)
REYES (VAN PERSIE 71)

Other Results:

	P	W	D	L	F	A	Pts
*Bolton Wanderers 1–1 Middlesbrough							
†Sunderland 2–1 Fulham							

Table position	P	W	D	L	F	A	Pts
5	37	19	7	11	64	29	64

*Played on Wednesday †Played on Thursday

JOSÉ ANTONIO REYES came off the bench to fire two late goals at the City of Manchester Stadium and kept Arsenal's hopes of finishing in fourth place alive.

It was a good night's work all round. Arsenal celebrated their second away win in four days, England left-back Ashley Cole came through a full 90 minutes for the first time since October, and, again, Thierry Henry was in majestic form – and had a hand in the opening goal after half an hour.

DID YOU KNOW?
Manchester City haven't beaten the Gunners in 19 attempts.

After a strong surge the Frenchman held off three City defenders and slipped the ball through to Fredrik Ljungberg, who ignored the attentions of Micah Richards to finish expertly into the far corner. It was, incredibly, the Super Swede's first Premiership goal of the season.

However, City were anxious to avoid a club record fifth successive home loss at their magnificent stadium and levelled seven minutes before the break, when David Sommeil stabbed the ball home after Jens Lehmann fumbled Trevor Sinclair's header.

Arsenal desperately wanted to ensure they still had a chance of going into the final Highbury match against Wigan with a chance of taking fourth spot from Tottenham, and after the break they looked brighter and fresher.

Ljungberg hit the post and substitute Cesc Fabregas, celebrating his 19th birthday, was introduced, but it was Fabregas' compatriot

"I was nervous before this game, because we have had a horrendous season up north this season. I shouldn't have worried as the boys turned it on in the second half and Pires and Reyes came on to kill off City in the last 15 minutes. The win put the pressure back on Spurs who, despite being seven points clear just three days earlier, now had to win their final game to be sure of fourth." OLIVER JAMES, WATFORD, HERTS

"It was tight, but I was always confident. City gave everything and Jens Lehmann had to make two good saves at 1–1. Ashley Cole had 90 minutes of high pace and came through well."
ARSÈNE WENGER

"Reyes lights up Arsenal." DAILY TELEGRAPH

Reyes who made the biggest impact. He came on for van Persie, and started and finished a three-man move that culminated in a decisive strike past David James from Emmanuel Eboue's cut-back. He added his second when he swept home Henry's unselfish pass to seal Arsenal's sixth and final away win of the Premiership season.

Above Thierry Henry prepares to congratulate Fredrik Ljungberg on the Swede's goal.
Opposite José Antonio Reyes hits a sweet left-foot shot to restore Arsenal's lead.
Top, right Ashley Cole made a welcome return to the starting line-up.

MAN OF THE MATCH

THIERRY HENRY

Mins on pitch	90
Tackles won	0
Passes completed	33 (70%)
Shots on target	1
Shots off target	2

GAME STATISTICS

MANCHESTER CITY		ARSENAL
1	GOALS	3
1	1ST HALF GOALS	1
6	SHOTS ON TARGET	9
5	SHOTS OFF TARGET	6
6	BLOCKED SHOTS	3
12	CORNERS	6
23	FOULS	10
6	OFFSIDES	4
3	YELLOW CARDS	0
0	RED CARDS	0
69.0	PASSING SUCCESS	80.2
33	TACKLES	26
75.8	TACKLES SUCCESS	61.5
43.4	POSSESSION	56.6
55.7	TERRITORIAL ADVANTAGE	44.3

ARSENAL 4
PIRES 8,
HENRY 35, 56, 76 (PEN)

Wigan Athletic 2
SCHARNER 10,
THOMPSON 34

DATE **SUNDAY 7 MAY 2006**
VENUE **HIGHBURY**
ATTENDANCE **38,359**
REFEREE **URIAH RENNIE**

FORM		
W 3–1	(H)	Prem
W 1–0	(H)	CL
D 1–1	(H)	Prem
D 0–0	(A)	CL
W 3–0	(A)	Prem
W 3–1	(A)	Prem

Other Results: Sunday

Aston Villa	2–1	Sunderland
Blackburn Rovers	2–0	Manchester City
Bolton Wanderers	1–0	Birmingham City
Everton	2–2	West Bromwich Alb.
Fulham	1–0	Middlesbrough
Manchester United	4–0	Charlton Athletic
Newcastle United	1–0	Chelsea
Portsmouth	1–3	Liverpool
West Ham United	2–1	Tottenham Hotspur

Table position	P	W	D	L	F	A	Pts
4	38	20	7	11	68	31	67

WHAT A WAY TO SAY GOODBYE! In a thrilling win, Thierry Henry scored a hat-trick and Arsenal leapfrogged arch rivals Spurs into fourth spot to earn a place in next season's Champions League qualifiers.

In Highbury's wonderful 93-year history, very few games can have matched this for sheer drama and emotion. The fans were in celebratory mood for the last ever competitive game at the old stadium before the summer move to Emirates Stadium, and they were on cloud nine when Robert Pires fired Arsenal ahead on eight minutes and news filtered through that Spurs were 1–0 down at West Ham.

But the game was turned on its head when, after dithering in the Arsenal defence, Paul Scharner levelled for Wigan and then the visitors took a shock lead through David Thompson's cheeky 35-yard free-kick, beating out-of-position Jens Lehmann at his near post.

Spurs had levelled at Upton Park by half-time, but so had Arsenal when Henry side-footed past Mike Pollitt. Teddy Sheringham – of all people – then had the chance to give West Ham the lead, but missed from the spot.

Back at Highbury, Henry edged Arsenal ahead on 56 minutes when he intercepted Thomspon's backpass, rounded Pollitt and tapped into the empty net. And the Frenchman, who has scored more goals than another player at Highbury in Arsenal's history, rounded off another virtuoso performance with a hat-trick.

Andreas Johansson and Fredrik Ljungberg had only just come off their respective benches when the Wigan player hauled down the Arsenal midfielder in the area. Johansson was shown a straight red and Henry further punished him with an assured finish from the spot.

A few miles away in east London, West Ham had also scored a decisive second against Spurs to win their match – and by then the Highbury farewell party was in full swing...

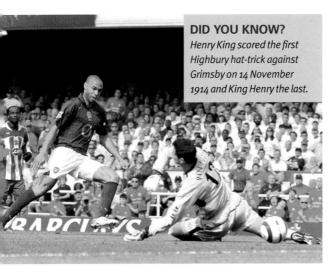

Above *Thierry Henry pulls Arsenal level before the break with an assured finish past Mike Pollitt.*
Opposite *Robert Pires fires Arsenal ahead after only eight minutes.*
Below *The post-match celebrations will live long in the memory of all those at Highbury.*

FINAL THOUGHTS

"What an incredible day! It doesn't seem real. I have been going to Highbury since 1991 and I have never heard an atmosphere like that... it was just buzzing from start to finish. I also want to say 'well done' to the Club for such a magnificent closing ceremony. It was all just perfect and done with such class... but then we wouldn't expect it any other way, would we?"
CRAIG MADLEY, BICESTER, OXON

"I felt that Wigan gave us a hard time, but we had to deal with nerves as well. I feel that we did it in a fantastic manner, because we scored 10 goals in the last three games, and all three teams gave us a very hard time. I'm very proud for my team, because they did it in an exceptional way with a lot of character."
ARSÈNE WENGER

"Henry signs off at old stadium on a hat-trick high." THE GUARDIAN

MAN OF THE MATCH

THIERRY HENRY

Mins on pitch	90
Tackles won	0
Passes completed	36 (69%)
Shots on target	3
Shots off target	0
Goals	3

GAME STATISTICS

ARSENAL		WIGAN ATHLETIC
4	GOALS	2
2	1ST HALF GOALS	2
7	SHOTS ON TARGET	3
7	SHOTS OFF TARGET	6
3	BLOCKED SHOTS	1
5	CORNERS	1
13	FOULS	17
2	OFFSIDES	2
1	YELLOW CARDS	1
0	RED CARDS	1
76.9	PASSING SUCCESS	68.3
28	TACKLES	25
82.1	TACKLES SUCCESS	68.0
60	POSSESSION	40
52.4	TERRITORIAL ADVANTAGE	47.6

Light Relief: Emmanuel Eboue is mobbed after scoring with a 30-yard drive at Sunderland's Stadium of Light in the Carling Cup.

DOMESTIC CUPS

Arsène Wenger maintained his policy of blooding rising stars in the Carling Cup and it almost paid dividends as the young guns fought their way to the semi-finals with fine 3–0 wins at Sunderland and then against runaway Championship leaders Reading, who fielded a full-strength side, at Highbury.

Doncaster, who had beaten Aston Villa and Manchester City in the previous rounds, were then beaten on penalties in Yorkshire after a battling 2–2 draw, but surprise-package Wigan proved too strong in the two-legged semi final. A 1–0 win at the JJB was followed by a narrow 1–2 reverse at Highbury, with Jason Roberts scoring in the last minute in north London to pull the tie level at 2–2 and put Wigan through on away goals.

The FA Cup holders began their defence with a 2–1 Highbury win over Cardiff in the third round, before Bolton snatched a late winner at the Reebok Stadium through Stelios Giannakopoulos in the fourth round to end the Gunners' interest in the competition.

Pre-match banter: Arsenal prepare to start the second leg of the Carling Cup semi-final against Wigan. Arsenal won 2–1 on the night but it was Wigan who went on to the final, winning on the away goals rule having won the first leg 1–0.

MATCHES

MATCHES PLAYED	7
PLAYERS USED	27

GOALS

SCORED	12 (+3 PENS)
Per game	1.71
CONCEDED	6 (+1 PEN)
Per game	0.86

ATTENDANCE

AT HOME	107,381
Average home gate	35,793

Memorable moments

- Gilberto sliding home a last-gasp equaliser away to Doncaster Rovers to send the tie to penalties
- Van Persie's stunning free kick at home against Wigan that looked like it was enough to earn a place in the Carling Cup final
- Emmanuel Eboue's 30-yard net-buster that opened the scoring against Sunderland
- Almunia's save from Paul Green that sealed plucky Doncaster's fate and won an absorbing tie
- Arturo Lupoli's stylish finish for the third goal that put the tie beyond Reading

ARSENAL 2 <small>PIRES 6, 18</small>
Cardiff City 1 <small>JEROME 86</small>

DATE SATURDAY 7 JANUARY 2006
VENUE HIGHBURY
ATTENDANCE 36,552
REFEREE MARTIN ATKINSON

FORM

L	0–2 (H)	Prem
D	2–2 (A)	C Cup
	(won 3–1 on pens)	
W	1–0 (A)	Prem
W	4–0 (H)	Prem
D	0–0 (A)	Prem
D	0–0 (H)	Prem

OWUSU-ABEYIE (REYES 45) LARSSON (VAN PERSIE 77)

ALMUNIA

LAUREN SENDEROS DJOUROU GILBERT

PIRES GILBERTO FLAMINI REYES

BERGKAMP VAN PERSIE

JEROME

ARDLEY LEDLEY COX COOPER

WHITLEY

WESTON PURSE LOOVENS BARKER

ALEXANDER

KOSKELA (LOOVENS 64) LEE (COOPER 89)

A ROBERT PIRES DOUBLE put the holders through to the next round in a rerun of the 1927 Cup final. On that occasion, the Cup left England for the only time, and the Welsh side were hoping to heap another embarrassing defeat on the Gunners, but it was not to be.

For this clash, Thierry Henry was rested, but it didn't matter as Pires scored twice in the opening 18 minutes. Just six minutes had elapsed when a flowing Arsenal move opened up the Cardiff defence and José Antonio Reyes demonstrated quick footwork to release Pires. who swept home a low shot into the corner.

This came after Cardiff's leading scorer Cameron Jerome had spurned a superb opportunity to give his side the lead, lifting the ball over the advancing Manuel Almunia – and fortunately over the bar – but the Championship side could not contain Arsène Wenger's side and they soon fell further behind.

Robin van Persie, playing against his former neighbour and Feyenoord team-mate Glenn Loovens, was pivotal in a neat passing move as he picked out Dennis Bergkamp, who squared the ball to Pires to slot home.

Robert Pires keeps his head down as he steers in Reyes' pass with a low right-foot shot.

However, without Reyes, who had come off at the break, the Gunners lost some of their attacking impetus and with four minutes left Jerome tapped in a consolation for the Bluebirds. At that point Cardiff's 6,500 travelling fans smelt a possible replay, but it was too little, too late.

DID YOU KNOW?

Arsenal haven't been put out of the FA Cup in the Third round since 1996 (Sheffield Utd).

GAME STATISTICS

ARSENAL		CARDIFF CITY
2	GOALS	1
3	SHOTS ON TARGET	3
4	SHOTS OFF TARGET	1
0	BLOCKED SHOTS	2
7	CORNERS	5
11	FOULS	10
0	OFFSIDES	6
1	YELLOW CARDS	2
0	RED CARDS	0
57%	POSSESSION	43%

Left, above José Antonio Reyes holds off the challenge of Bluebirds midfielder Jeff Whitley.
Left Lauren leaps and heads the ball clear from the challenge of Neil Ardley.

Bolton Wanderers 1 GIANNAKOPOULOS 84
ARSENAL 0

DATE   SATURDAY 28 JANUARY 2006
VENUE   REEBOK STADIUM
ATTENDANCE   13,326
REFEREE   MIKE DEAN

PERFORMANCE IN THE PREMIERSHIP YEARS	FORM	
	D 0–0 (H) Prem	
Reebok Stadium	W 2–1 (H) FA Cup	
PLAYED	8	L 0–1 (A) C Cup
WON	2	W 7–0 (H) Prem
DRAWN	3	L 0–1 (A) Prem
LOST	2	W 2–1 (H) C Cup
FOR	8	
AGAINST	9	

VAZ TE (CAMPO 54)   JANSEN (BORGETTI 73)   HUNT (GIANNAKOPOULOS 90)

JAASKELAINEN

O'BRIEN   BEN HAIM   N'GOTTY   GARDNER

NAKATA   CAMPO   NOLAN

GIANNAKOPOULOS   DAVIES   BORGETTI

VAN PERSIE

HLEB

LJUNGBERG   DIABY   FLAMINI   REYES

GILBERT   CAMPBELL   DJOUROU   SENDEROS

ALMUNIA

FA Cup Final		
Millennium Stadium		
	Liverpool 3–3 West Ham United	
	Liverpool won 3–1 on penalties	

THE TRIP TO THE REEBOK was rewarded with yet more awayday agony for the Gunners, with Stelios Giannakopoulos heading an 84th-minute winner to leave the holders reeling from a double cup shock inside five days.

The Greece international, who was fast developing a scoring touch against Arsenal, struck with a full-length diving header just as the tie looked to be heading back to north London for a replay.

This game had taken on greater significance after Wigan scraped into the Carling Cup final at Highbury in the Gunners' last game, but boss Arsène Wenger opted to rest the likes of Thierry Henry, Robert Pires, Gilberto and Dennis Bergkamp, who had played two hours of football against the Latics.

With Arsenal on the back foot, Bolton, unbeaten at the Reebok Stadium in 14 games, carved out three half-chances in the opening 20 minutes, but it wasn't all one-way traffic as the Gunners probed a Bolton defence that had only conceded seven goals at home all season.

Indeed, José Antonio Reyes had a brilliant chance to put the Londoners in front on the stroke of half-time, when Hleb teed him up, but the Spaniard took his eye off the ball and mishit his effort.

Bolton midfielder Kevin Nolan (left) pursues Alexander Hleb.

Arsenal moved up a gear in the second half with some delightful build-up play, although Trotters' sub Ricardo Vaz Te should have broken the deadlock when he dragged his shot wide.

Robin van Persie's header grazed the bar shortly afterwards, before Stelios eluded Sol Campbell to head powerfully past Almunia and end Arsenal's cup dream for another year.

FINAL THOUGHTS

"It's sad to lose, but we fought to the end. That hasn't always been the case this season, but today we had a real go at them. This is a tough place to come to, but we matched them."

JUSTIN BAILEY, BROXBOURNE, HERTS

"We should have won by three goals. The boys in the dressing room are destroyed."

ARSÈNE WENGER

"To be fair to the FA Cup holders, they did not deserve to lose."

DAILY STAR

DID YOU KNOW?

This is the first time Arsenal have failed to reach the semi-finals of the FA Cup in five years.

GAME STATISTICS

BOLTON WANDERERS		ARSENAL
1	GOALS	0
4	SHOTS ON TARGET	2
5	SHOTS OFF TARGET	4
2	BLOCKED SHOTS	5
3	CORNERS	10
11	FOULS CONCEDED	19
7	OFFSIDES	2
1	YELLOW CARDS	5
0	RED CARDS	0
47%	POSSESSION	53%

Opposite *Swiss youngster Johan Djourou heads the ball clear.*

Sunderland 0
ARSENAL 3
EBOUE 61,
VAN PERSIE 67 (PEN), 87

DATE   TUESDAY 25 OCTOBER 2005
VENUE   STADIUM OF LIGHT
ATTENDANCE   47,366
REFEREE   MATT MESSIAS

PERFORMANCE IN THE PREMIERSHIP YEARS		FORM	
Stadium of Light		D 0–0 (A) Prem	
		W 2–1 (A) CL	
PLAYED	6	W 1–0 (H) Prem	
WON	2		
DRAWN	2	L 1–2 (A) Prem	
LOST	2	W 2–0 (A) CL	
FOR	7	W 1–0 (H) Prem	
AGAINST	3		

WHAT A NIGHT AT THE STADIUM OF LIGHT! A sell-out crowd of over 47,000 witnessed the Young Guns of the future win an entertaining encounter on Wearside.

Sunderland's enterprising policy of selling tickets at a maximum of £5 – with some as cheap as £1 – gave genuine football fans the opportunity to see some of English football's rising talent, and it made for a sensational atmosphere in a ground which already enjoys a great reputation, even when half-full.

Again, Arsène Wenger used the competition to blood his talented youth and reserve players and Black Cats manager Mick McCarthy also allowed several of his promising youngsters to sample a big match atmosphere.

Fabrice Muamba was the latest Arsenal player to make his debut and he put in a mature performance, while Justin Hoyte, on-loan to Sunderland from Highbury, denied his employers the first goal of the game when he diverted wide Robin van Persie's close-range effort.

The relatively open game still didn't have a goal by the hour mark, but just a minute later it was the Londoners who took the lead when Emmanuel Eboue sent a 30-yards howitzer flying into the Sunderland net for his first Arsenal goal.

DID YOU KNOW?
Fabrice Muamba makes his first-team debut and £5-a-ticket ensures a sellout crowd.

Even many of the home fans applauded a brilliant strike – and within six minutes Arsenal were 2–0 up. Arturo Lupoli's progress was halted illegally by Dan Smith and van Persie smashed the penalty into the top corner. The ex-Feyenoord man then sealed a comprehensive win when he picked up Larsson's through ball and finished easily.

Above Robin van Persie was outstanding at the Stadium of Light. Here he troubles the Black Cats defence.
Opposite Emmanuel Eboue unleashes a stunning strike to open the scoring just after the hour mark.

FINAL THOUGHTS

"The Carling Cup is becoming must-see football for us Gooners. It was a really enjoyable game and some of those lads have got a big, big future. I thought Eboue was very impressive; he had great composure and scored a beauty. I also think it was brilliant that Sunderland charged so little, Arsenal do it, too, and more clubs should. Surely it's better to have a packed stadium than a half-full one?" STEVE DEACON, GUILDFORD, SURREY

"I was happy with the performance of the boys and their spirit on the night. I was pleased with the fact that they could cope with a big crowd and a team who are totally committed." ARSÈNE WENGER

"Wengers boys spot-on... with no trick shots." DAILY EXPRESS

GAME STATISTICS

SUNDERLAND		ARSENAL
0	GOALS	3
0	1ST HALF GOALS	0
3	SHOTS ON TARGET	7
4	SHOTS OFF TARGET	6
1	BLOCKED SHOTS	1
4	CORNERS	3
12	FOULS	15
3	OFFSIDES	4
1	YELLOW CARDS	0
0	RED CARDS	0
52	POSSESSION	48

ARSENAL 3
Reading 0

REYES 12, VAN PERSIE 42, LUPOLI 65

DATE **TUESDAY 29 NOVEMBER 2005**
VENUE **HIGHBURY**
ATTENDANCE **36,137**
REFEREE **LEE MASON**

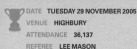

FORM

D	1–1 (A)	Prem
W	3–0 (H)	CL
W	3–1 (H)	Prem
W	3–2 (A)	Prem
W	1–0 (A)	CL
W	3–0 (H)	Prem

ARSENAL'S YOUNG GUNS – average age 19, if you take out goalkeeper Manuel Almunia – gave Highbury a glimpse of the future with an assured display that disposed of the Championship leaders.

For three of the Reading side, it was an emotional return 'home', goalkeeper Graham Stack and midfield duo James Harper and Steven Sidwell all having been products of the Arsenal youth system and crucial in their new club's rise to the summit.

Hammersmith-born right-back Kerrea Gilbert, making his first-team debut, takes a throw-in under the watchful eye of Arsène Wenger.

Yet Arsenal made short work of a Royals team who arrived in north London on the back of an impressive 23-game unbeaten run, stretching back to the opening day of the season.

The Gunners didn't look back after taking a 12th-minute lead when Spaniard José Antonio Reyes pounced on Quincy Owusu-Abeyie's pass to take the ball around Stack and slide home from a tight angle.

Reading nearly levelled, only for stand-in skipper Almunia, the veteran of the side at 28, to save Dave Kitson's effort, but the keeper was called into action moments later to deny England Under-21 striker Leroy Lita after Philippe Senderos made a hash of his clearance.

However, just as the visitors, roared on by 7,000 visiting fans, sensed an equaliser, Robin van Persie broke their hearts three minutes from the break with a devastating second. The Dutch striker pounced on Reyes' neat lay-off to hit his eighth goal in eight games with an unstoppable left-foot drive.

Arsenal sealed the victory with 25 minutes remaining, when 18-year-old Italian striker Arturo Lupoli, a replacement for van Persie, pounced on Ibrahima Sonko's poor control to race through, sidestep Stack and score.

GAME STATISTICS

ARSENAL		READING
3	GOALS	0
2	1ST HALF GOALS	0
6	SHOTS ON TARGET	6
5	SHOTS OFF TARGET	4
0	BLOCKED SHOTS	0
9	CORNERS	8
11	FOULS	4
2	OFFSIDES	3
1	YELLOW CARDS	0
0	RED CARDS	0
50.3%	POSSESSION	49.7%

FINAL THOUGHTS

"The difference was our finishing. Reading looked a very decent side, but it's all about taking your chances, isn't it? For us, I thought Quincy was outstanding. He looks better and better every time I see him." MATTHEW CULLEY, BUCKS

"José needed that goal. I called him into the team because he needed to score to find his confidence again." ARSÈNE WENGER

"The future is bright. The future is redcurrant." THE SUN

Substitute Arturo Lupoli rounds former Arsenal 'keeper Graham Stack.

DID YOU KNOW?
Arsenal have never been beaten by Reading – this was their fifth meeting.

Doncaster Rovers 2
McINDOE 4,
GREEN 104

ARSENAL 2
OWUSU-ABEYIE 63,
GILBERTO 120

ARSENAL WON 3–1 ON PENALTIES

DATE **WEDNESDAY 21 DECEMBER 2005**

VENUE **BELLEVUE STADIUM**

ATTENDANCE **10,006**

REFEREE **PHIL DOWD**

PERFORMANCE IN THE PREMIERSHIP YEARS	FORM	
Bellevue Stadium	W 3–0	(H) Prem
This was Arsenal's first visit to this ground in Carling Cup history	W 3–0	(H) C Cup
	L 0–2	(A) Prem
	D 0–0	(H) CL
	L 0–1	(A) Prem
	L 0–2	(H) Prem

GILBERTO snatched a last-gasp equaliser to save Arsenal's blushes and Manuel Almunia completed the job with a brilliant display in the penalty shoot-out to secure a place in the last four.

The struggling League One side had already claimed the scalps of Premiership sides Manchester City and Aston Villa in the previous rounds, and they lead again here after just four minutes when Michael McIndoe ran through the static Gunners' defence, skipped past Almunia and squeezed the ball home.

Arsenal had to wait until the 63rd minute for an equaliser when Quincy Owusu-Abeyie cut in from the left and let fly to beat Doncaster goalkeeper Jan Budtz via a deflection off Sean Thornton.

The game went to extra-time and Doncaster hit a second when a mix-up between Almunia and Philippe Senderos allowed Paul Green to stab the ball home.

Arsenal fans' minds now turned back 14 years to a cold day in Wrexham, when the Division Four strugglers caused the shock of the round with a 2–1 win over

> **DID YOU KNOW?**
> *This was the fourth consecutive penalty shoot-out won by the Gunners and the eighth in the history of the Club.*

the reigning Division One champions, but with Arsenal heading for an embarrassing defeat, Samba star Gilberto forced the ball home.

He then kicked off the shoot-out with a comfortable finish, but McIndoe immediately replied for Doncaster. Pascal Cygan scored, but Neil Roberts struck a post with his effort: 2–1 Arsenal.

Sebastian Larsson netted to put Arsenal in the driving seat and when Almunia stopped Paul Heffernan's effort it looked to be all over, but Alexander Hleb saw his penalty saved and it was left to the outstanding Almunia to beat out Green's strike.

FINAL THOUGHTS

"Our support was fantastic and it was great to stand on terraces again, maybe for the last time. It was a real baptism for some of the younger lads and I'm sure they'll benefit from it. Our superior fitness made a difference and, thankfully, luck was on our side at the end." MICHAEL BOWLES, NEWCASTLE-UNDER-LYME, STAFFS

"When there are 60 seconds to go and you are 2–1 down away from home, 99% of the time you're out. Doncaster have some players with a future in the Premiership." ARSÈNE WENGER

"Manuel to the rescue after Doncaster force Arsenal to work overtime." THE INDEPENDENT

GAME STATISTICS

DONCASTER ROVERS		ARSENAL
2	GOALS	2
1	1ST HALF GOALS	0
7	SHOTS ON TARGET	11
4	SHOTS OFF TARGET	10
0	BLOCKED SHOTS	2
3	CORNERS	8
22	FOULS	16
10	OFFSIDES	0
3	YELLOW CARDS	2
0	RED CARDS	0
51.0	POSSESSION	49.0

Opposite Manuel Almunia makes a superb save at the feet of Lewis Guy.
Below Gilberto Silva arrives right on time to bundle home a late equaliser for Arsenal.

Wigan Athletic 1 SCHARNER 77
ARSENAL 0

DATE TUESDAY 10 JANUARY 2006
VENUE JJB STADIUM
ATTENDANCE 12,181
REFEREE HOWARD WEBB

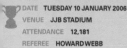

PERFORMANCE IN THE PREMIERSHIP YEARS		FORM	
JJB Stadium		D 2-2 (A) C Cup (won 3-1 on pens)	
PLAYED	10	W 1-0 (A) Prem	
WON	5	W 4-0 (H) Prem	
DRAWN	4	D 0-0 (A) Prem	
LOST	1	D 0-0 (H) Prem	
FOR	16	W 2-1 (H) FA Cup	
AGAINST	8		

WIGAN TOOK A SLIGHT ADVANTAGE into the second leg courtesy of a thumping header from debut boy Paul Scharner. The £2.5 million purchase from Brann Bergen scored the only goal of this semi-final first leg, after the JJB Stadium was plunged into darkness due to a power cut that held the game up for 14 minutes.

As in previous rounds, Arsène Wenger rested many of his experienced players and stayed loyal to the young guns who carried his side to the last four. In fact, just three players – Fredrik Ljungberg, Pascal Cygan and Gilberto – had started in Arsenal's thrilling 3–2 Premiership win over Wigan in November.

Arsenal had the first chance when Mathieu Flamini played a through ball into Ljungberg, but with a clear sight of goal he scooped his shot over the advancing Mike Pollitt and the bar. Jason Roberts then went close for the hosts with a glancing header and Graham Kavanagh's low 20-yard free-kick was superbly dealt with by Manuel Almunia.

Wigan then received a double blow when striker David Connolly limped off injured and a groin strain saw Lee McCulloch depart proceedings. The latter would be replaced by Scharner, sporting blue and white striped hair in honour of his new employers.

The JJB's lights went out nine minutes into the second half, but when they came back on the Latics stepped up a gear and won the game in the 77th minute when Scharner powered into the six-yard box to send a downward header under Almunia.

FINAL THOUGHTS

"I was extremely disappointed with the performance. I'd give us a four out of ten tonight. In fact, at times it was turgid. We needed a physical presence up front and we didn't have it. I do think the defence played very well, and Almunia was excellent, but we offered nothing up front and that isn't good enough."

MARK CURTIN, RUISLIP, MIDDX

"In the second half they were on top. We did not create enough going forward." ARSÈNE WENGER

"Austrian is bright spark for Wigan as Gunners see their Cup hopes dim." DAILY MIRROR

GAME STATISTICS

WIGAN ATHLETIC		ARSENAL
1	GOALS	0
0	1ST HALF GOALS	0
3	SHOTS ON TARGET	1
3	SHOTS OFF TARGET	2
2	BLOCKED SHOTS	1
6	CORNERS	1
11	FOULS	11
7	OFFSIDES	2
1	YELLOW CARDS	0
0	RED CARDS	0
44%	POSSESSION	56%

DID YOU KNOW?
This was Wigan's first major domestic cup semi-final... Arsenal's 36th.

Above Mathieu Flamini leaps high to head the ball clear under the challenge of Wigan's lively midfielder Jimmy Bullard.
Opposite Philippe Senderos manages to hold off Latics striker Jason Roberts.

ARSENAL 2
HENRY 65,
VAN PERSIE 108

Wigan Athletic 1
ROBERTS 120

2–2 ON AGGREGATE, WIGAN ATHLETIC WON ON AWAY GOALS RULE

JASON ROBERTS denied Arsenal their first League Cup final appearance in 13 years when he struck with just 65 seconds to go of a pulsating match at Highbury. It continued the fairytale season for newly-promoted Wigan, but for the Gunners it was a devastating goal, after they controlled much of this game and looked to have all but booked their place in Cardiff at the end of February.

With the game in its final throes, the burly striker, who impressed all night with his willingness to chase lost causes, took full advantage of a disastrous mix-up between Philippe Senderos and Sol Campbell to pounce on the loose ball and tuck his shot under Jens Lehmann.

Arsenal had been impressive up to that stage as they overturned a 1–0 deficit from the first leg to lead 2–0 – and 2–1 on aggregate. Thierry Henry had taken the tie to extra-time when he headed in the excellent Kerrea Gilbert's cross with 25 minutes remaining of the full 90. And then Robin van Persie produced another moment of magic with his trusty left boot, curling a stupendous free-kick past Mike Pollitt in the Wigan goal 18 minutes into extra-time.

DATE **TUESDAY 24 JANUARY 2006**
VENUE **HIGHBURY**
ATTENDANCE **34,692**
REFEREE **PHIL DOWD**

FORM	
D	0–0 (A) Prem
D	0–0 (H) Prem
W	2–1 (H) FA Cup
L	0–1 (A) C Cup
W	7–0 (H) Prem
L	0–1 (A) Prem

FLAMINI (DIABY 45) PIRES (HLEB 69) VAN PERSIE (HENRY 79)

ALMUNIA

GILBERT SENDEROS CAMPBELL LAUREN

HLEB GILBERTO DIABY REYES

BERGKAMP HENRY

MELLOR ROBERTS

BAINES KAVANAGH BULLARD TEALE

BAINES HENCHOZ SCHARNER CHIMBONDA

POLLITT

JOHANSSON (MELLOR 60) ZIEGLER (MAHON 63)

Carling Cup Final

Millennium Stadium

Manchester United 4–0 Wigan Athletic

Above *Stephane Henchoz can't stop Thierry Henry (partially obscured) from heading the Gunners into the lead on the night, and pulling the tie level.*
Opposite *Robin van Persie smashes a fantastic free-kick past Mike Pollitt to make it 2–0 on the night.*

Those two goals had been no more than Arsenal had deserved after Pollitt had single-handedly denied the hosts a cricket score with a brilliant display of goalkeeping. The pick of the bunch was an exceptional save from José Antonio Reyes' first-half spot-kick, the journeyman keeper flying across his goal to tip the Spaniard's effort around the post.

However, as the crowd smelt another day out in Wales, Roberts turned the tie on its head with his late moment of glory. It was so very, very close.

GAME STATISTICS

ARSENAL		WIGAN ATHLETIC
2	GOALS	1
0	1ST HALF GOALS	0
11	SHOTS ON TARGET	6
5	SHOTS OFF TARGET	6
2	BLOCKED SHOTS	2
10	CORNERS	8
21	FOULS	23
1	OFFSIDES	5
2	YELLOW CARDS	3
0	RED CARDS	0
52%	POSSESSION	48%

FINAL THOUGHTS

"I just had a feeling that there'd be a twist in the tale. We played so well, but it was always so tight and Wigan had a lot of belief. When the crowd starting doing oles when we were 2–0 up I got very worried, but we were unlucky tonight – and Wigan have been good." JOHN COLLINS, STOKE NEWINGTON, LONDON

"You cannot complain with the spirit. When you can complain is with the goal we conceded." ARSÈNE WENGER

"Highbury staged its last ever League Cup tie and it is doubtful the old stadium has ever witnessed such drama."

DAILY EXPRESS

PRE-SEASON

FAREWELL TO A HIGHBURY HERO

Arsenal entered their final season at Highbury without inspirational skipper Patrick Vieira. The France midfielder finally agreed a five-year deal with Serie A giants Juventus, after successive summers of speculation about a move.

"When you have had nine years at a club, like I have had, it is a difficult decision," explained an emotional Vieira, as he said his goodbyes at the London Colney training ground, "but I can go with my head held high. I left shaking the hands of Arsène Wenger and David Dein. That was very important to me."

THE COMINGS AND GOINGS

Edu was the other major summer departure after he signed for Valencia CF in Spain on a Bosman free transfer, while long-serving reserve goalkeeper Stuart Taylor left for Aston Villa in search of first-team football.

Jeremie Aliadiere and England Under-21 starlets Justin Hoyte and David Bentley were loaned out, the latter making his move to Blackburn permanent later in the season.

Belarus international midfielder Alexander Hleb was the big summer signing when he arrived from VfB Stuttgart, while Mart Poom was drafted in from Sunderland as goalkeeping cover. Bastia's defensive midfielder Alex Song was also brought in on loan.

PRE-SEASON FORM

The fleet-footed Hleb took only three minutes to make an impact in a Gunners shirt, scoring the opener in a 4–1 win in the traditional first pre-season match at north London neighbours Barnet.

Three matches at a training camp in Austria against locals sides Weiz and Ritzing, and Dutch outfit FC Utrecht, yielded 13 goals and three wins, before the Gunners travelled to the Netherlands where they beat 2004 Champions League winners Porto and hosts Ajax to win the Amsterdam Tournament, with an admiring Diego Maradona watching from the stands.

An Arsenal XI travelled to KSK Beveren in Belgium where they drew 3–3 and rounded off the pre-season preparations with a 6–2 win at Boreham Wood with José Antonio Reyes claiming a hat-trick in Hertfordshire.

THE COMMUNITY SHIELD

Sandwiched between those two matches, the FA Cup holders met league champions Chelsea in the Community Shield in Cardiff. In a tight encounter, Ivory Coast striker Didier Drogba edged the Blues in front after seven minutes and doubled their advantage early in the second half.

Arsenal, though, were impressive against José Mourinho's side and Cesc Fabregas pulled a goal back with 25 minutes remaining. The Gunners searched for an equaliser and Thierry Henry went close with eight minutes remaining, but Chelsea held on – and laid down a marker for the rest of the season.

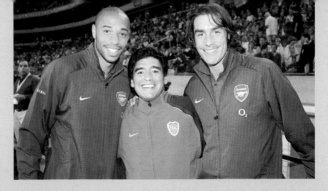

FRIENDLY

Barnet 1

Arsenal 4 (Hleb 3, Henry 15 (pen), Bergkamp 28, Hoyte 35)

Saturday 16 July 2005

Underhill Stadium

Team: Howard (Mannone 45), Hoyte, Christanval, Cygan (Connolly 45), Lauren (Eboue 45), Reyes (Stokes 45), Hleb (Bendtner 67), Flamini (Muamba 67), Henry (Lupoli 45), Bergkamp (Bentley 45), Pires (Gilbert 67)

FRIENDLY

SC Weiz 0

Arsenal 5 (Flamini 1, Henry 4, 37, Bentley 15, Bergkamp 50)

Wednesday 20 July 2005

Weiz, Austria

Team: Howard (Mannone 45), Lauren (Cole 45), Cygan (Toure 45), Senderos (Djourou 45), Hoyte, Pires (Ljungberg 45), Flamini (Larsson 45), Song, Hleb (Bergkamp 45), Bentley, Henry (Reyes 45), (Flamini 78)

FRIENDLY

SC Ritzing 2

Arsenal 5 (Bergkamp 10, Henry 17, Reyes 35 (pen), Hleb 79, Larsson 90)

Sunday 24 July 2005

Ritzing, Austria

Team: Howard (Mannone 45), Lauren (Senderos 45), Christanval, Toure (Cygan 45), Hoyte, Ljungberg (Hleb 45), Song, Flamini (Larsson 62), Reyes, Bergkamp (Bentley 45), Henry (Pires 45)

FRIENDLY

FC Utrecht 0

Arsenal 3 (Pires 13 (pen), Reyes 54, Henry 77)

Tuesday 26 July 2005

Bad Waltersdorf, Austria

Team: Howard, Lauren (Eboue 45), Senderos (Christanval 45), Cygan, Cole, Ljungberg (Bentley 45), Song, Hleb (Hoyte 76), Pires, Bergkamp (Reyes 45), Henry

AMSTERDAM TOURNAMENT

Ajax 0

Arsenal 1 (Lupoli 87)

Friday 29 July 2005

Amsterdam Arena

Team: Lehmann, Lauren (Eboue 60), Cole (Hoyte 71), Senderos (Cygan 45), Toure, Flamini, Ljungberg (Bentley 71), Pires, Bergkamp (Hleb 60), Henry, Reyes

AMSTERDAM TOURNAMENT

Porto 1

Arsenal 2 (Ljungberg 49, 58)

Sunday 31 July 2005

Amsterdam Arena

Team: Lehmann, Lauren (Eboue 72), Cole, Senderos (Toure 64), Cygan, Flamini, Bentley (Ljungberg 45), Pires (Djourou 80), Reyes (Bergkamp 45), Hleb, Henry

FRIENDLY

Beveren 3

Arsenal 3 (Lupoli 19, van Persie 74, 79)

Tuesday 2 August 2005

Freethiel Stadium

Team: Howard, Hoyte (Connolly 60), Djourou, Clichy, Larsson (Muamba 60), Owusu-Abeyie (Bendtner 85), Fabregas, van Persie, Lupoli (Smith 60), Bentley (Cregg 85), Eboue

COMMUNITY SHIELD

Chelsea 2

Arsenal 1 (Fabregas 65)

Sunday 7 August 2005

Millennium Stadium

Team: Lehmann, Lauren (Hoyte 78), Cole, Senderos (Cygan 72), Toure, Flamini (Gilberto 45), Ljungberg (Reyes 72), Pires (Hleb 45), Fabregas, Henry, Bergkamp (van Persie 45)

FRIENDLY

Boreham Wood 2

Arsenal 6 (van Persie 6, 11, Reyes 33 (pen), 45, 71 (pen), Pires 39)

Wednesday 10 August 2005

Meadow Park

Team: Jordan, Eboue (Kelly 64), Hoyte, Flamini (Smith 68), Cygan, Djourou (Connolly 45), Pires (Lupoli 68), Larsson (Owusu-Abeyie 45), Reyes, Hleb (Muamba 68), van Persie (Cregg 68)

Left Belarus international midfielder Alexander Hleb, signed for Arsenal from Stuttgart in the summer of 2005, took only three minutes to open his account for the Gunners. *Top* Diego Maradona, pictured with Thierry Henry and Robert Pires, was watching some of the games at the Ajax Tournament.

SEASON SUMMARY

FIRST-TEAM STATISTICS 2005/2006

- ● Own Goal
- ★ First sub
- ❖ Fourth Sub

- 1 or 2 Goalscorer
- ✚ Second sub
- ◆ Fifth Sub

- (p) Penalty
- ▲ Third sub
- ■ Sixth Sub

Home matches in RED type

PREMIERSHIP

Sunday 14 August 2005 v Newcastle United (H) 2–0 Att: 8,072
Lehmann, Lauren, Cole, Senderos, Toure, Ljungberg, Fabregas ★, Gilberto, Pires ▲, Bergkamp ✚, **Henry 1** (p), Hleb ★ (72), **van Persie 1** ✚ (72), Flamini ▲ (82), Cygan, Almunia

Sunday 21 August 2005 v Chelsea (A) 0–1 Att: 42,136,
Lehmann, Lauren, Cole, Senderos, Toure, Ljungberg ★, Fabregas ✚, Gilberto, Hleb, Pires, Henry, van Persie ★ (26), Flamini ★ (85), Bergkamp, Cygan, Almunia

Wednesday 24 August 2005 v Fulham (H) 4–1 Att: 37,867
Lehmann, Lauren, Cole, **Cygan 2**, Toure, Hleb ✚, Fabregas, Gilberto, Reyes ★, Bergkamp, **Henry 2**, Flamini ★ (79), Clichy ✚ (86), van Persie, Pires, Almunia

Saturday 10 September 2005 v Middlesbrough (A) 1–2 Att: 28,075
Lehmann, Lauren, Cole, Cygan, Toure, Hleb, Flamini ★, Gilberto, Pires ✚, Bergkamp, **Reyes1**, Fabregas ★ (60), van Persie ✚ (72), Senderos, Clichy, Almunia

Monday 19 September Everton (H) 2–0 Att: 38,121
Lehmann, Lauren, Cole, **Campbell 2**, Toure, Ljungberg, Gilberto, Pires ★, van Persie ✚, Reyes ▲, Hleb ★ (29), Bergkamp ✚ (66), Song ▲ (85), Senderos, Almunia

Saturday 24 September 2005 v West Ham United (A) 0–0 Att: 34,742
Lehmann, Lauren, Cole, Campbell, Toure, Ljungberg, Fabregas, Gilberto ★, Hleb, van Persie ▲, Reyes ✚, Flamini ★ (72), Owusu-Abeyie ✚ (73), Clichy ▲ (82), Cygan, Almunia

Sunday 2 October 2005 v Birmingham City (H) 1–0 ● Att: 37,891
Lehmann, Lauren, Cole, Campbell, Toure, Hleb ★, Fabregas, Gilberto, Pires ✚, Ljungberg ▲, Reyes, Bergkamp ★ (61), van Persie ✚ (70), Flamini ▲ (87), Cygan, Almunia

Saturday 15 October 2005 v West Bromwich Albion (A) 1–2 Att: 26,604
Lehmann, Lauren, Clichy, **Senderos 1**, Toure, Ljungberg ★, Fabregas, Flamini ✚, Pires, Bergkamp, Reyes, Eboue ★ (37), Owusu-Abeyie ✚ (77), Cygan, Song, Almunia

Saturday 22 October 2005 Manchester City (H) 1–0 Att: 38,189
Lehmann, Lauren, Clichy, Cygan, Toure, Fabregas, Flamini, Gilberto, **Pires 1** (p), Bergkamp, Henry, Eboue, Owusu-Abeyie, van Persie, Senderos, Almunia

Saturday 29 October 2005 v Tottenham Hotspur (A) 1–1 Att: 36,154
Lehmann, Lauren, Clichy, Campbell, Toure, Fabregas, Flamini ★, Gilberto, Ljungberg ✚, Bergkamp, Reyes ▲, **Pires 1** ★ (45), van Persie ✚ (65), Cygan ▲ (90), Eboue, Almunia,

Saturday 5 November 2005 v Sunderland (H) 3–1 Att: 38,210
Lehmann, Lauren, Clichy, Campbell, Toure, Pires, Fabregas, Gilberto, Reyes ★, **van Persie 1** ✚, **Henry 2**, Eboue ★ (65), Bergkamp ✚ (71), Senderos, Flamini, Almunia

Saturday 19 November 2005 v Wigan Athletic (A) 3–2 Att: 25,004
Lehmann, Lauren, Cygan, Campbell, Toure, Ljungberg, Fabregas ▲, Gilberto, Pires ★, **van Persie 1** ✚, **Henry 2**, Flamini ★ (75), Bergkamp ✚ (75), Senderos ▲ (90), Reyes, Almunia

Saturday 26 November 2005 v Blackburn Rovers (H) 3–0 Att: 38,192
Lehmann, Lauren, Cygan, Campbell, Toure, Pires ✚, **Fabregas 1**, Gilberto, Reyes ★, Bergkamp ▲, **Henry 1**, Ljungberg ★ (72), Flamini ✚ (77), **van Persie 1** ▲ (82), Senderos, Almunia,

Saturday 3 December 2005 v Bolton Wanderers (A) 0–2 Att: 26,792
Lehmann, Lauren ▲, Cygan, Campbell, Toure, Ljungberg, Fabregas ★, Gilberto, Pires, van Persie ✚, Henry, Reyes ★ (69), Bergkamp ✚ (69), Eboue ▲ (74), Senderos, Almunia,

Saturday 10 December 2005 v Newcastle United (A) 0–1 Att: 52,297
Lehmann, Toure, Lauren, Campbell, Senderos, Ljungberg, Fabregas ★, Gilberto, Hleb ★, van Persie ✚, Henry, Flamini ★ (63), Pires ✚ (85), Owusu-Abeyie ▲ (85), Eboue, Almunia

Sunday 18 December 2005 v Chelsea (H) 0–2 Att: 38,347
Lehmann, Lauren, Cole, Campbell, Senderos, Ljungberg ★, Fabregas, Flamini, Hleb ✚, van Persie ▲, Henry, Bergkamp ★ (70), Pires ✚ (70), Owusu-Abeyie ▲ (81), Eboue, Almunia

Monday 26 December 2005 v Charlton Athletic (A) 1–0 Att: 27,111
Lehmann, Lauren, Cygan, Campbell, Toure, Ljungberg, Fabregas, Gilberto, Hleb ★, **Reyes 1** ✚, Henry, Pires ★ (75), Flamini ✚ (80), Senderos, Eboue, Almunia

Wednesday 28 December 2005 v Portsmouth (H) 4–0 Att: 38,223
Lehmann, Lauren, Cygan, Campbell, Toure, Pires, Flamini, Gilberto ✚, **Reyes 1** ★, Bergkamp 1, **Henry 2** (1p), Eboue ✚ (67), Fabregas ✚ (72), Ljungberg, Senderos, Almunia

Saturday 31 December 2005 v Aston Villa (A) 0–0 Att: 37,114
Lehmann, Lauren, Cygan, Campbell, Toure, Ljungberg ▲, Fabregas, Flamini, Hleb ✚, van Persie ★, Henry, Bergkamp ★ (68), Reyes ✚ (76), Pires ▲ (78), Senderos, Almunia,

Tuesday 3 January 2006 v Manchester United (H) 0–0 Att: 38,313
Lehmann, Lauren, Cygan, Campbell, Toure, Pires, Fabregas ✚, Gilberto, Hleb ★, Reyes ▲, Henry, Bergkamp ★ (73), Flamini ✚ (80), Eboue ▲ (90), Senderos, Almunia

Saturday 14 January 2006 v Middlesbrough (H) 7–0 Att: 38,186
Lehmann, Lauren, Cygan ★, Djourou, **Senderos 1**, Ljungberg, Fabregas, **Gilberto 1** ✚, **Pires 1** ▲, Reyes, **Henry 3**, Cole ★ (34), Flamini ✚ (69), **Hleb 1** ▲ (69), Lupoli, Almunia

Saturday 21 January 2006 Everton (A) 0–1 Att: 36,920
Lehmann, Gilbert ★, Lauren, Campbell, Senderos, Ljungberg, Fabregas, Gilberto, Pires ✚, Reyes, Henry, Hleb ★ (73), Diaby ✚ (82), Flamini, Djourou, Almunia

Wednesday 1 February 2006 v West Ham United (H) 2–3 Att: 38,216
Lehmann, Gilbert ★, Senderos, Campbell ✚, Djourou, Ljungberg, Diaby ▲, Gilberto, **Pires 1**, van Persie, **Henry 1**, Flamini ★ (27), Larsson ✚ (45), Bergkamp ▲ (71), Hleb, Almunia

Saturday 4 February 2006 v Birmingham City (A) 2–0 Att: 27,075
Lehmann, Flamini, Larsson, Djourou, Senderos, Fabregas, Diaby, Gilberto, Reyes ★, **Adebayor 1**, **Henry 1**, Hleb ★ (80), Pires, Bergkamp, Walcott, Almunia

Saturday 11 February 2006 v Bolton Wanderers (H) 1–1 Att: 38,193
Lehmann, Flamini, Larsson ▲, Djourou, Senderos, Fabregas, Diaby ✚, **Gilberto 1**, Reyes ✚, Adebayor, Henry, Pires ★ (32), Ljungberg ✚ (45), Bergkamp ▲ (73), Song, Almunia

Tuesday 14 February 2006 v Liverpool (A) 0–1 Att: 44,065
Lehmann, Eboue, Flamini, Senderos, Toure, Ljungberg, Fabregas, Gilberto, Pires ★, Adebayor, Henry, Hleb ★ (79), Diaby, Larsson, Djourou, Almunia

Saturday 25 February 2006 v Blackburn Rovers (A) 0–1 Att 22,504
Lehmann, Eboue, Flamini, Senderos, Toure, Fabregas, Diaby ✚, Gilberto ▲, Reyes ★, Adebayor, Henry, Pires ★ (45), Hleb ✚ (65), Lupoli ▲ (82), Djourou, Almunia

Saturday 4 March 2006 v Fulham (A) 4–0 Att: 22,397
Lehmann, Eboue, Flamini, Senderos, Toure, Ljungberg, Diaby, Gilberto, Hleb ✚, **Adebayor 1** ★, **Henry 2** ▲, Bergkamp ★ (72), **Fabregas 1** ✚ (79), Reyes ▲ (83), Djourou, Poom

Sunday 12 March 2006 v Liverpool (H) 2–1 Att: 38,221
Lehmann, Eboue, Flamini, Senderos, Toure, Ljungberg★, Fabregas, Gilberto, Hleb,
Adebayor✚, **Henry 2**, Pires★(15), Bergkamp✚(68), Song, Djourou, Almunia

Saturday 18 March 2006 v Charlton Athletic (H) 3–0 Att: 38,223
Lehmann, Eboue, Flamini, Senderos, Toure, **Hleb 1**★, Fabregas▲, Gilberto,
Pires 1, **Adebayor 1**✚, Henry, Bergkamp✚(68), van Persie✚(68),
Song▲(78), Djourou, Almunia

Saturday 1 April 2006 v Aston Villa (H) 5–0 Att: 38,183
Lehmann, Eboue▲, Flamini, Senderos, Toure, Pires, Fabregas★, Gilberto,
Reyes, **Adebayor 1**, **Henry 2**✚, **Diaby 1**★(16), **van Persie 1**✚(64),
Djourou▲(67), Hleb, Almunia

Sunday 9 April 2006 v Manchester United (A) 0–2 Att: 70,908
Lehmann, Eboue, Flamini, Senderos, Toure, Pires, Fabregas✚, Gilberto,
Hleb▲, Adebayor, van Persie★, Henry★(70), Diaby★(70), Ljungberg▲(73),
Djourou, Poom

Wednesday 12 April 2006 v Portsmouth (A) 1–1 Att: 20,230
Lehmann, Djourou, Flamini, Campbell▲, Toure, Ljungberg, Diaby, Song,
Reyes✚, Adebayor★, **Henry 1**, van Persie★(75), Hleb★(80), Eboue▲(90),
Bergkamp, Poom

Saturday 15 April 2006 v West Bromwich Albion (H) 3–1 Att: 38,167
Lehmann, Eboue, Flamini, Senderos, Toure, **Hleb 1**✚, Diaby, Gilberto, Reyes,
van Persie▲, Henry★, Adebayor★(62), **Pires 1**✚(71), **Bergkamp 1**▲(71),
Djourou, Poom

Saturday 22 April 2006 v Tottenham Hotspur (H) 1–1 Att: 38,326
Lehmann, Djourou, Flamini, Senderos★, Toure, Pires, Diaby✚, Gilberto,
Reyes, Adebayor, van Persie▲, Eboue★(54), Fabregas✚(62), **Henry 1**▲(62),
Song, Almunia

Monday 1 May 2006 v Sunderland (A) 3–0● Att: 44,003
Lehmann, Eboue, Clichy, Campbell, Toure, **Fabregas 1**, Diaby, Song, Pires★,
Adebayor✚, **Henry 1**▲, Cole★(64), van Persie✚(64), Bergkamp▲(71),
Djourou, Poom

Thursday 4 May 2006 v Manchester City (A) 3–1 Att: 41,875
Lehmann, Eboue, Cole, Campbell, Toure, **Ljungberg 1**, Song★, Gilberto,
Hleb✚, van Persie▲, Henry, Fabregas★(58), Pires✚(72), **Reyes 2**▲(72),
Djourou, Almunia

Sunday 7 May 2006 v Wigan Athletic (H) 4–2 Att: 38,359
Lehmann, Eboue, Cole, Campbell, Toure, **Pires 1**★, Fabregas, Gilberto,
Hleb▲, Reyes✚, **Henry 3**, Ljungberg▲(73), Bergkamp✚(78), van
Persie▲(78), Djourou, Almunia

UEFA CHAMPIONS LEAGUE

Wednesday 14 September 2005v FC Thun (H) 2–1 Att: 34,498,
Almunia, Lauren, Campbell, Toure, Cole, Ljungberg✚, Fabregas★, **Gilberto 1**,
Pires, van Persie, Reyes▲, **Bergkamp 1**▲(72), Hleb✚(80), Owusu-
Abeyie▲(80), Song, Senderos, Clichy, Poom

Tuesday 27 September 2005 v Ajax (A) 2–1 Att: 50,000
Almunia, Lauren, Campbell, Toure, Cole, Hleb▲, Fabregas, Flamini, **Pires 1**(p)✚,
Ljungberg 1, Reyes★, Owusu-Abeyie★(80), Clichy✚(88), Cygan▲(90),
Song, Lupoli, Eboue, Poom

Tuesday 18 October 2005 v Sparta Prague (A) 2–0 Att: 12,128
Lehmann, Lauren, Cygan, Toure, Clichy, Fabregas▲, Flamini, Gilberto, Pires,
van Persie✚, Reyes★, **Henry 2**★(16), Eboue✚(73), Owusu-Abeyie▲(89),
Song, Larsson, Senderos, Almunia

Wednesday 2 November 2005 v Sparta Prague (H) 3–0 Att: 35,115
Almunia, Lauren, Campbell, Toure, Clichy, Pires✚, Flamini, Gilberto,
Reyes▲, Bergkamp, **Henry 1**★, **van Persie 2**★(66), Fabregas✚(73),
Eboue▲(83), Song, Cygan, Senderos, Poom

Tuesday 22 November 2005 v FC Thun (A) 1–0 Att: 31,300
Almunia, Eboue, Campbell, Senderos, Cygan✚, Ljungberg, Flamini, Song★,
Reyes, van Persie, Henry▲, Fabregas▲(56), Lauren✚(67), **Pires 1**▲(p)(70),
Lupoli, Bendtner, Djourou, Poom

Wednesday 7 December 2005 v Ajax (H) 0–0 Att: 35,376
Almunia, Eboue, Senderos, Toure, Lauren▲, Hleb★, Flamini, Larsson,
Owusu-Abeyie, Reyes✚, Henry, Fabregas★(62), van Persie✚(65),
Gilberto▲(73), Lupoli, Djourou, Cygan, Poom

Tuesday 21 February 2006 v Real Madrid (A) 1–0 Att: 80,000
Lehmann, Eboue, Senderos, Toure, Flamini, Ljungberg▲, Fabregas, Gilberto,
Hleb★, Reyes✚, **Henry 1**, Pires★(76), Diaby✚(80), Song▲(90), Lupoli,
Walcott, Djourou, Almunia

Wednesday 8 March 2006 v Real Madrid (H) 0–0 Att: 35,487
Lehmann, Eboue, Senderos, Toure, Flamini, Ljungberg, Fabregas, Gilberto,
Hleb✚, Reyes★, Henry, Pires★(68), Bergkamp✚(86), Diaby, Song, Walcott,
Djourou, Almunia

Tuesday 28 March 2006 v Juventus (H) 2–0 Att: 35,472
Lehmann, Eboue, Senderos, Toure, Flamini, Pires, **Fabregas 1**, Gilberto,
Hleb, Reyes▲, **Henry 1**, van Persie★(82), Bergkamp, Diaby, Song, Walcott,
Djourou, Almunia

Wednesday 5 April 2006 v Juventus (A) 0–0 Att: 50,000
Lehmann, Eboue, Senderos, Toure, Flamini, Ljungberg, Fabregas, Gilberto,
Hleb✚, Reyes★, Henry, Pires★(62), Diaby✚(86), Campbell, Song, Walcott,
van Persie, Almunia

Wednesday 19 April 2006 v Villarreal (H) 1–0 Att: 35,438
Lehmann, Eboue, Senderos, **Toure 1**, Flamini, Ljungberg★, Fabregas,
Gilberto, Hleb✚, Pires, Henry, van Persie★(80), Bergkamp✚(80), Diaby,
Song, Walcott, Djourou, Almunia

Tuesday 25 April 2006 v Villarreal (A) 0-0 Att: 23,000
Lehmann, Eboue, Campbell, Toure, Flamini★, Ljungberg, Fabregas, Gilberto,
Hleb, Reyes✚, Henry, Clichy★(8), Pires✚(69), Diaby, Song, van Persie,
Djourou, Almunia

Wednesday 17 May 2006 v Barcelona (N) 1–2 Att: 79,500
Lehmann, Eboue, **Campbell 1**, Toure, Cole, Ljungberg, Fabregas✚, Gilberto,
Hleb▲, Pires★, Henry, Almunia▲(19), Flamini✚(74), Reyes▲(84), van
Persie, Bergkamp, Senderos, Clichy (at Stade de France, Paris)

THE FA CUP

Saturday 7 January 2006 v Cardiff City (H) 2–1 Att: 36,552
Almunia, Gilbert, Senderos, Djourou, Lauren, **Pires 2**, Flamini, Gilberto,
Reyes★, van Persie✚, Bergkamp, Owusu-Abeyie★(45), Larsson✚(77),
Hleb, Lupoli, Poom

Saturday 28 January 2006 v Bolton Wanderers (A) 0–1 Att: 13,325
Almunia, Gilbert, Campbell, Djourou, Senderos, Hleb, Flamini, Diaby,
Ljungberg, van Persie, Reyes, Bendtner, Larsson, Muamba, Lupoli, Poom

THE CARLING CUP

Tuesday 25 October 2005 v Sunderland (A) 3–0 Att: 47,366
Almunia, **Eboue 1**, Campbell, Senderos, Cygan, Muamba, Song, Larsson★,
Owusu-Abeyie▲, **van Persie 2**(1p), Lupoli✚, Cregg★(89), Stokes✚(89),
Bendtner▲(90), Connolly, Poom

Tuesday 29 November 2005 v Reading (H) 3–0 Att: 36,137
Almunia, Eboue, Djourou, Senderos, Gilbert, Muamba, Flamini, Larsson,
Owusu-Abeyie▲, **van Persie 1**★, **Reyes 1**✚, **Lupoli 1**★(63), Cygan✚(75),
Bendtner▲(83), Connolly, Poom

Wednesday 21 December 2005 v Doncaster (A) 2–2 Att: 10,006
Almunia, Eboue, Djourou, Senderos, Cygan, **Gilberto 1**, Song, Hleb, Owusu-
Abeyie 1✚, van Persie★, Lupoli▲, Bendtner★(33), Larsson✚(78),
Gilbert▲(106), Muamba, Poom, (AET) (Arsenal won 3–1 on penalties)

Tuesday 10 January 2006 v Wigan Athletic (A) 0–1 Att: 12,181
Almunia, Gilbert▲, Djourou, Senderos, Cygan, Gilberto, Flamini, Hleb,
Ljungberg, Owusu-Abeyie★, Reyes✚, Lupoli★(72), Fabregas✚(72),
Larsson▲(75), Bendtner, Poom

Tuesday 24 January 2006 v Wigan Athletic (H) 2–1 Att: 34,692
Almunia, Gilbert, Campbell, Senderos, Lauren, Gilberto, Diaby★, Hleb✚,
Reyes, Bergkamp, **Henry 1**▲, Flamini★(45), Pires✚(69), **van Persie
1**▲(79), Djourou, Poom, (AET)

THE FA COMMUNITY SHIELD

Sunday 7 August 2005 v Chelsea (N) 1–2 Att: 58,014
Lehmann, Lauren■, Toure, Senderos◆, Cole, Flamini★, Pires✚,
Ljungberg❖, **Fabregas 1**, Bergkamp▲, Henry, Hleb★(46), Gilberto✚(46),
van Persie▲(46), Reyes❖(72), Cygan◆(73), Hoyte■(78) (at the Millennium
Stadium, Cardiff)

APPEARANCES AND GOALS 2005/2006

	PREM APPS(SUB) GLS	CL	FAC	CC	CS
JENS LEHMANN	38	8	-	-	1
GILBERTO	33 2	10 1	1	3 1	(1)
KOLO TOURE	33	12 1	-	-	1
FRANCESC FABREGAS	30(5) 3	10(3) 1	-	(1)	1 1
THIERRY HENRY	30(2) 27	10(1) 5	-	1 1	1
ROBERT PIRES	23(10) 7	7(5) 2	1 2	(1)	1
JOSÉ ANTONIO REYES	22(4) 5	11(1)	2	3 1	(1)
LAUREN	22	5(1)	1	1	1
FREDRIK LJUNGBERG	21(4) 1	9 1	1	1	1
SOL CAMPBELL	20 2	6 1	1	2	-
MATHIEU FLAMINI	19(12)	11(1)	2	2(1)	1
PHILIPPE SENDEROS	19(1) 2	7	2	5	1
ALEXANDER HLEB	17(8) 3	9(1)	1	3	(1)
ROBIN VAN PERSIE	13(11) 5	3(4) 2	2	3(14)	(1)
EMMANUEL ADEBAYOR	12(1) 4	-	-	-	-
EMMANUEL EBOUE	11(7)	9(2)	-	3 1	-
PASCAL CYGAN	11(1) 2	2(1)	-	3(1)	(1)
ABOU DIABY	9(3) 1	(2)	1	1	-
ASHLEY COLE	9(2)	3	-	-	1
DENNIS BERGKAMP	8(16) 2	1(3) 1	1	1	1
JOHAN DJOUROU	6(1)	-	2	3	-
GAEL CLICHY	5(2)	2(2)	-	-	-
ALEXANDRE SONG	3(2)	1(1)	-	2	-
SEBASTIAN LARSSON	2(1)	1	(1)	2(2)	-
KERREA GILBERT	2	(1)	2	3(1)	-
QUINCY OWUSU-ABEYIE	(4)	1(3)	(1)	4 1	-
ARTURO LUPOLI	(1)	-	-	2(2) 1	-
MANUEL ALMUNIA	-	5(1)	2	5	-
FABRICE MUAMBA	-	-	-	2	-
NICKLAS BENDTNER	-	-	-	(3)	-
PATRICK CREGG	-	-	-	(1)	-
ANTHONY STOKES	-	-	-	(1)	-
JUSTIN HOYTE	-	-	-	-	(1)
OWN GOALS	2				

LEAGUE STATISTICS

	ARSENAL	LEAGUE RANK
GAMES	38	
GOALS	68	3
SHOTS	444	4
CONVERSION %	15%	1
PASSES	17,903	1
PASS %	81%	2
CROSSES	617	20
CROSS %	26%	7
TACKLES	1,151	15
TACKLE %	72%	6
FOULS	516	15
YELLOW CARDS	54	12
RED CARDS	2	13

ARSENAL TOP FIVES

SHOOTING	NO.	%
THIERRY HENRY	102	52%
JOSÉ ANTONIO REYES	49	49%
ROBIN VAN PERSIE	41	56%
ROBERT PIRES	36	58%
FRANCESC FABREGAS	33	48%

PASSING	NO.	%
FRANCESC FABREGAS	1,957	76%
GILBERTO	1,820	74%
ROBERT PIRES	1,370	74%
KOLO TOURE	1,357	78%
THIERRY HENRY	1,088	76%

CROSSING	NO.	%
THIERRY HENRY	120	30%
JOSÉ ANTONIO REYES	89	24%
ROBERT PIRES	54	23%
ROBIN VAN PERSIE	50	19%
FREDRIK LJUNGBERG	48	26%

TACKLING	NO.	%
GILBERTO	135	69%
FRANCESC FABREGAS	124	73%
KOLO TOURE	112	69%
LAUREN	84	64%
MATHIEU FLAMINI	62	73%

DRIBBLING	NO.	%
THIERRY HENRY	263	53%
JOSÉ ANTONIO REYES	218	54%
ROBERT PIRES	171	54%
ALEXANDER HLEB	159	75%
FREDRIK LJUNGBERG	133	59%

FOULS WON

FRANCESC FABREGAS	66
JOSÉ ANTONIO REYES	65
FREDRIK LJUNGBERG	50
ALEXANDER HLEB	45
THIERRY HENRY	37

FOULS LOST

GILBERTO	64
FRANCESC FABREGAS	44
JOSÉ ANTONIO REYES	40
THIERRY HENRY	36
LAUREN	31

CARDS

	YELLOW	RED
FRANCESC FABREGAS	5	1
GILBERTO	4	1
LAUREN	6	0
JOSÉ ANTONIO REYES	5	0
PASCAL CYGAN	4	0

GOALS (HOW)

	FOR	AGAINST
LEFT FOOT	16	9
RIGHT FOOT	43	17
HEAD	7	5
OTHER	0	0
OWN GOAL	2	0

GOALS (WHEN)

	FOR	AGAINST
0–15 MINUTES	8	3
16–30 MINUTES	12	6
31–45 MINUTES	16	8
46–60 MINUTES	6	2
61–75 MINUTES	4	7
76–90 MINUTES	22	5

GOALS (WHERE)

	FOR	AGAINST
INSIDE BOX	55	27
OUTSIDE BOX	9	4
PENALTY	4	0

GOALS (WHO)

	FOR	AGAINST
GOALKEEPER	0	0
DEFENDER	6	3
MIDFIELDER	20	18
STRIKER	40	10
OWN GOAL	2	0

PLAYERS' PREMIERSHIP STATISTICS

	STARTS (AS SUB)	GOALS (CONC)	GOAL ASST	CARDS Y	R
EMMANUEL ADEBAYOR	12 (1)	4	4	0	0
DENNIS BERGKAMP	8 (16)	2	1	2	0
SOL CAMPBELL	20 (0)	2	2	1	0
GAEL CLICHY	5 (2)	0	0	2	0
ASHLEY COLE	9 (2)	0	0	3	0
PASCAL CYGAN	11 (1)	2	0	4	0
ABOU DIABY	9 (3)	1	1	2	0
JOHAN DJOUROU	6 (1)	0	0	0	0
EMMANUEL EBOUE	11 (7)	0	2	0	0
FRANCESC FABREGAS	30 (5)	3	5	5	1
MATHIEU FLAMINI	19 (12)	0	3	4	0
KERREA GILBERT	2 (0)	0	0	0	0
GILBERTO	33 (0)	2	0	4	1
THIERRY HENRY	30 (2)	27	8	2	0
ALEXANDER HLEB	17 (8)	3	0	0	0
SEBASTIAN LARSSON	2 (1)	0	0	2	0
LAUREN	22 (0)	0	1	6	0
JENS LEHMANN	38 (0)	(31)	0	1	0
FREDRIK LJUNGBERG	21 (4)	1	3	2	0
ROBERT PIRES	23 (10)	7	4	2	0
JOSÉ ANTONIO REYES	22 (4)	5	10	5	0
PHILIPPE SENDEROS	19 (1)	2	0	2	0
KOLO TOURE	33 (0)	0	1	3	0
ROBIN VAN PERSIE	13 (11)	5	1	2	0

THE NUMBERS GAME 2005/2006

1,044,266

the number of fans through the turnstiles at Highbury for first-team matches in all competitions

7,562*

the total number of air miles clocked up by Arsenal travelling to Champions League away games

75

the number of ex-players involved in the 'Legends Parade' at the final match at Highbury against Wigan Athletic on 7 May 2006

16

the number of Arsenal players who were involved in the 2006 World Cup

4,158

the number of minutes on the pitch clocked up by Jens Lehmann – Arsenal's most constant presence over the season – in all competitions

818**

the combined age of Arsenal's 34 first-team squad members

2.3 million

the number of page impressions on the Arsenal website on 7 May, the day of the final game at Highbury against Wigan – the most ever in a single day

3

the number of tonnes of fertiliser used on the Highbury pitch during the campaign

24**

the average age of Arsenal's first-team squad

14

the number of times Arsenal hit the woodwork in the Premiership – more than any other club

470

the total number of shots on goal that Arsenal managed in the Premiership

3.21

the average number of goals per match at Highbury – the highest in the Premiership

600

the number of litres of white paint used to produce the pitch markings throughout the season

23

the number of cleans sheets kept by Jens Lehmann in all competitions

800

the number of kilograms of grass seed used to maintain the Arsenal pitch during the season

17

different scorers for the first team in all competitions

7.34

Thierry Henry's Actim Index rating for the season – the highest in the Premiership

16

the number of different nationalities represented in the first-team squad

2,700

the number of lots that went under the hammer at the auction of Highbury memorabilia on 29 July 2006

includes the final in Paris ** as of 1 August 2006 *** not including injury time*

60

the number of countries in which Arsenal TV broadcasts were viewed in 2005/2006

97

the total number of goals scored by Arsenal in all competitions

995***

the number of minutes that Arsenal went without conceding a goal in the Champions League – a competition record

72,000

the quantity of official matchday programmes produced for the final game at Highbury against Wigan Athletic

104

the number of minutes between each Thierry Henry goal in the Premiership

711

the number of apartments due to be created as a result of the development of the East and West Stands at Highbury

9

the number of Premiership assists by José Antonio Reyes

PLAYER PROFILES

EMMANUEL ADEBAYOR

POSITION FORWARD
SQUAD NUMBER 25
BORN LOME, TOGO, 26 FEBRUARY 1984

OTHER CLUBS Metz, Monaco
JOINED ARSENAL from Monaco in January 2006
SENIOR ARSENAL DEBUT 4 February 2006 v
Birmingham City at St Andrew's (League)
ARSENAL RECORD **League** 12 (1) games, 4 goals;
Total 12 (1) games, 4 goals
TOGO CAPS 15
IN 2005/06 Tall and leggy, quick and skilful, the
Togolese international marksman gave Arsenal an
extra attacking option with his power in the air after
arriving at Highbury during the January transfer
window. Emmanuel scored on his debut and
showed encouraging signs of gelling effectively
with Thierry Henry.

JEREMIE ALIADIERE

POSITION FORWARD
SQUAD NUMBER NONE
BORN RAMBOUILLET, FRANCE, 30 MARCH 1983

OTHER CLUBS Celtic on loan, West Ham United on
loan, Wolverhampton Wanderers on loan
JOINED ARSENAL as scholar in summer 1999,
professional in March 2000
SENIOR ARSENAL DEBUT 27 November 2001 v
Grimsby Town at Highbury (League Cup, as substitute)
ARSENAL HONOURS **League Championship** 03/04
ARSENAL RECORD **League** 3 (15) games, 1 goal;
FA Cup 1 (2) games, 0 goals; **League Cup** 3 (2)
games, 4 goals; **Europe** 0 (1) game, 0 goals;
Community Shield 0 (1) game, 0 goals; **Total** 7 (21)
games, 5 goals
IN 2005/06 The pacy, stylish French under-21

FIRST-TEAM STATISTICS IN THE PREMIERSHIP 2005/06

	Adebayor		Adebayor
Games	12 (1)	Headed goals	2
Goals	4	Left-foot goals	1
Penalty goals	0	Right-foot goals	1
Set-piece goals	0	Goal attempts	23
Goals from inside box	4	Accuracy	48%
Goals from outside box	0	Conversion	17%

international striker spent the season on loan at three clubs. First came a brief stint at Celtic during which he saw service in the European Cup, then a fleeting spell at West Ham was followed by a more active sojourn with Championship promotion hopefuls Wolves.

MANUEL ALMUNIA
POSITION GOALKEEPER
SQUAD NUMBER 24
BORN PAMPLONA, SPAIN, 19 MAY 1977

OTHER CLUBS Osasuna B, Cartagonova, Sabadell, Celta Vigo, Eibar on loan, Recreativo Huelva on loan, Albacete on loan
JOINED ARSENAL from Celta Vigo in July 2004
SENIOR ARSENAL DEBUT 27 October 2004 v Manchester City at City of Manchester Stadium (League Cup)
ARSENAL RECORD **League** 10 games, 0 goals; **FA Cup** 4 games, 0 goals; **League Cup** 8 games, 0 goals; **Europe** 6 (1) games, 0 goals; **Total** 28 (1) games, 0 goals

IN 2005/06 The oft-underrated Spanish custodian provided solid cover for Jens Lehmann, not least in the European Cup final in which he pulled off a series of fine saves. He didn't make a single Premiership start, which must have been frustrating for a 'keeper both competent and courageous.

NICKLAS BENDTNER
POSITION FORWARD
SQUAD NUMBER 33
BORN COPENHAGEN, DENMARK, 16 JANUARY 1988

JOINED ARSENAL as scholar in summer 2004
Senior Arsenal debut 25 October 2005 v Sunderland at Stadium of Light (League Cup, as substitute)
ARSENAL RECORD **League Cup** 0 (3) games, 0 goals; **Total** 0 (3) games, 0 goals
IN 2005/06 The rookie Danish sharpshooter made massive strides, scoring freely for the reserves and suggesting that he has a bright future at the top level. The 6ft 3in dasher is quick and powerful, a menace in aerial combat and capable of picking out astute passes to his fellow attackers. Watch this space.

	Adebayor			Adebayor
Offsides	17	Tackles		29
Assists	4	Tackle success		69%
Chances created	18	Clearances		5
Pass completion own half	84%	Fouls		15
Pass completion opp half	77%	Free-kicks won		15
Cross completion	33%			

Totals of international caps correct to 17 May 2006

DENNIS BERGKAMP

POSITION FORWARD
SQUAD NUMBER 10
BORN AMSTERDAM, 10 MAY 1969

OTHER CLUBS Ajax, Internazionale
JOINED ARSENAL from Internazionale in July 1995
SENIOR ARSENAL DEBUT 20 August 1995 v
Middlesbrough at Highbury (League)
ARSENAL HONOURS League Championship 97/8,
01/02, 03/04; FA Cup 01/02, 02/03, 04/05
ARSENAL RECORD League 253 (62) games, 87
goals; FA Cup 34 (5) games, 14 goals; League Cup
16 games, 8 goals; Europe 37 (11) games, 11 goals;
Charity/Community Shield 5 games, 0 goals;
Total 345 (78) games, 120 goals
HOLLAND CAPS 79
IN 2005/06 The Dutch maestro continued to make
football connoisseurs drool with frequent touches of
exquisite class throughout his valedictory campaign
as a Gunner. His place in folklore as one of the most
brilliant performers in the history of Arsenal –
indeed, of the English game – is utterly secure.

SOL CAMPBELL

POSITION DEFENDER
SQUAD NUMBER 23
BORN NEWHAM, LONDON, 18 SEPTEMBER 1974

OTHER CLUB Tottenham Hotspur
Joined Arsenal from Tottenham Hotspur in July 2001
SENIOR ARSENAL DEBUT 18 August 2001
v Middlesbrough at The Riverside (League)
ARSENAL HONOURS League Championship 01/02,
03/04; FA Cup 01/02

ARSENAL RECORD League 133 (2) games, 8 goals;
FA Cup 19 games, 2 goals; League Cup 2 games,
0 goals; Europe 39 games, 1 goal; Community Shield
2 games, 0 goals; Total 195 (2) games, 11 goals
ENGLAND CAPS 66
IN 2005/06 The imposing England stopper endured
a difficult campaign in which he was ravaged by
injuries, but he returned in the spring to stamp his
authority on the Arsenal rearguard and to re-enter
the international reckoning. His majestic header in
the European Cup final was a memorable highlight.

FIRST-TEAM STATISTICS IN THE PREMIERSHIP 2005/06

	Bergkamp	Campbell	Clichy	Cole		Bergkamp	Campbell	Clichy	Cole
Games	8 (16)	20	5 (2)	9 (2)	Headed goals	0	2	-	-
Goals	2	2	0	0	Left-foot goals	0	0	-	-
Penalty goals	0	0	-	-	Right-foot goals	2	0	-	-
Set-piece goals	0	0	-	-	Goal attempts	22	12	1	4
Goals from inside box	1	2	-	-	Accuracy	64%	17%	0%	0%
Goals from outside box	1	0	-	-	Conversion	9%	17%	0%	0%

GAEL CLICHY

POSITION DEFENDER
SQUAD NUMBER 22
BORN TOULOUSE, FRANCE, 26 JULY 1985

OTHER CLUB Cannes
JOINED ARSENAL from Cannes in August 2003
SENIOR ARSENAL DEBUT 28 October 2003 v
Rotherham United at Highbury (League Cup)
ARSENAL HONOURS **League Championship** 03/04
ARSENAL RECORD **League** 19 (15) games, 0 goals;
FA Cup 6 (3) games, 0 goals; **League Cup** 6 games,
0 goals; **Europe** 4 (3) games, 0 goals; **Community
Shield** 0 (1) game, 0 goals; **Total:** 35 (22) games,
0 goals
IN 2005/06 The nippy, skilful Frenchman was doubly
unfortunate in that he was sidelined by injury for
many months and also missed the opportunity to
capitalise on the prolonged absence of Ashley Cole.
But Gael is a left-back of the highest quality and can
be expected to shine in the years ahead.

ASHLEY COLE

POSITION DEFENDER
SQUAD NUMBER 3
BORN STEPNEY, LONDON, 20 DECEMBER 1980

OTHER CLUB Crystal Palace on loan
JOINED ARSENAL as trainee in summer 1997,
professional in November 1998
SENIOR ARSENAL DEBUT 30 November 1999
v Middlesbrough at The Riverside (League Cup,
as substitute)
ARSENAL HONOURS **League Championship** 01/02,
03/04; **FA Cup** 01/02, 02/03, FA Cup 04/05.
ARSENAL RECORD **League** 151 (5) games, 8 goals;
FA Cup 19 (1) games, 0 goals; **League Cup** 2 (1)
games, 0 goals; **Europe** 42 (3) games, 1 goal;
Community Shield 4 games, 0 goals; **Total** 218 (10)
games, 9 goals
ENGLAND CAPS 44
IN 2005/06 Just as poor Ashley was entering his
prime, he was condemned by injury to sit out most
of the season. However, he fought back to fitness in
time for the climax of a tumultuous term, proving
that he remains one of the classiest full-backs in the
world – and, all being well, his best is yet to come.

	Bergkamp	Campbell	Clichy	Cole		Bergkamp	Campbell	Clichy	Cole
Offsides	13	0	0	2	Tackles	9	44	24	38
Assists	1	2	0	0	Tackle success	67%	61%	88%	71%
Chances created	13	6	1	7	Clearances	3	243	29	17
Pass completion own half	88%	89%	90%	91%	Fouls	22	18	5	11
Pass completion opp half	74%	60%	80%	85%	Free-kicks won	19	17	6	4
Cross completion	26%	0%	29%	18%					

Totals of international caps correct to 17 May 2006

PATRICK CREGG

POSITION MIDFIELDER
SQUAD NUMBER 35
BORN DUBLIN, 21 FEBRUARY 1986

JOINED ARSENAL as scholar in summer 2002, professional in July 2003, transferred to Falkirk in January 2006
SENIOR ARSENAL DEBUT 9 November 2004 v Everton at Highbury (League Cup, as substitute)
ARSENAL RECORD **League Cup** 0 (3) games, 0 goals; **Total** 0 (3) games, 0 goals
IN 2005/06 The sparky young Irish midfielder confirmed the early promise demonstrated in Arsenal's junior ranks, but proved unable to make a long-term senior breakthrough. Patrick moved to Falkirk in the January transfer window, featuring prominently in the Bairns' successful campaign to avoid relegation from the Scottish top flight.

PASCAL CYGAN

POSITION CENTRAL DEFENDER
SQUAD NUMBER 18
BORN LENS, FRANCE, 29 APRIL 1974

OTHER CLUBS Valenciennes, ES Wasquehal, Lille
JOINED ARSENAL from Lille in July 2002
SENIOR ARSENAL DEBUT 1 September 2002 v Chelsea at Stamford Bridge (League, as substitute)
ARSENAL HONOURS **League Championship** 03/04
ARSENAL RECORD **League** 52 (11) games, 3 goals; **FA Cup** 4 (1) games, 0 goals; **League Cup** 7 (1) games, 0 goals; **Europe** 16 (4) games, 0 goals; **Community Shield** 1 (1) games, 0 goals; **Total** 80 (18) games, 3 goals
IN 2005/06 The unflappable French defender made a doughty contribution in the first half of the campaign, but then a hamstring strain ended his season in mid-January. Thought the development of Kolo Toure and Philippe Senderos has limited his opportunities, Pascal remains a valuable member of the squad.

FIRST-TEAM STATISTICS IN THE PREMIERSHIP 2005/06

	Cygan	Diaby	Djourou		Cygan	Diaby	Djourou
Games	11 (1)	9 (3)	6 (1)	Headed goals	1	0	-
Goals	2	1	0	Left-foot goals	1	0	-
Penalty goals	0	0	-	Right-foot goals	0	1	-
Set-piece goals	0	1	-	Goal attempts	4	7	5
Goals from inside box	2	0	-	Accuracy	50%	29%	60%
Goals from outside box	0	0	-	Conversion	50%	14%	0%

JOHAN DJOUROU

POSITION **DEFENDER/MIDFIELDER**
SQUAD NUMBER **36**
BORN **IVORY COAST, 18 JANUARY 1987**

OTHER CLUB Etoile
JOINED ARSENAL as scholar in summer 2003, professional January 2005
SENIOR ARSENAL DEBUT 27 October 2004 v Manchester City at City of Manchester Stadium (League Cup, as substitute)
ARSENAL RECORD **League** 6 (1) games, 0 goals; **FA Cup** 2 games, 0 goals; **League Cup** 5 (1) games, 0 goals; **Total** 13 (2) games, 0 goals
SWITZERLAND CAPS 1
IN 2005/06 The versatile naturalised Swiss international, primarily a centre-half, stepped out of the junior ranks on a dozen occasions and made the most of his extended opportunity. Johan showed composure, intelligence and maturity to match his all-round ability, and can be expected to progress further in 2006/07.

ABOU DIABY

POSITION **MIDFIELDER**
SQUAD NUMBER **2**
BORN **PARIS, 11 MAY 1986**

OTHER CLUB Auxerre
JOINED ARSENAL from Auxerre in January 2006
SENIOR ARSENAL DEBUT 21 January 2006 v Everton at Goodison Park (League, as substitute)
ARSENAL RECORD **League** 9 (3) games, 1 goal; **FA Cup** 1 game, 0 goals; **League Cup** 1 game, 0 goals; **Europe** 0 (2) games, 0 goals; **Total** 11 (5) games, 1 goal
IN 2005/06 The towering Parisian bore eloquent testimony to Arsène Wenger's judgement, revealing a comprehensive range of midfield attributes before being cut down and grievously injured against Sunderland in May. In the long term, his power, desire and not-to-be-underrated dexterity on the ball should play a key part in Arsenal's future.

	Cygan	Diaby	Djourou
Offsides	1	0	0
Assists	0	1	0
Chances created	3	6	1
Pass completion own half	89%	87%	95%
Pass completion opp half	76%	76%	78%
Cross completion	0%	0%	0%

	Cygan	Diaby	Djourou
Tackles	47	27	12
Tackle success	81%	74%	92%
Clearances	81	18	52
Fouls	20	23	6
Free-kicks won	3	13	8

Totals of international caps correct to 17 May 2006

EMMANUEL EBOUE

POSITION DEFENDER
SQUAD NUMBER 27
BORN ABIDJAN, IVORY COAST, 4 JUNE 1983

OTHER CLUBS Abidjan, Beveren
JOINED ARSENAL from Beveren in January 2005
SENIOR ARSENAL DEBUT 9 January 2005 v Stoke City
at Highbury (FA Cup)
ARSENAL RECORD League 11 (8) games, o goals;
FA Cup 3 games, o goals; League Cup 3 games,
1 goal; Europe 9 (2) games, o goals; Total 26 (10)
games, 1 goal
IVORY COAST CAPS 11
IN 2005/06 Emmanuel emerged as one of the most
sensational finds of the season, arguably the most
exciting right-back prospect in the European game.
Flinty and uncompromising in defence, he thrilled the
fans as a swashbuckling attacker, employing his pace
and flair down the right flank to run opponents ragged.

CESC FABREGAS

POSITION MIDFIELDER
SQUAD NUMBER 15
BORN VILESSOC DE MAR, SPAIN, 4 MAY 1987

OTHER CLUB Barcelona
JOINED ARSENAL from Barcelona in September 2003
SENIOR ARSENAL DEBUT 28 October 2003 v
Rotherham United at Highbury (League Cup)
ARSENAL HONOURS FA Cup 04/05
ARSENAL RECORD League 54 (14) games, 5 goals;
FA Cup 4 (2) games, o goals; League Cup 3 (2)
games, 1 goal; Europe 14 (4) games, 2 goals;
Community Shield 2 games, 1 goal; Total 77 (22)
games, 9 goals
SPAIN CAPS 1
IN 2005/06 Arsenal's youthful play-maker bestrode
both the Premiership and Champions League as a
truly exceptional talent. With his vision, imagination
and immaculate touch, he lit up the game, and
seems set for a glorious future as the creative hub
of Arsène Wenger's beautifully fluent young team.

FIRST-TEAM STATISTICS IN THE PREMIERSHIP 2005/06

	Eboue	Fabregas	Flamini		Eboue	Fabregas	Flamini
Games	11 (7)	30 (5)	19 (12)	Headed goals	-	1	-
Goals	0	3	0	Left-foot goals	-	1	-
Penalty goals	-	0	-	Right-foot goals	-	3	-
Set-piece goals	-	0	-	Goal attempts	6	33	9
Goals from inside box	-	2	-	Accuracy	33%	48%	33%
Goals from outside box	-	1	-	Conversion	0%	9%	0%

MATHIEU FLAMINI

POSITION **MIDFIELDER OR LEFT-BACK**
SQUAD NUMBER **16**
BORN **MARSEILLE, FRANCE, 7 MARCH 1984**

JOINED ARSENAL from Olympique Marseille in July 2004
SENIOR ARSENAL DEBUT 15 August 2004 v Everton at Goodison Park (League, as substitute)
ARSENAL RECORD **League** 28 (24) games, 1 goal; **FA Cup** 6 games, 0 goals; **League Cup** 5 (1) games, 0 goals; **Europe** 13 (3) games, 0 goals; **Community Shield** 1 game, 0 goals; **Total** 53 (28) games, 1 goal
IN 2005/06 Mathieu can be proud of a magnificent contribution to the team effort, stepping in at left-back when both Ashley Cole and Gael Clichy were injured, and barely putting a foot wrong. Quick and brave, tenacious and skilful, he seems capable of flourishing either in defence or midfield. A colossal asset.

RYAN GARRY

POSITION **DEFENDER**
SQUAD NUMBER **NONE**
BORN **HORNCHURCH, 29 SEPTEMBER 1983**

JOINED ARSENAL as scholar in summer 2000, professional in summer 2001
SENIOR ARSENAL DEBUT 6 November 2002 v Sunderland at Highbury (League Cup, as substitute)
ARSENAL RECORD **League** 1 game, 0 goals; **League Cup** 0 (1) game, 0 goals; **Total** 1 (1) games, 0 goals
IN 2005/06 Ryan endured serial agony with a shin condition which relegated him to the sidelines for most of the season. After returning from one lengthy lay-off in August, the talented England Youth international soon suffered further problems, but was hoping for a return to meaningful action in 2006/07.

	Eboue	Fabregas	Flamini
Offsides	1	3	1
Assists	2	5	3
Chances created	10	32	11
Pass completion own half	88%	92%	89%
Pass completion opp half	78%	78%	82%
Cross completion	18%	30%	25%

	Eboue	Fabregas	Flamini
Tackles	41	124	62
Tackle success	80%	69%	69%
Clearances	38	30	63
Fouls	13	44	26
Free-kicks won	23	66	24

Totals of international caps correct to 17 May 2006

GILBERTO SILVA

POSITION MIDFIELDER
SQUAD NUMBER 19
BORN LAGOA DA PRATA, BRAZIL, 7 OCTOBER 1976

OTHER CLUBS America MG, Atletico Mineiro
JOINED ARSENAL from Atletico Mineiro in July 2002
SENIOR ARSENAL DEBUT 11 August 2002 v Liverpool
at Millennium Stadium (Community Shield, as
substitute)
ARSENAL HONOURS League Championship 03/04;
FA Cup 02/03, 04/05
ARSENAL RECORD League 107 (6) games, 6 goals;
FA Cup 7 (2) games, o goals; League Cup 4 games,
1 goal; Europe 27 (4) games, 3 goals; Community
Shield 2 (2) games, 2 goals; Total 147 (14) games,
12 goals
BRAZIL CAPS 35
IN 2005/06 Given extra responsibility following the
departure of Patrick Vieira, Gilberto responded with
the finest form of his career to date, emerging as
one of the most influential holding midfielders in
Europe. Whether protecting his back four or probing
in support of the attack, the Brazilian World Cup
winner was a study in poise and resolution.

KERREA GILBERT

POSITION DEFENDER
SQUAD NUMBER 38
BORN HAMMERSMITH, LONDON, 28 FEBRUARY 1987

JOINED ARSENAL as scholar in summer 2003,
professional in summer 2005
SENIOR ARSENAL DEBUT 29 November 2005 v
Reading at Highbury (League Cup)
ARSENAL RECORD League 2 games, o goals; FA Cup
2 games, o goals; League Cup 3 (1) games, o goals;
Europe o (1) game, o goals; Total 7 (2) games, o goals
IN 2005/06 Kerrea impressed mightily in both full-
back berths when given a clutch of mid-season
opportunities. The powerful, athletic youngster set
up a rare headed goal for Thierry Henry in the
League Cup semi-final against Wigan, then he was
unlucky to suffer a back injury just as he was
thriving. Another one for the future.

FIRST-TEAM STATISTICS IN THE PREMIERSHIP 2005/06

	Gilbert	Gilberto	Henry	Hleb		Gilbert	Gilberto	Henry	Hleb
Games	2	33	30 (2)	17 (8)	Headed goals	-	1	0	0
Goals	0	2	27	3	Left-foot goals	-	0	3	1
Penalty goals	-	0	3	0	Right-foot goals	-	1	24	2
Set-piece goals	-	0	2	0	Goal attempts	0	27	102	10
Goals from inside box	-	2	22	3	Accuracy	-	33%	52%	50%
Goals from outside box	-	0	5	0	Conversion	-	7%	26%	30%

THIERRY HENRY

POSITION FORWARD
SQUAD NUMBER 14
BORN PARIS, 17 AUGUST 1977

OTHER CLUBS AS Monaco, Juventus
JOINED ARSENAL from Juventus in August 1999
SENIOR ARSENAL DEBUT 7 August 1999 v Leicester
City at Highbury (League, as substitute)
ARSENAL HONOURS League Championship 01/02,
03/04; FA Cup 01/02, 02/03
ARSENAL RECORD League 219 (18) games, 164
goals; FA Cup 15 (6) games, 6 goals; League Cup
3 games, 2 goals; Europe 72 (6) games, 41 goals;
Community Shield 4 games, 1 goal; Total 313 (30)
games, 214 goals
FRANCE CAPS 76
IN 2005/06 The record-breaking marksman, new
Arsenal skipper and PFA Footballer of the Year was
a realistic candidate for the title of the world's top
player, thanks to a combination of searing pace,
mesmerising skill and lethal finishing ability. In the
wake of European Cup final defeat, his signing of a
new contract offered the best possible boost for
the Gunners.

ALEXANDER HLEB

POSITION MIDFIELDER
SQUAD NUMBER 13
BORN MINSK, BELARUS, 1 MAY 1981

OTHER CLUBS BATE Borisov, VfB Stuttgart
JOINED ARSENAL 27 June 2005 from VfB Stuttgart
SENIOR ARSENAL DEBUT 7 August 2005 v Chelsea at
the Millennium Stadium (Community Shield)
ARSENAL RECORD League 17 (8) games, 3 goals; FA
Cup 1 game, 0 goals; League Cup 3 games, 0 goals;
Europe 9 (1) games, 0 goals; Community Shield 0 (1)
game, 0 goals; Total 30 (10) games, 3 goals
BELARUS CAPS 22
IN 2005/06 The twinkling feet and prodigious work-
rate of Alexander Hleb was an enduring feature of the
Gunners' roller-coaster of a campaign. His impetus
was jolted by injury in the autumn, but on recovery he
began to show consistent form and built a productive
understanding with his fellow attackers.

	Gilbert	Gilberto	Henry	Hleb
Offsides	1	1	39	0
Assists	0	0	8	0
Chances created	2	11	63	25
Pass completion own half	77%	88%	79%	88%
Pass completion opp half	93%	80%	70%	78%
Cross completion	67%	22%	31%	32%

	Gilbert	Gilberto	Henry	Hleb
Tackles	4	135	45	55
Tackle success	50%	67%	67%	80%
Clearances	5	65	16	9
Fouls	2	64	36	24
Free-kicks won	2	35	37	45

Totals of international caps correct to 17 May 2006

JUSTIN HOYTE

POSITION DEFENDER
SQUAD NUMBER NONE
BORN WALTHAM FOREST, 20 NOVEMBER 1984

OTHER CLUB Sunderland on loan
JOINED ARSENAL as scholar in summer 2001, as professional in July 2002
SENIOR ARSENAL DEBUT 7 May 2003 v Southampton at Highbury (League, as substitute)
ARSENAL RECORD League 4 (3) games, 0 goals; **FA Cup** 0 (1) game, 0 goals; **League Cup** 5 games, 0 goals; **Europe** 1 (1) games, 0 goals; **Community Shield** 0 (2) games, 0 goals; **Total** 10 (7) games, 0 goals
IN 2005/06 Justin spent the entire season battling unsuccessfully against relegation on loan at Sunderland, but he will have benefited enormously from the regular top-flight action. Despite the incessant pressure, often the tall, speedy England under-21 defender was one of the Wearsiders' most polished and reliable performers.

SEBASTIAN LARSSON

POSITION MIDFIELDER
SQUAD NUMBER 29
BORN ESKILTUNA, SWEDEN, 6 JUNE 1985

JOINED ARSENAL as scholar in summer 2001, professional in July 2002
SENIOR ARSENAL DEBUT 27 October 2004 v Manchester City at City of Manchester Stadium (League Cup)
ARSENAL RECORD League 2 (1) games, 0 goals; **FA Cup** 0 (1) game, 0 goals; **League Cup** 4 (3) games, 0 goals; **Europe** 1 game, 0 goals; **Total** 7 (5) games, 0 goals
IN 2005/06 The classy Sweden Under-21 international midfielder made marked progress, being awarded five senior starts. Versatile enough to double confidently as a left-back if needed, as he did on his three Premiership outings, he offered Arsène Wenger a viable option when the squad was ravaged by injuries.

FIRST-TEAM STATISTICS IN THE PREMIERSHIP 2005/06

	Larsson	Lauren	Lehmann		Larsson	Lauren	Lehmann
Games	2 (1)	22	38	Headed goals	-	-	-
Goals Saves	0	0	91	Left-foot goals	-	-	-
Penalty goals Save success rate	-	-	75%	Right-foot goals	-	-	-
Set-piece goals	-	-	-	Goal attempts Catches	0	4	93
Goals from inside box	-	-	-	Accuracy Catch completion rate	-	100%	94%
Goals from outside box	-	-	-	Conversion Punches	-	0%	31

LAUREN

POSITION DEFENDER OR MIDFIELDER
SQUAD NUMBER 12
BORN LONDI KRIBI, CAMEROON, 19 JANUARY 1977

OTHER CLUBS Utrera, Seville, Levante, Real Mallorca
JOINED ARSENAL from Real Mallorca in May 2000
SENIOR ARSENAL DEBUT 19 August 2000 v
Sunderland at the Stadium of Light (League,
as substitute)
ARSENAL HONOURS **League Championship** 01/02,
03/04; **FA Cup** 01/02, 02/03, 04/05
ARSENAL RECORD **League** 152 (7) games, 6 goals;
FA Cup 23 games, 2 goals; **League Cup** 2 games,
0 goals; **Europe** 46 (7) games, 1 goal; **Community
Shield** 4 games, 0 goals; **Total** 227 (14) games,
9 goals
CAMEROON CAPS 22
IN 2005/06 Lauren suffered interminable frustration
after falling prey to injury in January. Not only did
the stalwart right-back miss out on the Gunners'
tumultuous progress to the European Cup final, but
he could only look on helplessly as the ebullient
Emmanuel Eboue laid persuasive claim to his first-
team berth.

JENS LEHMANN

POSITION GOALKEEPER
SQUAD NUMBER 1
BORN ESSEN, GERMANY, 10 NOVEMBER 1969

OTHER CLUBS DJK Heisingen, Schwarz-Weiss Essen,
FC Schalke, AC Milan, Borussia Dortmund
JOINED ARSENAL from Borussia Dortmund in
July 2003
SENIOR ARSENAL DEBUT 10 August 2003 v
Manchester United at the Millennium Stadium
(Community Shield)
ARSENAL HONOURS **League Championship** 03/04;
FA Cup 04/05
ARSENAL RECORD **League** 104 games, 0 goals;
FA Cup 10 games, 0 goals; **Europe** 25 games,
0 goals; **Community Shield** 3 games, 0 goals;
Total 142 games, 0 goals
GERMANY CAPS 29
IN 2005/06 The tempestuous German played the
finest football of his life, particularly during the
Champions League campaign in which the Gunners
went ten matches without conceding a goal. His late
penalty save ensured semi-final victory and it was
a shame that his wonderful season should climax
with dismissal in Paris.

	Larsson	Lauren	Lehmann
Offsides	0	0	-
Assists	0	1	0
Chances created	0	8	1
Pass completion own half	90%	91%	82%
Pass completion opp half	69%	82%	26%
Cross completion	50%	15%	-

	Larsson	Lauren	Lehmann
Tackles	5	84	1
Tackle success	80%	71%	0%
Clearances	12	88	23
Fouls	3	31	0
Free-kicks won	2	36	23

Totals of international caps correct to 17 May 2006

FREDRIK LJUNGBERG

POSITION MIDFIELDER

SQUAD NUMBER 8

BORN HALMSTADS, SWEDEN, 16 APRIL 1977

OTHER CLUB Halmstads

JOINED ARSENAL from Halmstads in September 1998

SENIOR ARSENAL DEBUT 20 September 1998 v
Manchester United at Highbury (League,
as substitute)

ARSENAL HONOURS **League Championship** 01/2,
03/04; **FA Cup** 01/02, 02/03, 04/05

ARSENAL RECORD **League** 172 (26) games, 46
goals; **FA Cup** 26 (4) games, 10 goals; **League Cup**
3 games, 0 goals; **Europe** 59 (9) games, 14 goals;
Charity/Community Shield 3 games, 0 goals;
Total 263 (39) games, 70 goals

SWEDEN CAPS 56

IN 2005/06 Like so many of his colleagues he suffered
from niggling injuries, but the Gunners invariably
looked more convincing when Freddie was beavering
away on one of the midfield flanks. Previously noted
for his crucial goals, he fell short in that department
this time, hitting the target only twice all season.

ARTURO LUPOLI

POSITION FORWARD

SQUAD NUMBER 41

BORN BRESCIA, ITALY, 24 JUNE 1987

OTHER CLUB Parma

JOINED ARSENAL as scholar in summer 2004,
professional September 2004

SENIOR ARSENAL DEBUT 27 October 2004
v Manchester City at City of Manchester Stadium
(League Cup)

ARSENAL RECORD **League** 0 (1) game, 0 goals;
FA Cup 1 game, 0 goals; **League Cup** 5 (2) games,
3 goals; **Total** 6 (3) games, 3 goals

IN 2005/06 Arturo proved himself a smoothly
efficient marksman, finishing joint top-scorer for
the reserves with Nicklas Bendtner and looking
both stylish and sharp. The Italian Under-19
international, who hit the target in the Carling Cup
triumph over Reading, appeared ready to take the
next step up the football ladder.

FIRST-TEAM STATISTICS IN THE PREMIERSHIP 2005/06

	Ljungberg	Lupoli	Owusu -Abeyie		Ljungberg	Lupoli	Owusu -Abeyie
Games	21 (4)	0 (1)	0 (4)	Headed goals	0	-	-
Goals	1	0	0	Left-foot goals	1	-	-
Penalty goals	0	-	-	Right-foot goals	0	-	-
Set-piece goals	0	-	-	Goal attempts	24	0	0
Goals from inside box	1	-	-	Accuracy	54%	-	-
Goals from outside box	0	-	-	Conversion	4%	-	-

FABRICE MUAMBA

POSITION MIDFIELDER
SQUAD NUMBER 44
BORN DR CONGO, 6 APRIL 1988

JOINED ARSENAL as scholar in summer 2004
SENIOR ARSENAL DEBUT 25 October 2005 v
Sunderland at Stadium of Light (League Cup)
ARSENAL RECORD **League Cup** 2 games, 0 goals;
Total 2 games, 0 goals
IN 2005/06 The England Youth international holding
midfielder gave a positive account of himself in
League Cup encounters with Sunderland and
Reading, only to be ruled out of the Doncaster
quarter-final through injury. Fabrice tackled
abrasively and looked comfortable on the ball. His
role model, Patrick Vieira, would have approved.

QUINCY OWUSU-ABEYIE

POSITION FORWARD
SQUAD NUMBER 26
BORN AMSTERDAM, HOLLAND, 15 APRIL 1986

JOINED ARSENAL as scholar in September 2002;
transferred to Spartak Moscow in January 2006
SENIOR ARSENAL DEBUT 28 October 2003
v Rotherham United at Highbury (League Cup,
as substitute)
ARSENAL RECORD **League** 1 (4) games, 0 goals;
FA Cup 0 (3) games, 0 goals; **League Cup** 6 (4)
games, 2 goals; **Europe** 1 (4) games, 0 goals;
Total 8 (15) games, 2 goals
IN 2005/06 Quicksilver raider Quincy appeared
on the verge of claiming a regular berth in the
Gunners' senior squad, but then accepted a move
to Spartak Moscow during the January transfer
window. The Holland Under-21 international
made five senior starts and rose from the bench
eight times.

	Ljungberg	Lupoli	Owusu -Abeyie		Ljungberg	Lupoli	Owusu -Abeyie
Offsides	4	0	0	Tackles	59	0	0
Assists	3	0	0	Tackle success	71%	0%	0%
Chances created	32	0	1	Clearances	4	0	0
Pass completion own half	89%	0%	100%	Fouls	25	0	0
Pass completion opp half	79%	0%	55%	Free-kicks won	50	0	0
Cross completion	27%	0%	0%				

Totals of international caps correct to 17 May 2006

the bench than in previous campaigns, he had lost none of his customary fluency, whether operating in central midfield, on one of the flanks or just behind the main striker. Yet again his goal tally reached double figures, a tribute to his enduring class. Robert joined Villarreal in May 2006.

MART POOM

POSITION GOALKEEPER
SQUAD NUMBER 21
BORN TALLINN, ESTONIA, 3 MARCH 1972

OTHER CLUBS FC Wil, Portsmouth, Derby County, Sunderland
JOINED ARSENAL from Sunderland on loan in August 2005, transferred in January 2006
ARSENAL RECORD no senior appearances
ESTONIA CAPS 103

IN 2005/06 At many clubs Mart Poom would have been first-choice custodian, but at Highbury the man who amassed a century of caps for Estonia had to be content with the role of third string. Still, he performed splendidly for the reserves and set a fine example for the Gunners' clutch of rookie 'keepers.

ROBERT PIRES

POSITION MIDFIELDER
SQUAD NUMBER 7
BORN REIMS, FRANCE, 29 JANUARY 1973

OTHER CLUBS Stade de Reims, FC Metz, Olympique Marseille
JOINED ARSENAL from Olympique Marseille in July 2000
SENIOR ARSENAL DEBUT 19 August 2000 v Sunderland at the Stadium of Light (League, as substitute)
ARSENAL HONOURS **League Championship** 01/02, 03/04; **FA Cup** 02/03, 04/05
ARSENAL RECORD **League** 159 (30) games, 62 goals; **FA Cup** 22 (6) games, 10 goals; **League Cup** 1 (1) games, 1 goal; **Europe** 55 (8) games, 11 goals; **Community Shield** 1 (1) games, 0 goals; **Total** 238 (46) games, 84 goals
FRANCE CAPS 79

IN 2005/06 Though Robert started more games from

FIRST-TEAM STATISTICS IN THE PREMIERSHIP 2005/06

	Pires	Reyes	Senderos		Pires	Reyes	Senderos
Games	23 (10)	22 (4)	19 (1)	Headed goals	0	0	1
Goals	7	5	2	Left-foot goals	1	3	0
Penalty goals	1	0	0	Right-foot goals	6	2	1
Set-piece goals	0	0	0	Goal attempts	36	49	6
Goals from inside box	7	5	2	Accuracy	58%	49%	50%
Goals from outside box	0	0	0	Conversion	19%	10%	33%

JOSÉ ANTONIO REYES

POSITION **FORWARD**

SQUAD NUMBER **9**

BORN **UTRERA, SPAIN, 1 SEPTEMBER 1983**

OTHER CLUBS Sevilla, Spain

JOINED ARSENAL from Sevilla in January 2004

SENIOR ARSENAL DEBUT 1 February 2004 v
Manchester City at Highbury (League, as substitute)

ARSENAL HONOURS **League Championship** 03/04;
FA Cup 04/05

ARSENAL RECORD **League** 54 (15) games, 16 goals;
FA Cup 10 (1) games, 3 goals; **League Cup** 4 games,
1 goal; **Europe** 20 (4) games, 2 goals; **Community
Shield** 1 (1) games, 1 goal; **Total** 89 (21) games,
23 goals

SPAIN CAPS 16

IN 2005/06 José appeared at his penetrative best
against Real Madrid at the Bernabeu, but overall he
did not quite equal the consistency of his previous
campaign, halving his goal tally to six. Sometimes
the mercurial young attacker had to absorb cruel
physical punishment, but he bore it manfully and
remains a golden prospect.

PHILIPPE SENDEROS

POSITION **DEFENDER**

SQUAD NUMBER **20**

BORN **SWITZERLAND, 14 FEBRUARY 1985**

OTHER CLUB Servette

JOINED ARSENAL from Servette in June 2003

SENIOR ARSENAL DEBUT 27 October 2004 v
Manchester City at City of Manchester Stadium
(League Cup)

ARSENAL HONOURS **FA Cup** 04/05

ARSENAL RECORD **League** 31 (2) games, 2 goals;
FA Cup 8 games, 0 goals; **League cup** 8 games,
0 goals; **Europe** 8 games, 0 goals; **Community
Shield** 1 game, 0 goals; **Total** 56 (2) games,
2 goals

SWITZERLAND CAPS 10

IN 2005/06 Philippe made the most of Sol Campbell's
protracted absences to establish himself as a
centre-half of colossal class. He proved a solid and
courageous partner for Kolo Toure throughout most
of the fabulous Champions League run, and appears
to be one of Arsène Wenger's principal building
blocks for the future.

	Pires	Reyes	Senderos
Offsides	5	5	0
Assists	4	10	0
Chances created	26	44	2
Pass completion own half	93%	83%	90%
Pass completion opp half	81%	67%	62%
Cross completion	13%	34%	33%

	Pires	Reyes	Senderos
Tackles	51	51	56
Tackle success	76%	71%	73%
Clearances	14	3	219
Fouls	25	40	20
Free-kicks won	29	65	26

Totals of international caps correct to 17 May 2006

ALEXANDRE SONG

POSITION MIDFIELDER OR DEFENDER
SQUAD NUMBER 17
BORN DOUALA, CAMEROON, 9 APRIL 1987

OTHER CLUB Bastia
JOINED ARSENAL summer 2005 on loan from Bastia
ARSENAL RECORD **League** 3 (2) games, o goals;
League Cup 2 games, o goals; **Europe** 1 (1) games,
o goals; **Total** 6 (3) games, o goals
IN 2005/06 The all-action Cameroonian midfielder
performed creditably when given first-team
opportunities in both the League Cup and the
Champions League, and Arsène Wenger
demonstrated further faith by awarding him three
Premiership starts in the spring. Alex is the nephew
of ex-Liverpool defender Rigobert Song.

RYAN SMITH

POSITION MIDFIELDER
SQUAD NUMBER 47
BORN ISLINGTON, LONDON, 10 NOVEMBER 1986

OTHER CLUB Leicester City on loan
JOINED ARSENAL as scholar in summer 2003,
professional in November 2004
SENIOR ARSENAL DEBUT 28 October 2003 v
Rotherham United at Highbury (League Cup, as
substitute)
ARSENAL RECORD **League Cup** 2 (4) games, o goals;
Total 2 (4) games, o goals
IN 2005/06 Needing wider experience, the fleet-
footed, tricky England Youth international accepted
a loan stint with Championship club Leicester City.
But Ryan, who helped the Foxes to eject Tottenham
Hotspur from the FA Cup in January, later lost his
place and opted to return to Highbury in March.

FIRST-TEAM STATISTICS IN THE PREMIERSHIP 2005/06

	Song	Toure		Song	Toure
Games	3 (2)	33	Headed goals	-	-
Goals	0	0	Left-foot goals	-	-
Penalty goals	-	-	Right-foot goals	-	-
Set-piece goals	-	-	Goal attempts	1	18
Goals from inside box	-	-	Accuracy	0%	33%
Goals from outside box	-	-	Conversion	0%	0%

ANTHONY STOKES

POSITION FORWARD
SQUAD NUMBER 45
BORN DUBLIN, 25 JULY 1988

JOINED ARSENAL as scholar in summer 2004
SENIOR ARSENAL DEBUT 25 October 2005 v
Sunderland at Stadium of Light (League Cup)
ARSENAL RECORD **League Cup** 0 (1) game, 0 goals;
Total 0 (1) game, 0 goals
IN 2005/06 The Republic of Ireland Under-19
international front-man cum midfielder was
granted a fleeting taste of the big time, rising from
the bench for the last two minutes of the League
Cup triumph over Sunderland. An accomplished
finisher, Anthony is blessed with boundless
enthusiasm and endeavour.

KOLO TOURE

POSITION DEFENDER
SQUAD NUMBER 28
BORN IVORY COAST, 19 MARCH 1981

OTHER CLUB ASEC Mimosas
JOINED ARSENAL from ASEC Mimosas in February 2002
SENIOR ARSENAL DEBUT 11 August 2002 v Liverpool
at Millennium Stadium (Community Shield, as
substitute)
ARSENAL HONOURS **League Championship** 03/04;
FA Cup 04/05
ARSENAL RECORD **League** 113 (18) games, 3 goals;
FA Cup 12 (4) games, 2 goals; **League Cup** 3 games,
0 goals; **Europe** 33 (4) games, 2 goals; **Community
Shield** 3 (1) games, 0 goals; **Total** 164 (27) games,
7 goals
IVORY COAST CAPS 45
IN 2005/06 Kolo enjoyed another barnstorming
season at the heart of the Gunners' rearguard, his
commanding presence proving of enormous value
to callow colleagues such as Senderos, Eboue and
Flamini. Endlessly dynamic and almost terrifyingly
courageous, the Ivorian has matured into one of the
Premiership's most compelling performers.

	Song	Toure		Song	Toure
Offsides	0	1	Tackles	15	112
Assists	0	1	Tackle success	67%	79%
Chances created	1	5	Clearances	6	299
Pass completion own half	87%	93%	Fouls	3	18
Pass completion opp half	79%	67%	Free-kicks won	2	23
Cross completion	0%	14%			

Totals of international caps correct to 17 May 2006

but he proved himself an extravagantly gifted and immensely resilient attacker. He is capable of transforming a match with a sudden flash of brilliance and much is expected of him in the years ahead.

THEO WALCOTT

POSITION FORWARD
SQUAD NUMBER 32
BORN STANMORE, LONDON, 16 MARCH 1989

OTHER CLUB Southampton
JOINED ARSENAL from Southampton in January 2006
ARSENAL RECORD no senior appearances.
IN 2005/06 Theo cut his professional teeth at Southampton, allying verve and skill to extreme pace, but Arsenal fans did not see him in senior action following his arrival in the January transfer window. However, his shock selection for England's World Cup squad spoke volumes for the youngster's limitless potential.

ROBIN VAN PERSIE

POSITION FORWARD
SQUAD NUMBER 11
BORN ROTTERDAM, HOLLAND, 6 AUGUST 1983

OTHER CLUB Feyenoord
JOINED ARSENAL from Feyenoord in May 2004
SENIOR ARSENAL DEBUT 8 August 2004 v Manchester United at Millennium Stadium (Community Shield, as substitute)
ARSENAL HONOURS FA Cup 04/05
ARSENAL RECORD League 25 (25) games, 10 goals; FA Cup 5 (2) games, 3 goals; League Cup 6 (1) games, 5 goals; Europe 3 (10) games, 3 goals; Community Shield 0 (2) games, 0 goals; Total 39 (40) games, 21 goals
HOLLAND CAPS 7
IN 2005/06 The contribution of Robin van Persie has tended to be overshadowed by the stars around him,

FIRST-TEAM STATISTICS IN THE PREMIERSHIP 2005/06

	van Persie		van Persie
Games	13 (11)	Headed goals	0
Goals	5	Left-foot goals	5
Penalty goals	0	Right-foot goals	0
Set-piece goals	0	Goal attempts	41
Goals from inside box	4	Accuracy	56%
Goals from outside box	1	Conversion	12%

ARSÈNE WENGER Manager

BORN STRASBOURG, FRANCE, 22 OCTOBER 1949

CLUBS AS PLAYER Mutzig, Mulhouse, Strasbourg
CLUBS AS MANAGER/COACH Strasbourg (youth section), Cannes (assistant), Nancy, AS Monaco, Grampus Eight Nagoya
HONOURS AS MANAGER/COACH with AS Monaco – **French League Championship** 87/8, **French Cup** 90/1, **France Manager of the Year** 87/8; with Grampus Eight Nagoya – **Emperor's Cup** 1996, **Japan Super Cup** 1996, **Japan Manager of the Year** 1995; with Arsenal – **League Championship** 97/8, 01/02, 03/04; **FA Cup** 97/8, 01/02, 02/03, 04/05; **Manager of the Year** 97/8, 01/02, 03/04
JOINED ARSENAL 1996

YOUTH DEVELOPMENT STAFF

LIAM BRADY Head of Youth Development and Academy Manager
Born Dublin, 13 February 1956
Clubs as player Arsenal, Juventus, Sampdoria, Internazionale, Ascoli, West Ham United
Honours as player with Arsenal – **FA Cup** 78/9; with Juventus – **Italian Championship** 81/2. Won 72 caps for Republic of Ireland
Clubs as coach/manager Celtic, Brighton and Hove Albion
Joined Arsenal coaching staff 1996

DAVID COURT Assistant Head of Youth Development and Assistant Academy Manager
Born Mitcham, 1 March 1944
Clubs as player Arsenal, Luton Town
Joined Arsenal coaching staff 1996

STEVE BOULD Under-18s Coach
Born Stoke, 16 November 1962
Clubs as player Stoke City, Torquay United (loan), Arsenal, Sunderland
Honours as player with Arsenal – **European Cup-Winners' Cup** 93/4; **League title** 88/9, 90/1, 97/8. Won 2 England caps
Joined Arsenal coaching staff 2001

DERMOT DRUMMY Youth Coach
Born Hackney, 16 January 1961
Clubs as player Arsenal, Blackpool
Joined Arsenal coaching staff 1996

DAVID WALES Youth Team Physiotherapist
Born Gateshead, 24 August 1972
Joined Arsenal 2001

JON COOKE Youth Team Physiotherapist
Born Colchester, 24 September 1976
Joined Arsenal September 2002

SENIOR OFFICIALS 2005/2006

PAT RICE Assistant Manager
Born Belfast, 17 March 1949
Clubs as player Arsenal, Watford
Honours as player **League Championship** 70/1; **FA Cup** 70/1, 78/9. Won 49 caps for Northern Ireland
Joined Arsenal as coach 1984
Honours as Arsenal coach **FA Youth Cup** 87/8, 93/4; **League Championship** 97/8, 01/02, 03/04; **FA Cup** 97/8, 01/02, 02/03, 04/05

BORO PRIMORAC First Team Coach
Born Mostar, Yugoslavia (now Bosnia), 5 December 1954
Clubs as player Hajduk Split, Cannes, Lille
Honours as player Captained Yugoslavia, 18 caps
Clubs as coach Cannes, Valenciennes, Grampus Eight Nagoya
Joined Arsenal 1997
Honours as Arsenal coach **League Championship** 97/8, 01/02, 03/04; **FA Cup** 97/8, 01/02, 02/03, 04/05

NEIL BANFIELD Reserves Coach
Born Poplar, 20 January 1962
Clubs as player Crystal Palace, Adelaide City, Leyton Orient

Clubs as coach Charlton Athletic
Joined Arsenal 1997

GERRY PEYTON Goalkeeping Coach
Born Birmingham, 20 May 1956
Clubs as player Fulham, Southend United (loan), Bournemouth, Everton, Bolton Wanderers (loan), Brentford, Chelsea (loan), West Ham United
Honours as player won 33 caps for Republic of Ireland
Clubs as coach Vissel Kobe of Japan, AIK Solna of Sweden, Fulham
Joined Arsenal July 2003

GARY LEWIN Physiotherapist
Born East Ham, London, 16 May 1964
Clubs as player Arsenal (youth), Barnet
Joined Arsenal as physio 1983
England physio since 1996

COLIN LEWIN Assistant Physiotherapist
Born Plaistow, London, 15 September 1973
Joined Arsenal 1995

TONY COLBERT Fitness Coach
Born Paddington, London, 29 May 1963
Joined Arsenal 1998

CRAIG GANT Assistant Fitness Coach/Masseur
Born London, 27 February 1970
Joined Arsenal part-time 2000, full-time 2001

JOEL HARRIS Sports Therapist
Born Wimbledon, London, 28 August 1961
Joined Arsenal part-time 1994, full-time 1998

JOHN KELLY Masseur
Born Barking, 18 March 1957
Joined Arsenal August 2002

STEVE ROWLEY Chief Scout
Born Romford, 2 December 1958
Joined Arsenal 1980

VIC AKERS Kit Manager
Born Islington, London, 24 August 1946
Clubs as player Slough Town, Cambridge United, Watford
Joined Arsenal as reserve team physio and kit manager 1986. General manager of Arsenal Ladies

PAUL AKERS Assistant Kit Manager
Born Bromley, 3 February 1976
Joined Arsenal 2001

PAUL JOHNSON Equipment Manager
Born Hackney, 14 March 1961
Joined Arsenal 1981

LADIES OFFICIALS

VIC AKERS General Manager
CLARE WHEATLEY Development Manager
CIARA GRANT Assistant Development Officer
FAYE WHITE Assistant Development Officer
JAYNE LUDLOW Medical Officer
FRED DONNELLY Academy Director
KELLY SMITH Assistant Academy Director

	van Persie			van Persie
Offsides	11	Tackles		21
Assists	1	Tackle success		62%
Chances created	15	Clearances		4
Pass completion own half	85%	Fouls		22
Pass completion opp half	76%	Free-kicks won		20
Cross completion	22%			

Totals of international caps correct to 17 May 2006

RESERVES 2005/2006

BARCLAYS PREMIERSHIP RESERVE LEAGUE SOUTH

MON 8 AUG	WEST HAM UNITED	H	3–2	TUE 17 JAN	LEICESTER CITY	A	4–1
TUE 16 AUG	COVENTRY CITY	A	0–1	MON 30 JAN	NORWICH CITY	A	5–0
TUE 30 AUG	LEICESTER CITY	H	5–2	THUR 7 FEB	PORTSMOUTH	A	2–3
MON 5 SEP	IPSWICH TOWN	A	4–2	MON 13 FEB	CHELSEA	A	0–0
MON 12 SEP	CRYSTAL PALACE	H	2–2	MON 27 FEB	TOTTENHAM HOTSPUR	H	1–2
WED 21 SEP	PORTSMOUTH	H	5–3	MON 6 MAR	FULHAM	H	0–1
MON 3 OCT	CHELSEA	H	0–0	THUR 9 MAR	CRYSTAL PALACE	A	2–2
MON 10 OCT	TOTTENHAM HOTSPUR	A	2–0	MON 20 MAR	CHARLTON ATHLETIC	H	2–0
TUE 18 OCT	FULHAM	A	3–1	WED 29 MAR	SOUTHAMPTON	A	1–5
WED 9 NOV	CHARLTON ATHLETIC	A	3–0	MON 3 APR	NORWICH CITY	H	2–2
MON 14 NOV	SOUTHAMPTON	H	2–2	MON 10 APR	WATFORD	H	1–1
MON 5 DEC	WATFORD	A	2–1	WED 19 APR	COVENTRY CITY	H	4–0
WED 4 JAN	IPSWICH TOWN	H	2–0	THUR 27 APR	WEST HAM UNITED	A	3–1

BARCLAYS PREMIERSHIP RESERVE LEAGUE SOUTH FINAL TABLE

	P	W	D	L	F	A	PTS
TOTTENHAM HOTSPUR	26	20	3	3	52	13	63
SOUTHAMPTON	26	16	3	7	50	26	51
ARSENAL	26	14	7	5	60	34	49
CHARLTON ATHLETIC	26	14	4	8	38	29	46
COVENTRY CITY	26	13	1	12	30	36	40
CHELSEA	26	10	9	7	34	24	39
FULHAM	26	11	3	12	26	32	36
CRYSTAL PALACE	26	10	5	11	43	42	35
IPSWICH TOWN	26	10	1	15	44	54	31
WEST HAM UNITED	26	7	8	11	37	38	29
LEICESTER CITY	26	7	7	12	38	57	28
WATFORD	26	8	3	15	25	51	27
PORTSMOUTH	26	6	4	16	35	54	22
NORWICH CITY	26	4	6	16	19	46	18

Right Defender Matthew Connolly played superbly for the Reserves this season and will be knocking strongly on the first-team door in 2006/07.

Far right, top Nicklas Bendtner was the Reserves leading appearance maker this season as well as being joint top-scorer with Arturo Lupoli (below).

LEAGUE APPEARANCES AND GOALS

	APPS (AS SUB)	GOALS
NICKLAS BENDTNER	23 (2)	18
FABRICE MUAMBA	21 (3)	1
MATTHEW CONNOLLY	21 (1)	0
ANTHONY STOKES	18 (4)	3
ARTURO LUPOLI	16	18
SEBASTIAN LARSSON	16	5
KERREA GILBERT	16	0
SEAN KELLY	14 (2)	0
MART POOM	11	0
ALEXANDRE SONG	11	0
PATRICK CREGG	10 (1)	1
RYAN SMITH	10 (1)	1
PAUL RODGERS	9 (1)	0
JAY SIMPSON	8 (6)	6
MITCHELL MURPHY	8 (2)	0
GIORGOS EFREM	7 (3)	2
VITO MANNONE	7	0
JOHAN DJOUROU	6	0
ARMAND TRAORE	6	0
QUINCY OWUSU-ABEYIE	4	1
MANUEL ALMUNIA	4	0
THEO WALCOTT	3	2
SOL CAMPBELL	3	0
ASHLEY COLE	3	0
EMMANUEL EBOUE	3	0
MARC ELSTON	2 (6)	1
SHANE TRACY	2 (6)	0
MARK RANDALL	2 (5)	0
GAEL CLICHY	2	0
ABOU DIABY	2	0
MATTHIEU FLAMINI	2	0
RYAN GARRY	2	0
MARK HOWARD	2	0
MICHAEL JORDAN	2	0
JOSEPH O'CEARULL	2	0
PHILIPPE SENDEROS	2	0
RENE STEER	1 (4)	0
GAVIN HOYTE	1 (2)	0
CARL PARISIO	1 (1)	0
DAVID BENTLEY	1	0
JORDAN FOWLER	1	0
ROBIN VAN PERSIE	1	0
OWN GOALS		1

YOUTH 2005/2006

FA ACADEMY LEAGUE UNDER-18

FRI 19 AUG	CREWE ALEXANDRA	H	2–0		SAT 10 DEC	IPSWICH TOWN	H	3–0
WED 31 AUG	BIRMINGHAM CITY	A	0–3		SAT 21 JAN	MILLWALL	H	0–2
SAT 3 SEP	BRISTOL CITY	A	3–2		SAT 4 FEB	FULHAM	A	1–0
SAT 10 SEP	CARDIFF CITY	H	0–0		SAT 11 FEB	SOUTHAMPTON	A	1–2
SAT 17 SEP	COVENTRY CITY	A	3–2		SAT 18 FEB	CHELSEA	H	0–3
SAT 24 SEP	IPSWICH TOWN	A	2–2		SAT 25 FEB	CHARLTON ATHLETIC	H	5–2
SAT 1 OCT	WEST HAM UNITED	H	0–2		SAT 4 MAR	WEST HAM UNITED	A	0–2
SAT 8 OCT	NORWICH CITY	A	5–1		SAT 11 MAR	LEICESTER CITY	H	1–3
SAT 15 OCT	CRYSTAL PALACE	H	1–0		SAT 18 MAR	TOTTENHAM HOTSPUR	A	2–1
SAT 22 OCT	MILLWALL	A	2–2		SAT 25 MAR	CRYSTAL PALACE	A	2–2
SAT 5 NOV	FULHAM	H	2–3		SAT 1 APR	WATFORD	H	0–2
SAT 12 NOV	SOUTHAMPTON	H	1–2		SAT 8 APR	ASTON VILLA	A	5–1
SAT 19 NOV	CHELSEA	A	1–3		THUR 13 APR	NORWICH CITY	H	0–0
SAT 3 DEC	CHARLTON ATHLETIC	A	2–1		SAT 22 APR	MILTON KEYNES DONS	H	3–4

FA YOUTH CUP

THUR 15 DEC	BRENTFORD	H	2–2	ARSENAL LOST ON PENALTIES

FA ACADEMY LEAGUE UNDER-18 GROUP A

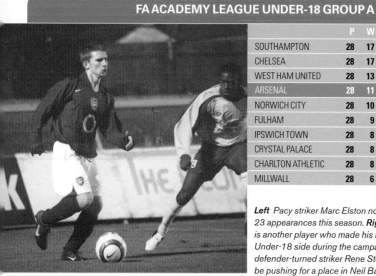

	P	W	D	L	F	A	PTS
SOUTHAMPTON	28	17	5	6	72	35	56
CHELSEA	28	17	5	6	45	21	56
WEST HAM UNITED	28	13	6	9	51	41	45
ARSENAL	28	11	5	12	47	47	38
NORWICH CITY	28	10	6	12	31	34	36
FULHAM	28	9	5	14	30	46	32
IPSWICH TOWN	28	8	7	13	53	64	31
CRYSTAL PALACE	28	8	6	14	54	59	30
CHARLTON ATHLETIC	28	8	4	16	36	52	28
MILLWALL	28	6	8	14	30	52	26

*Left Pacy striker Marc Elston notched 11 goals in his 23 appearances this season. **Right** Midfielder Jay Simpson is another player who made his mark in Steve Bould's Under-18 side during the campaign and, along with defender-turned striker Rene Steer (**Far right**), looks to be pushing for a place in Neil Banfield's Reserve side.*

LEAGUE AND FA YOUTH CUP APPEARANCES AND GOALS

	APPS (AS SUB)	GOALS		APPS (AS SUB)	GOALS
SHANE TRACY	27 (2)	2	ABU AGOG	7 (4)	1
JAY SIMPSON	23 (1)	2	CEDRIC EVINA	7 (3)	1
MARC ELSTON	23	11	MATTHEW CONNOLLY	7 (2)	2
RENE STEER	21 (6)	1	KIERAN GIBBS	3 (5)	1
SEAN KELLY	19	0	RHYS MURPHY	3 (5)	0
GIORGOS EFREM	16 (1)	3	BILLY COYN	3 (3)	0
LEE BUTCHER	16	0	ARMAND TRAORE	3	0
PAUL RODGERS	15 (2)	0	MOSES BARNETT	2 (3)	0
PEGGY LOKANDO	14 (8)	0	MARK HOWARD	2	0
FABRICE MUAMBA	13 (2)	1	JAMES DUNNE	1 (1)	0
ANTHONY STOKES	13	5	EMMANUEL FRIMPONG	1 (1)	0
HENRI LANSBURY	11 (2)	2	SANCHEZ WATT	1 (1)	0
MITCHELL MURPHY	11	0	ALEXANDRE SONG	1	1
VITO MANNONE	11	0	JOHAN DJOUROU	1	0
MARK RANDALL	10	2	MICHAEL UWEZ	0 (4)	1
JEFFREY IMUDIA	9 (8)	1	KIERAN AGARD	0 (4)	0
GAVIN HOYTE	9 (2)	0	AHMAD ABDILLAHI	0 (1)	0
NICKLAS BENDTNER	8 (2)	9			
CARL PARISIO	8	0	OWN GOALS		2

ARSENAL LADIES 2005/2006

FIRST-TEAM FIXTURES

THUR 4 AUG	CHARLTON ATHLETIC	CS	*	4–0		SUN 8 JAN	CARDIFF CITY	FAC R4	A	4–1
SUN 14 AUG	CHELSEA	PL	A	2–0		THUR 19 JAN	WIMBLEDON	CC QF	A	9–0
SUN 21 AUG	LEEDS UNITED	PL	H	4–3		SUN 22 JAN	LEEDS UNITED	PL	A	4–1
SUN 28 AUG	BRISTOL ACADEMY	PL	A	5–1		SUN 29 JAN	ASTON VILLA	FAC R5	A	3–0
SUN 4 SEP	FULHAM	PL	A	6–1		SUN 5 FEB	SUNDERLAND	PL	A	6–1
TUE 13 SEP	KS AZS WROCLAW	UC	+	3–1		SUN 19 FEB	CHELSEA	FAC R6	A	6–1
THUR 15 SEP	LADA TOLIATTI	UC	+	1–0		WED 22 FEB	ADDEYAN	CC SF	H	9–1
SAT 17 SEP	BRONDBY	UC	+	0–1		SUN 26 FEB	FULHAM	PL	H	5–1
SUN 2 OCT	WOLVERHAMPTON W	LC R1	H	5–0		SUN 5 MAR	CHARLTON ATHLETIC	LCF	A	1–2
SAT 8 OCT	FRANKFURT	UC QF	H	1–1		SUN 19 MAR	CHARLTON ATHLETIC	FAC SF	A	2–1
SAT 15 OCT	FRANKFURT	UC QF	A	1–3		WED 22 MAR	CHARLTON ATHLETIC	CC F		3–4
THUR 20 OCT	CHARLTON ATHLETIC	PL	A	3–3		THUR 30 MAR	BIRMINGHAM CITY	PL	H	4–2
SUN 23 OCT	MANCHESTER CITY	LC R24	A	4–0		SUN 2 APR	SUNDERLAND	PL	H	7–0
SUN 30 OCT	EVERTON	PL	A	3–3		SUN 9 APR	EVERTON	PL	H	5–0
SUN 6 NOV	BRISTOL CITY	LC QF	A	5–0		THUR 13 APR	CHARLTON ATHLETIC	PL	H	2–0
SUN 13 NOV	BIRMINGHAM CITY	PL	A	7–0		SUN 16 APR	DONCASTER ROVERS BELLES	PL	A	5–3
SUN 27 NOV	DONCASTER ROVERS BELLES	PL	H	4–0		MON 1 MAY	LEEDS UNITED	FAC F	^	5–0
SUN 4 DEC	CHELSEA	PL	H	6–0						
SUN 11 DEC	EVERTON	LC SF	A	2–0						
SUN 18 DEC	BRISTOL ACADEMY	PL	H	5–1						

CS Charity Shield *PL* Premier League *UC* UEFA Cup *LC* League Cup *FAC* FA Cup
CC County Cup *QF* Quarter-final *SF* Semi-final *F* Final

* National Hockey Stadium, Milton Keynes + Denmark ^ New Den, Millwall

FA WOMEN'S NATIONAL PREMIER LEAGUE FINAL TABLE

	P	W	D	L	F	A	PTS
ARSENAL	18	16	0	2	83	20	50
EVERTON	18	14	2	2	46	20	44
CHARLTON ATHLETIC	18	12	3	3	41	13	39
DONCASTER BELLES	18	7	9	2	32	34	23
BRISTOL ACADEMY	18	4	6	8	19	29	20
BIRMINGHAM CITY	18	6	10	2	24	40	20
LEEDS UNITED	18	4	8	6	27	36	18
FULHAM	18	4	12	2	24	45	14
SUNDERLAND	18	3	11	4	22	57	13
CHELSEA	18	3	12	3	22	46	12

Right Another year, another league and FA Cup (opposite, bottom right) double for Vic Akers' Ladies. *Opposite* Strikers Kelly Smith (left) and Rachel Yankey both scored in the 5–0 FA Cup final defeat of Leeds United at the New Den.

APPEARANCES AND GOALS

	APPS (AS SUB)	GOALS		APPS (AS SUB)	GOALS
EMMA BYRNE	35	0	CORI DANIELS	8 (2)	0
MARY PHILLIP	34	0	HAYLEY KEMP	7 (1)	0
LIANNE SANDERSON	33 (2)	25	GEMMA DAVISON	5 (9)	3
JAYNE LUDLOW	30 (2)	24	SIAN LARKIN	2 (7)	1
RACHEL YANKEY	30 (1)	10	CHARLOTTE GURR	2	2
FAYE WHITE	27	2	REBECCA SPENCER	2 (1)	0
CIARA GRANT	26 (6)	15	DANIELLE BUET	1 (4)	1
KELLY SMITH	26 (2)	27	SARAH McGRATH	1	2
YVONNE TRACEY	25 (1)	2	BETH LLOYD	1 (2)	0
ANITA ASANTE	24 (2)	1	ASHLEY HUTTON	1 (1)	0
RACHEL McARTHUR	22 (8)	11	VAILA BARSLEY	1	0
ALEX SCOTT	19 (6)	2	KAREN RAY	0 (2)	1
LEANNE CHAMP	17 (3)	0	KAREN MARSH	0 (1)	0
JULIE FLEETING	15 (1)	17			
KIRSTY PEALLING	13 (8)	0	OWN GOALS		4

THE FA WOMEN'S CUP
IN PARTNERSHIP WITH NATIONWIDE
WINNERS 2006

THIERRY HENRY: THE MASTER

FACTFILE

HEIGHT **6' 2"**
BORN **17 AUGUST 1977,**
LES ULIS, PARIS, FRANCE
INTERNATIONAL
CAPS **76***
INTERNATIONAL
GOALS **31***
ARSENAL CAREER
313 APPEARANCES
214 GOALS

* Up to 17 May 2006,
excludes World Cup figures

ARSENAL CAREER ACHIEVEMENTS
Premiership 2000/01, 2002/03
FA Cup 2002, 2003, 2005
Professional Footballers' Association
Player of the Year 2003, 2004
Football Writers' Association Player
of the Year 2003, 2004, 2006
Golden Boot 2002, 2004, 2005, 2006
FIFA World Player of the Year runner-up
2003, 2004
INTERNATIONAL CAREER ACHIEVEMENTS
World Cup winner 1998
European Championship winner 2000
Confederations Cup winner 2003

SINCE HIS ARRIVAL IN NORTH LONDON IN 1999, Thierry Henry has proved himself to be the leading striker in the Premiership and, perhaps, world football. With explosive pace, sublime control and the kind of swagger that only truly great players possess, the France striker has helped make the last few years at Highbury some of the greatest in the stadium's 93-year history.

It was fitting that in the Club's last season at Highbury, Henry overtook Ian Wright's all-time Club goalscoring record when he scored both goals at Sparta Prague in September 2005 to go past the magic 185 mark. In a 7–0 drubbing of Middlesbrough in January 2006, he also equalled Cliff Bastin's club record of 150 league goals, achieving the milestone in just 220 Premiership games.

FIVE GREAT HENRY GOALS

1 4–2 v Wigan Athletic, May 2006
Henry netted the last ever goal at Highbury from the penalty spot (below left) in front of an adoring North Bank and claimed the matchball, too. It was the 126th and final hat trick scored by an Arsenal player at the stadium.

2 3–0 v Tottenham Hotspur, November 2002
The Gallic goal-getter embarked on a 70-yard run from deep inside his own half before finishing with aplomb for one of the greatest ever north London derby goals.

3 1–0 v Manchester United, October 2000
This is many fans' favourite ever Henry goal. With his back to goal, he chipped the ball up and then sent a magnificent overhead kick past Fabien Barthez and just under the bar for the winner.

4 4–2 v Liverpool, April 2004
Days after exiting the FA Cup and Champions League, Arsenal found themselves in trouble against Liverpool. Step forward Henry, with a brilliant individual goal en route to a timely hat-trick.

5 5–1 v Inter Milan, November 2003
Henry ran the Inter defence ragged and bewildered Javier Zanetti before firing in his second and Arsenal's third.

"When I was in Spain I thought Zinedine Zidane was the best in the world, but playing alongside Thierry made me realise that I was playing with the best footballer in the planet." JOSÉ ANTONIO REYES

"Ronaldinho is a special player, but Thierry Henry is probably technically the most gifted footballer ever to play the beautiful game." ZINEDINE ZIDANE

"People say he doesn't score a lot of goals with his head, but does he really have to with the ability he has in his feet? He makes spectacular goals look easy. His technique is fantastic." ALAN SHEARER

"I tell my kids in the Academy at Newcastle to watch Henry. Talk about cars going from 0 to 60 in a matter of seconds and he is like that. He just explodes. I could watch him for hours." PETER BEARDLSEY

No other Arsenal player has scored as many goals at the stadium and Henry is the only player in Premiership history to have netted 20 League goals in five successive seasons. In seven seasons he has never scored less than 22 goals, hitting 20 or more at Highbury alone in the last three campaigns.

He has won the Professional Footballers' Association Player of the Year Award twice and the Football Writers' Association Player of the Year Award a unique three times.

KEY DATES

DENNIS BERGKAMP: THE ICEMAN

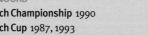

BORN 10 MAY 1969, AMSTERDAM, NETHERLANDS
HEIGHT 6'
WEIGHT 12st 5lb
INTERNATIONAL CAPS 79
INTERNATIONAL GOALS 37
PREVIOUS CLUBS
AJAX AMSTERDAM (1981–93)
185 GAMES, 103 GOALS
INTERNAZIONALE (1993–95)
52 GAMES, 11 GOALS
SIGNED FOR ARSENAL
28 JUNE 1995
ARSENAL CAREER
(IN ALL COMPETITIONS)
345 APPEARANCES (78 SUB)
120 GOALS

HONOURS
Dutch Championship 1990
Dutch Cup 1987, 1993
European Cup-Winners' Cup 1987
UEFA Cup 1992, 1994
Premiership 1998, 2002, 2004
FA Cup 1998, 2002, 2003, 2005
PERSONAL AWARDS
Dutch Topscorer 1991, 1992, 1993
Dutch Player of the Year 1992, 1993
European Footballer of the Year (third place) 1993
PFA Players' Player of the Year 1998
Football Writers' Player of the Year 1998
Goal of the Season Award 1998, 2002
Arsenal FC Player of the Year 1998
FIFA World Player of the Year (third place) 1993,
(third place) 1997

ARSENAL WAS A VERY DIFFERENT CLUB when Bergkamp signed in 1995. Bruce Rioch had just taken over as manager after the dark departure of George Graham and the Gunners had finished in mid-table the previous season.

Bergkamp had topped a fans' wish list just weeks before and his arrival, alongside England captain David Platt, brought unprecedented optimism to

Highbury. "It was a signal of intent from the board and from me," recalls Rioch. "Now we meant business." Arsenal had taken their first major step into a new era.

1969 Born Amsterdam
1981 Joins Ajax Youth
1986 Makes Ajax debut v Roda JC Kerkrade
in December

1995–96

1996–97

1997–98

1998–99

1999–2000

2000–01

2001–02

1987 Wins European Cup-Winners' Cup medal
1990 International debut for Netherlands v Italy
1990 Wins first Dutch title
1992 UEFA Cup winner
1993 Eredivisie topscorer for third successive season. Also voted Dutch Player of the Year for second successive year
1993 Signs for Internazionale in Milan. Voted third in FIFA World Player of the Year awards
1994 Wins UEFA Cup and is topscorer in competition
1995 Signs for Arsenal
1997 Scores last-minute winner against Bolton in May to help Arsenal qualify for Uefa Cup
1997 Voted third in FIFA World Player of the Year awards. In September takes the first three places in the Match of the Day goal of the month competition – a feat never equalled
1998 Wins Premiership title. Voted PFA Players' Player of the Year and Football Writers' Player Of The Year. Wins Premiership goal of the season
1998 Scores stunning winner against Argentina in World Cup to surpass Faas Wilkes' record as leading Netherlands scorer of all time
2000 Retires from international football with 37 goals in 79 appearances
2002 Wins Double and Premiership goal of the season gong for a second time
2003 Wins FA Cup
2004 Wins Double
2005 Wins FA Cup
2006 In April scores a stunning goal against West Bromwich Albion on a day designated by fans as Dennis Bergkamp Day – his last goal for the Gunners. Retires from football after final game at Highbury. Plays in testimonial – the first match at Emirates Stadium

2002–03

2003–04

2004–05

2005–06

Above and below One of the finest goals ever seen in Premiership history was scored by Dennis Bergkamp at St James' Park in March 2002. Leaving Newcastle defender Nikos Dabizas on his backside with dazzling footwork, the Dutchman drilled the ball past keeper Shay Given to set Arsenal on the way to a 2–0 victory.

THE GOALS

Throughout his career, Dennis Bergkamp has been a striker who stands out for the quality of his goals.

His coolness in front of goal and superior technique allowed him to score the kind of goals most other players could only dream about, earning him the nickname 'The Iceman'.

In 1997 he scored possibly the greatest hat-trick seen in the Premiership at Leicester with three strikes displaying his ample talents. One an arrowing shot into the roof of the net from the edge of the area; the second a calm chip over an advancing keeper and the hat-trick thanks to mesmerising control and a finish that he repeated against Argentina the following year.

A stunning sidefooted 25-yard strike at Sunderland drew gasps of astonishment from the Roker Park faithful. "I started clapping until I realised I was Sunderland's manager," confessed Peter Reid.

A repeat performance came in the form of the memorable winner against Argentina in World Cup '98, a worthy goal of the tournament.

And in 2002 he scored what many consider his best for Arsenal at Newcastle – earning him the Premiership goal of the season trophy.

Dennis plays keep-ball with Charlton keeper Dean Kiely in a 4–0 win in October 2004.

With his back to goal he flicked the ball over his and the defender's shoulder, span around in one movement and collected his own pass before delivering an exceptional finish past a bemused Shay Given. Pure genius.

His first and last goals for Arsenal both came at the Clock End – and were two beauties. In September 1995 against Southampton he opened

SEASON-BY-SEASON STATISTICS

YEAR	GAMES (AS SUB)	GLS
1995–96 LEAGUE	33	11
FA CUP	1	0
LEAGUE CUP	7	5
TOTAL	**41**	**16**
1996–97 LEAGUE	28 (1)	12
FA CUP	2	1
LEAGUE CUP	2	1
UEFA CUP	1	0
TOTAL	**33 (1)**	**14**
1997–98 LEAGUE	28	16
FA CUP	7	3
LEAGUE CUP	4	2
UEFA CUP	1	1
TOTAL	**40**	**22**
1998–99 LEAGUE	28 (1)	12
FA CUP	6	3
LEAGUE CUP	1	0
CHAMPIONS LEAGUE	3	1
CHARITY SHIELD	1	0
TOTAL	**39 (1)**	**16**

YEAR	GAMES (AS SUB)	GLS
1999–2000 LEAGUE	23 (5)	6
EUROPE	11	4
TOTAL	**34 (5)**	**10**
2000–01 LEAGUE	19 (6)	3
FA CUP	4 (1)	1
CHAMPIONS LGE	3 (2)	1
TOTAL	**26 (9)**	**5**
2001–02 LEAGUE	22 (11)	9
FA CUP	4 (2)	3
LEAGUE CUP	1	0
CHAMPIONS LGE	3 (3)	2
TOTAL	**30 (16)**	**14**
2002–03 LEAGUE	23 (6)	4
FA CUP	2 (2)	2
CHAMPIONS LGE	6 (1)	1
COMMUNITY SHLD	1	0
TOTAL	**32 (9)**	**7**
2003–04 LEAGUE	21 (7)	4
FA CUP	3	1
CHAMPIONS LGE	4 (2)	0

YEAR	GAMES (AS SUB)	GLS
COMMUNITY SHLD	1	0
TOTAL	**29 (9)**	**5**
2004–05 LEAGUE	20 (9)	8
FA CUP	4	0
CHAMPIONS LGE	4	0
COMMUNITY SHLD	1	0
TOTAL	**29 (9)**	**8**
2005–06 LEAGUE	8 (16)	2
FA CUP	1	0
LEAGUE CUP	1	0
CHAMPIONS LGE	1 (3)	1
COMMUNITY SHLD	1	0
TOTAL	**12 (19)**	**3**
1995–2006 (11 SEASONS)		
LEAGUE	253 (62)	87
FA CUP	34 (5)	14
LEAGUE CUP	16	8
CHAMPIONS LGE	37 (11)	11
COMMUNITY SHLD	5	0
TOTAL	**345 (78)**	**120**

his account with a controlled volley from a Glenn Helder cross. "Most players would have taken an extra touch – but not Dennis," said Helder. His last Gunners goal – against West Brom was also a delight. A quick change of feet gave him the required space 25 yards out to curl in a wonderful effort to the delight of Highbury – and his watching family in an executive box behind the goal.

Despite earning a reputation as a creator, he netted consistently in 11 years at Highbury, joining the exclusive 100 Club in January 2003 with a strike against Oxford United in the FA Cup.

Dennis's 120th goal came against West Brom in April 2006.

THE LEGACY

BERGKAMP ON BERGKAMP

"Other clubs never came into my thoughts once I knew Arsenal wanted to sign me."

"Behind every kick of the ball there has to be a thought."

"The normal things for professional players now, I already did when I was 12 years old. I didn't have time to go out. If we had a game on Saturday, I would stay in on Friday night. I didn't smoke, I didn't drink. I stayed in on Saturday nights and Sunday to do my homework, so I could train two or three times a week."

"Maybe I am a little different from other players..."

"Arsenal will be lucky if Bergkamp scores ten goals this season." MASSIMO MORATTI, PRESIDENT OF INTERNAZIONALE

"If Ryan Giggs is worth £20 million, Bergkamp is worth a hundred." MARCO VAN BASTEN

"Enn doelpunt van een andrer planeet."
[It's a goal from another planet.] LOUIS VAN GAAL, FORMER COACH DESCRIBING A BERGKAMP STRIKE

"He's one of the best players in the game today, but he doesn't get the publicity. It might be because he is quiet off the pitch and does not make dramatic statements to the press, and I think he likes it that way. Can you not say he is the best player in the world right now? If there is a better one, then I have not seen him."
ARSÈNE WENGER, 1998

"I started clapping myself until I realised that I was Sunderland's manager." PETER REID

"Bergkamp is someone special. I know him from the days when we played together. He was very young then. He was one of those players who made people turn up to the stadium just to watch him play. In a way he was making art, scoring beautiful goals. He has already left a mark on football."
FRANK RIJKAARD

"Intelligence and class: what he does, there's always a head and always a brain. And his technique allows him to do what he sees and what he decides to do." ARSÈNE WENGER, 2006

Clockwise from bottom left Dennis celebrates with Thierry Henry and Ashley Cole after scoring against Everton in May 2002: Signing autographs at a pre-season friendly against Barnet in 2005: Tapping in the fourth goal in a 5–1 FA Cup victory over Farnborough Town in January 2003: Celebrating the Double with Sol Campbell and Ashley Cole in 2002: Giving the thumbs up after receiving another great pass from a teammate.

CLUB RECORDS

APPEARANCES

OVERALL
DAVID O'LEARY **722**
LEAGUE
DAVID O'LEARY **558**
PREMIERSHIP
DAVID SEAMAN **344**
CONSECUTIVE
APPEARANCES
TOM PARKER **172**
(3/4/1926–26/12/1929)

YOUNGEST

FRANCESC FABREGAS
16 year, 177 days
(v Rotherham United (h)
Lge Cup 28/10/03)
LEAGUE
GERRY WARD
16 years 321 days
(v Huddersfield Town (h)
22/8/53)
PREMIERSHIP
FRANCESC FABREGAS
17 years, 103 days
(v Everton (a) 15/8/04)
EUROPE
FRANCESC FABREGAS
17 years, 169 days
(v Panathinaikos (a)
20/10/2004)
SCORER
FRANCESC FABREGAS
16 years, 212 days
(v Wolves (h) Lge Cup
2/12/03)

OLDEST

JOCK RUTHERFORD
41 years, 159 days

(v Manchester City (h)
League) 20/3/1926)
PREMIERSHIP
JOHN LUKIC
39 years, 336 days
(v Derby County (h)
11/11/2000)
EUROPE
JOHN LUKIC
39 years, 311 days
(v Lazio (a) UCL Grp
Stage 17/10/2000)

ATTENDANCES

HIGHEST OVERALL
73,295
(v Sunderland 9 /3/ 1935)
LEAGUE
73,295
(v Sunderland 9 /3/ 1935)
PREMIERSHIP
38,419
(v Leicester City
15/5/2004)
WEMBLEY STADIUM
73,707
(v RC Lens 25 /11/1998)
LOWEST OVERALL
4,554
(v Leeds United
5/5/1966)
LOWEST PREMIERSHIP
18,253
(v Wimbledon 10/2/1993)

VICTORIES

BIGGEST OVERALL
12–0
Loughborough Town (h)
(12/3/1900 Lge Div 2);

Ashford United (h)
(14/10/1893 FA Cup
first round)
AWAY
7–0 **Standard Liege**
(3/11/93, European
Cup- Winners' Cup
second round)
PREMIERSHIP
7–0
Everton (h) (12/5/05);
Middlesbrough (h)
(14/1/06)
PREMIERSHIP AWAY
6–1
Middlesbrough
(24/4/99)
CHAMPIONS LEAGUE
5–1
Rosenborg (h) (7/12/04);
Inter Milan (a) (25/11/03)

DEFEATS

BIGGEST OVERALL
0–8
Loughborough Town (a)
(12/12/1896, Lge Div 2)
HOME
0–6
Derby County (h)
28/1/1899, FA Cup
1st round)
PREMIERSHIP
1–6
Manchester United
(25/2/01)
EUROPE
2–5
Spartak Moscow
(29/9/82, UEFA Cup
1st round)

DRAWS

HIGHEST
6–6
Leicester City (a)
(21/4/30)

GOALSCORERS

OVERALL
THIERRY HENRY **214**
PREMIERSHIP
THIERRY HENRY **164**
FA CUP
CLIFF BASTIN **26**
LEAGUE CUP
IAN WRIGHT **29**
EUROPE
THIERRY HENRY **42**
CHAMPIONS
LEAGUE
THIERRY HENRY **31**
IN A SEASON
TED DRAKE **44**
(1934/35 42 Lge,
1 FA Cup,
1 C. Shield)
IN A PREMIERSHIP
SEASON
THIERRY HENRY **30**
(2003/04)
IN A SINGLE
MATCH
TED DRAKE **7**
(v Aston Villa (a)
14/12/1935
(7–1))
IN A SINGLE
EUROPEAN MATCH
ALAN SMITH **4**
(v FK Austria (h)
18/9/91
European Cup (6–1))

RUNS

CONSECUTIVE WINS 14
from 12/9/87 and
from 10/2/02
CONSECUTIVE DEFEATS 8
from 12/2/77
UNBEATEN RUN IN ALL COMPETITIONS 24
from 20/3/02 to 19/10/02
UNBEATEN PREMIERSHIP RUN 49
from 7/5/03 to 1/2/05
WITHOUT A WIN 23
from 28/9/12
CONSECUTIVE CLEAN SHEETS 8
from 10/4/03
CONSECUTIVE PREMIERSHIP MATCHES SCORING 55
(19/5/01 to 7/12/02)

CLUB HONOURS

LEAGUE CHAMPIONS
13 TIMES
1930/31, 1932/33, 1933/34,
1934/35, 1937/38, 1947/48,
1952/53, 1970/71, 1988/89,
1990/91, 1997/98, 2001/02,
2003/04
FA CUP WINNERS
10 TIMES
1930, 1936, 1950, 1971, 1979,
1993, 1998, 2002, 2003, 2005
LEAGUE CUP WINNERS
2 TIMES
1987, 1993
EUROPE
FAIRS CUP
1970
EUROPEAN CUP-WINNERS' CUP
1994
CHARITY/COMMUNITY SHIELD WINNERS
11 TIMES
1930, 1931, 1933, 1934, 1938,
1948, 1953, 1998, 1999, 2002,
2004

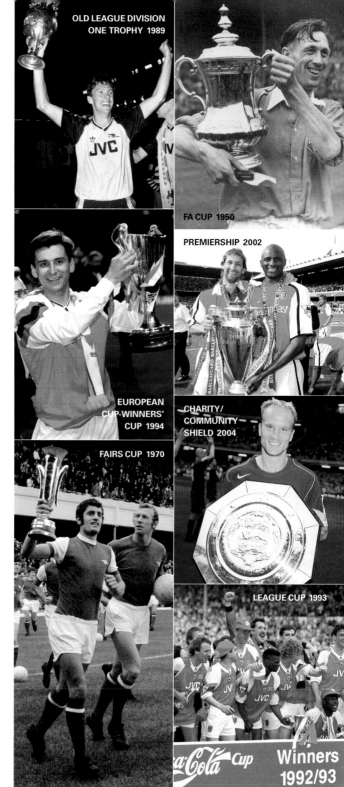

OLD LEAGUE DIVISION ONE TROPHY 1989

FA CUP 1950

PREMIERSHIP 2002

EUROPEAN CUP-WINNERS' CUP 1994

FAIRS CUP 1970

CHARITY/COMMUNITY SHIELD 2004

LEAGUE CUP 1993

Winners 1992/93

ARSENAL WERE DETERMINED to make the final season at Highbury live in the memory of all those who follow the Club. To this end they came up with a number of initiatives to see off the old stadium with a bang. A series of innovative ideas were devised under the banner of 'The Final Salute'. A new branding and crest were created and used throughout the season on everything, from the programme to the club gates. Key to this was a move away from the bright red shirts of recent decades to redcurrant.

ORIGINAL COLOURS

The reason for this surprising move was to be found in the kit design. In the summer of 2005, Arsenal launched a special home kit. The redcurrant design mirrored the first ever strip worn at Highbury back in 1913 when the Gunners opened their Highbury life with a 2–1 win over Leicester Fosse. It ended at Highbury with a 4–2 win over Wigan. The more familiar red and white strip will return at Emirates.

THEME DAYS

Every home game was given a special theme. They ranged from Wenger Day and Captains' Day, to Junior Gunners' Day and Home Grown Players' Day.

The visit of West Brom in April was designated Dennis Bergkamp Day. Thousands of fans wore the Dutch orange in homage to their hero and he obliged with a stunning goal to seal a 3–1 win.

Junior Gunners dressed in Edwardian style for 1913 Day.

PLAYERS' DAY
Sunday
14 August 2005
v Newcastle United

GOAL CELEBRATIONS'
DAY
Wednesday
24 August 2005
v Fulham

EUROPEAN NIGHT
Wednesday
14 September 2005
v FC Thun

DOUBLES DAY
Monday
19 September 2005
v Everton

INTERNATIONALS'
DAY
Sunday
2 October 2005
v Birmingham City

WENGER DAY
Saturday
22 October 2005
v Manchester City

EUROPEAN
NIGHT
Wednesday
2 November 2005
v Sparta Prague

MEMORIAL DAY
Saturday
5 November 2005
v Sunderland

49-ERS DAY
Saturday
26 November 2005
v Blackburn Rovers

LEAGUE CUP
NIGHT
Tuesday
29 November 2005
v Reading

BOXERS v
JOCKEYS DAY
Wednesday
7 December 2005
v Ajax

GREAT SAVES DAY
Sunday
18 December 2005
v Chelsea

HAT-TRICK
HEROES DAY
Wednesday
28 December 2005
v Portsmouth

BACK FOUR DAY
Tuesday
3 January 2006
v Manchester United

FA CUP DAY
Saturday
7 January 2006
v Cardiff City

1913 DAY
Saturday
14 January 2006
v Middlesbrough

A completely orange North Bank on Saturday 15 April 2006 – Dennis Bergkamp Day.

The Junior Gunners donned Edwardian clothing for 1913 Day, while Alan Smith led out former favourites on Players' Day.

One of the most emotional days was that of the 5–0 win over Aston Villa on 1 April 2006. It was designated David Rocastle Day in honour of the former star who died in 2001, aged 33.

The last ever match, against Wigan, was Goals' Day, when some of the scoring feats of the Gunners' top strikers through the years were remembered.

THE COUNTDOWN CLOCK

An electronic clock was erected in the stadium to count down the last season in N5. After the final match against Wigan, manager Arsène Wenger, whose vision and success has made the move to Emirates possible, counted down the last ten seconds with the 38,000 crowd. At 6.30pm on Sunday 7 May 2006 the counters hit zero, fireworks filled the sky and an emotional crowd bid farewell to Highbury.

Thierry Henry, Robert Pires and Ashley Cole unveiling the 52-metre mural depicting Arsenal's 93 years at Highbury, which was created by members of the community.

THE ARSENAL MURAL

A stunning 52-metre mural was unveiled in the main walkway of Arsenal Underground station on the Piccadilly Line on 12 January 2006. The mural was created by primary and secondary school children, local residents, disabled supporters and over-60s from the surrounding area. Each contributed

LEAGUE CUP NIGHT
Tuesday
24 January 2006
v Wigan Athletic

LONDON DERBIES' DAY
Wednesday
1 February 2006
v West Ham United

**HOME GROWN
PLAYERS' DAY**
Saturday
11 February 2006
v Bolton Wanderers

MANAGERS' DAY
Wednesday
8 March 2006
v Real Madrid

CAPTAINS' DAY
Sunday
12 March 2006
v Liverpool

**JUNIOR GUNNERS'
DAY**
Saturday
18 March 2006
v Charlton Athletic

DECADES' DAY
Tuesday
28 March 2006
v Juventus

DAVID ROCASTLE DAY
Saturday 1 April 2006
v Aston Villa

**DENNIS BERGKAMP
DAY**
Saturday
15 April 2006
v West Bromwich
Albion

RECORDS' DAY
Wednesday
19 April 2006
v Villarreal

KITS' DAY
Saturday
22 April 2006
v Tottenham Hotspur

GOALS' DAY
Sunday 7 May 2006
v Wigan Athletic

paintings, drawings and photographs depicting 93 glorious years at the old stadium. "It's wonderful that the Arsenal community has come together to depict Highbury's history and express in this way what the stadium means to them," said Thierry Henry.

THE PROGRAMME

Arsenal's matchday magazine played a major part in The Final Salute celebrations. Every issue had a special 16-page 'Historic Highbury' pullout with reproductions of former programmes, features on past games, Highbury memories from fans and journalists, and quirky tales from 93 years at Highbury.

'Hidden Highbury' also examined those areas deep in the stadium which fans do not get the opportunity to see, and the final programme of the season also contained an additional 'A–Z of Highbury'.

Publications manager Andy Exley and his team were rewarded with the coveted Premiership Programme of the Year Award, with the Historic Highbury section being singled out for particular praise.

The monthly official *Arsenal Magazine* also joined the countdown with former player, and their coach and manager Don Howe sharing Highbury tales in each issue, and comedian Paul Kaye giving his inimitable take on his final season as a West Stand season ticket holder.

THE SCOREBOARD

A welcome comeback was made by the old-style wooden scoreboard. Situated in the southeast corner of the stadium, it hadn't been seen at Highbury since the 1980s. Operated by selected membership holders, the half-time scores from other major games were shown at every match.

THE HIGHBURY AUCTION

Arsenal compiled a list of over 2700 historic items from the Club's famous stadium, which were sold in a special Highbury auction after the move to Emirates Stadium.

The wide-ranging items up for sale at the auction included the goalposts and nets, corner flags, the centre circle, Arsène Wenger's seat in the dug out, leather chairs and a table from the managing director's office, selected carpets from VIP areas, George Graham's old desk, a red double-decker bus used in the 1989 League Championship trophy parade, all the numbered boot pegs from the boot room, stadium turnstiles and even 20 red Arsenal wheelie bins!

However, not everything at Highbury was sold. Some items, including the famous Herbert Chapman bust and the clock from the Clock End, were taken to Emirates Stadium.

Fans could bid for all the items online. The first sale was followed by the main Highbury auction at the end of July, when over a thousand 'crown jewels' from the stadium were sold at a spectacular event that took place in front of the East Stand.

Admission to the Highbury auction was limited to 8000 people and was only gained through purchase of an event catalogue, but collectors from around the world also had the opportunity to buy items via a live webcast of the auction.

Fans salute the home of Arsenal for 93 years.

The 2700 Highbury auction lots included:

Both goalposts and nets from Highbury
The Arsenal and visitors' dugouts
Selected items from the Arsenal and
visitors' dressing rooms
The centre circle from the Highbury pitch
Both steel-framed electronic scoreboards
Both steel-framed 'Jumbotron'
big screens
Selected flagpoles and flags
Bow-fronted oak press conference desk,
used for all Highbury press conferences
since 1980
Red double-decker Routemaster bus,
used in the 1989 League Championship
trophy parade, formerly located in the
Highbury Museum
George Graham's original desk from
when he was manager of the club
All four corner flags
All Arsenal signage from inside
the stadium
A leather-bound copy of the last ever
matchday programme printed for a
competitive match at Highbury
Red leather upholstered chairs and
table, featuring the Arsenal crest, from
the managing director's office.
Red plastic wheelie bins with the
Arsenal crest
Selected carpets from throughout the
stadium with red trim, Arsenal cannons
and the Arsenal crest
All the numbered boot pegs from the
Highbury boot room
Over 300 photographs and prints (some
signed) from around the stadium
Sets of single and double entry
turnstiles
Over 5000 white ceramic wall tiles with
the Art Deco Arsenal crest
A marble plaque commemorating the
redevelopment of the South Stand,
officially opened by HRH the Duke of
Kent in February 1994.

HIGHBURY TIMELINE

1913 As Woolwich Arsenal, the club played its first match at Arsenal Stadium, Highbury, a 2–1 Division Two victory over Leicester Fosse. Later in 1913, the Club was renamed Arsenal Football Club.

1925 The Club bought the stadium site outright.

1931 Arsenal lifted their first title after a 3–1 Highbury win over Liverpool.

1932 The West Stand, with a capacity of 21,000, was opened in December by HRH Prince of Wales: Arsenal beat Sheffield United 9–2 with Jack Lambert hitting five, a Club record for a striker in one match at Highbury.

1935 A roof was erected over the Laundry End (later renamed the North Bank): Clock installed at back of southerly College End terrace (later called the Clock End).

1936 The Art Deco East Stand opened in October.

1939–45 Arsenal Stadium was transformed into an Air Raid Precautions (ARP) base and Arsenal had to play their wartime home fixtures at White Hart Lane!

1951 First official floodlight match as Hapoel Tel Aviv beaten 6–1.

1953 The Gunners beat Burnley 3–2 at Highbury on May Day to seal their seventh title.

1966 Muhammed Ali beat Henry Cooper in a heavyweight fight at the stadium.

1970 Arsenal beat Anderlecht 3–0 to win the Fairs Cup, the Club's first ever European trophy.

1989 Executive boxes and roof over Clock End erected.

1992 North Bank terrace demolished to make way for a 12,500-seater two-tiered North Stand.

1993 Highbury became an all-seater stadium on completion of the redevelopment of Clock End: Jumbotrons were installed in northwest and southeast corners of the stadium.

1998 Arsenal won their first Premiership title with a 4–0 Highbury demolition of Everton.

1999 In November, the Club announced proposals to move to a new stadium, situated at Ashburton Grove, N7.

2000 Highbury hosted its first ever Champions League match when Arsenal beat Shakhtar Donetsk 3–2 courtesy of two late Martin Keown goals.

2004 In February, the Club announced completion of funding for the stadium project and construction began at Ashburton Grove.

2005 Arsenal's last ever game in red and white at Highbury saw the Gunners beat Everton 7–0.

2006 In May, Arsenal played their last ever match at Highbury beating Wigan 4–2 to earn fourth place in the Premiership – at the expense of Tottenham: the new 60,000 seater Emirates Stadium is due to open in August and work is set to begin on Highbury Square development.

Fans in their red 'I was there' T-shirts for the final match at Highbury against Wigan Athletic on Sunday 7 May 2006.

HIGHBURY: THE STATISTICS

ARSENAL'S HIGHBURY RECORDS

LEAGUE	P	W	D	L	F	A
	1689	980	413	296	3372	1692

FA CUP	P	W	D	L	F	A
	142	92	32	18	305	123

FA CHARITY SHIELD	P	W	D	L	F	A
	5	4	0	1	13	6

(Played at Highbury in 1935, 1936, 1939, 1949 and 1954)

LEAGUE CUP	P	W	D	L	F	A
	98	69	14	15	195	74

EUROPEAN COMPETITIONS	P	W	D	L	F	A
	76	50	17	9	153	60

TOTAL	P	W	D	L	F	A
	2010	1195	476	339	4038	1955

156 different teams have played a competitive match at Highbury, with Everton, who ran out 83 times, the most frequent visitors (Arsenal won 57 of those encounters).

MANAGERS' RECORDS

GEORGE MORRELL (1913–1915)	P	W	D	L	F	A
	39	30	4	5	89	23

LESLIE KNIGHTON (1919–1925)	P	W	D	L	F	A
	133	66	34	33	201	132

HERBERT CHAPMAN (1925–1934)	P	W	D	L	F	A
	197	125	39	33	511	224

GEORGE ALLISON/ JOE SHAW	P	W	D	L	F	A
	13	9	1	3	28	15

(Caretaker Managers January–May 1934)

THE FINAL DAY

The last game, on Sunday 7 May 2006, saw Wigan as the final visitors to Highbury. Thierry Henry's hat-trick sealed a 4–2 win. After the game the Club held a closing ceremony hosted by matchday announcer Paul Burrell and actor and broadcaster Tom Watt.

The marching band – familiar to older fans – returned for one last time, as did PC Alex Morgan, the police tenor.

The largest collection of Arsenal legends paraded around the pitch and Who legend Roger Daltrey sang a special song he had written for the day, entitled 'Highbury Highs'.

Sir Henry Cooper also addressed the crowd before the first team did a final lap of honour, but it was left to Arsène Wenger to count down the Highbury clocks – sparking a magnificent firework display as the old stadium really did go out with a bang!

WHAT NEXT FOR HIGHBURY?

Demolition work will begin in the autumn of 2006 on the Clock End and North Bank stands, while the East and West Stands will be extensively renovated and turned into housing. When completed, the stadium will boast a wide selection of one-, two- and three-bedroom apartments and penthouses. The pitch will become an impressive landscaped garden with public access.

The Art Deco East Stand facade, however, will remain standing. Its listed building status means the next generations of fans will be able to enjoy its splendour long into the 21st century.

GEORGE ALLISON (1934–1947)	P	W	D	L	F	A
	135	78	36	21	312	128

TOM WHITTAKER (1947–1956)	P	W	D	L	F	A
	217	130	45	42	506	260

JACK CRAYSTON (1956–1958)	P	W	D	L	F	A
	37	20	8	9	82	55

GEORGE SWINDIN (1958–1962)	P	W	D	L	F	A
	88	46	19	23	185	136

BILLY WRIGHT (1962–1966)	P	W	D	L	F	A
	92	44	25	23	193	141

BERTIE MEE (1966–1976)	P	W	D	L	F	A
	265	155	66	44	430	197

TERRY NEILL (1976–1983)	P	W	D	L	F	A
	204	122	56	26	349	161

DON HOWE (DEC 1983–MAR 1986)	P	W	D	L	F	A
	56	36	15	5	107	46

STEVE BURTENSHAW	P	W	D	L	F	A
	5	1	2	2	5	6

(Caretaker Manager March–May 1986)

GEORGE GRAHAM (1986–1995)	P	W	D	L	F	A
	226	126	61	39	397	179

STEWART HOUSTON	P	W	D	L	F	A
	12	5	4	3	22	14

(Caretaker Manager February –May 1995
and August–September 1996)

BRUCE RIOCH (1995–1996)	P	W	D	L	F	A
	24	13	9	2	42	20

PAT RICE	P	W	D	L	F	A
	2	2	0	0	6	1

(Caretaker Manager September 1996)

ARSÈNE WENGER (1996–)	P	W	D	L	F	A
	237	166	47	24	510	201

PLAYERS

Top ten appearances at Highbury in
all competitions (as substitute in brackets)

1 David O'Leary 325 (23)
2 Tony Adams 330 (2)
3 George Armstrong 299 (9)
4 Lee Dixon 285 (14)
5 Nigel Winterburn 274 (4)
6 David Seaman 271
7 Pat Rice 253 (2)
8 Peter Storey 240 (5)
9 John Radford 234 (3)
10 Bob John 236

GOALSCORERS

Top ten Highbury goalscorers in
all competitions

1 Thierry Henry 137
2 Cliff Bastin 103
3 Ian Wright 97
4 Doug Lishman 94
5 Jimmy Brain 91
6 John Radford 88
7 Ted Drake 78
8 Joe Hulme 74
9 Reg Lewis 71
10= Dennis Bergkamp and David Herd 68

HAT-TRICKS

Top five (of 50) players who have scored
hat-tricks in competitive matches
at Highbury:

1 Jimmy Brain 11
2 Thierry Henry 8
3= Jack Lambert and Doug Lishman 7
4 Ted Drake 6
5= David Herd, David Jack, Ronnie Rooke
   and Ian Wright 5

Clockwise, from above Referee Uriah Rennie's whistle signals the beginning of the final fixture at Highbury: The match officials and the players of Arsenal and Wigan Athletic shake hands before the kick-off: Thierry Henry kisses the 'hallowed' Highbury turf after completing his hat-trick: Handshakes again, this time after the final whistle had been blown for the end of the game and the end of play at Highbury for the last time.

Clockwise, from top left *The brass band strikes up and the Final Salute to Highbury begins: The countdown clock displays the last few seconds of Arsenal's Highbury home: A helicopter flies over the ground with a banner unfurled declaring… 'Emirates Stadium… a bright new future': The closing ceremony comes to an end; let the fireworks and the party begin: A parade of Arsenal greats around the ground as part of the 'Final Salute' celebrations.*

A night view of the impressive new Emirates Stadium – work to clear the chosen site for Arsenal's new 60,000-seater home at Ashburton Grove first began back in January 2003.

NUTS AND BOLTS

Sir Robert McAlpine Ltd was appointed to build the new stadium in January 2002.

McAlpine's CV includes the Millennium Dome, the transformation of Birmingham city centre, the new Hampden Park Stadium in Glasgow and West Ham United's Centenary Stand at Upton Park.

The Emirates was designed by HOK Sport, whose credits include the English National Stadium at Wembley, Wimbledon's Centre Court, Stadium Australia in Sydney and the Royal Ascot Racecourse.

In excess of 60,000 cubic metres of concrete were used to build the Emirates. That's enough to fill the pitch area if it were three-storeys high, or to fill the team bath at Highbury more than 7,500 times!

The seating bowl is made up of 8,641 major pre-cast concrete units, and many more smaller units.

Approximately 10,000 tons of steel reinforcement is in place, weighing more than 300 team coaches.

Some 3,000 tons of tubular steel were used in the main roof, dwarfing the 100 tons in Highbury's North Bank.

Memories and mementos from Highbury past and present are buried in the time capsule which contains nearly 40 items, 25 of which were chosen by supporters.

The stadium's four tiers of seats are covered by a roof of around 30,000 square metres, about three and a half times the area of a football pitch The concrete terracing stretches to 33,000 metres. More than 30 companies provided materials and expertise in the massive fitting-out operation – and that's in addition to all the construction firms involved in the project.

The Emirates contains enough glass to cover two football pitches, some 15,000 square metres. The stadium's metal hand railings stretch for 4,500 metres.

There are more than 2,000 doors within the Emirates complex. The stadium contains 100 flights of stairs, enough to scale Canary Wharf twice over. For those who seek an easier way up, there are 13 elevators and five escalators.

More than 25,000 cubic metres of contamination was removed to clear the way for the stadium. The site of the Emirates Stadium is 17 acres. The grass area at the Emirates is bigger than at Highbury – 113 metres by 76 metres compared with 105 metres by 70 metres.

Top *July 2004 and construction work is well under way.*
Above *April 2006 and the foundations for the new pitch are starting to be laid down.*

It is expected that 1.14 million supporters will attend Premiership games each season at the Emirates, compared with a recent Highbury average of 722,795. The Emirates contains 150 executive boxes, more than three times as many as at Highbury. There is capacity for 250 wheelchairs, including positions at all public and corporate levels throughout the site. The Emirates contains more than 900 WCs, 370 metres of urinals and 113 toilets for the disabled. The highest point of the roof is 41.9 metres from pitch level. Around 1,000 construction workers were engaged on the project at the peak of activity. There are 41 TV camera positions in the stadium, plus 215 seats for the media. The Emirates is the first UK sports venue to feature permanently installed giant Diamond Vision video screens from Mitsubishi Electric, with the latest Japanese technology. Each weighs more than five tonnes and consist of 72 square metres, comapred to the 40 square metres of the Highbury screens. The quality of pre- and post-match entertainment at the Emirates will be superb. Arsenal have invested

in a network of 439 Sony LCD screens, which will be spread around the stadium, provinding football action, analysis and behind-the-scenes content. The main pitch floodlights consist of 196 2,000-watt bulbs, spread out over 144 sets at roof level. There are a further 12,000 light fittings around the stadium.

CLUB LEVEL: WHAT TO EXPECT ON MATCHDAY

CLUB LEVEL is a seating area which offers corporate hospitality at an affordable price. It consists of an eight-row ring of 6,700 seats offering halfway-line, midfield, behind-the-goals and corner views.

FOOD AND DRINK Thanks to the floor-to-ceiling glass facades, some of the Club Level bars and lounges enjoy panoramic views over London. Restaurant menus will range from a la carte international to English favourites.

THE MATCH Club Level seats have been ergonomically designed to make the viewing experience as enjoyable as possible. Sightlines will be outstanding, with fans able to survey every part of the pitch, thanks to the curved construction of the stadium. At half-time, guests return to the

May 2006: The lush, green turf is now down – it was specified that the pitch must be the equal of Highbury's impeccable and award-winning surface. Most of the seats are now in place but many remain under wraps for the time being.

restaurants and bars for complimentary drinks while LCD screens show match highlights.

POST-MATCH Bars and restaurants remain open so that guests can avoid crowds. Once the stadium has emptied, they can leave at their leisure.

CATERING

The Emirates boasts one of the finest cuisine operations in any football stadium.

There are more than 250 service points including:
Club Level restaurants and bars in each corner of the stadium with seating for a total of 7,000 supporters.
150 executive boxes, which will be served by eight kitchens and 75 pantries with a capacity to serve 2,000 meals on a matchday.
Kiosks throughout the concourse serving snacks, soft drinks and beer.
Delaware North Companies has a 20-year contract to operate corporate hospitality, casual dining and retail concessions.
Total turnover is estimated at £350 million.
DNC will contribute £12.5 million to the catering infrastructure budget.
DNC's previous contracts include the Kennedy Space Centre, Yosemite National Park and the Melbourne Park Stadium.

The catering operation was designed, supplied and installed by the Kent-based specialist company KCCJ. Nearly 2,000 computer drawings were needed for the design of 35 concessions, 18 kitchens, 22 bars and the main support kitchen.

KCCJ's other projects have included Wembley Arena, British Library, Scottish Exhibition and Conference Centre, Wales Millennium Centre and BBC White City.

THE PITCH

The playing surface is one of the most technically advanced in the world, truly the Rolls-Royce of pitches. It is enhanced by advanced ventilation and under-soil heating systems, ensuring superb conditions all-year-round.
Fresh air can be blown on to the pitch, supplying additional oxygen to the key area around the grass roots. Excess water can be drawn off by a vacuum system.
There will be a pop-up irrigation system, a dedicated running track and fully retractable advertising boards around the playing area.

TRAVEL AND TURNSTILES

ARRIVAL – There are multiple transport links through bus, tube and national rail. Currently more people arrive at Highbury by public transport than at any other club in the Premiership, and that trend will continue at the Emirates.

An automated access control system will allow supporters entry to the stadium with a Smartcard rather than a ticket.

The 104 fully automated and computer controlled turnstiles have been custom-made for the Club, encompassing aesthetics and modern technology in one compact double unit.

In addition there are nine double-gated entrances for the disabled, each featuring a lobby between the gates and the swipe card entry point.

Each turnstile unit is fitted with a state-of-the-art card reader system to allow for quick and efficient entry.

The turnstiles stand at 2 metres 30 cms from ground level.

REGENERATING ISLINGTON AND HIGHBURY

The redevelopment scheme, including work at Highbury Square, the Northern Triangle and nearby areas, is creating:

2,500 new homes, of which 1,000 are affordable housing.

2,600 new jobs.

A £60 million waste-recycling centre.

New public and green space.

40,000 square metres of new commercial space.

Four new health facilities.

At Highbury, the East and West Stand facades have been retained, while the North and South Stands have been replaced by apartment buildings.

The Art Deco West Stand is being converted into 116 studios, a mixture of one-, two- and three-bedroom apartments. Other areas of the ground, stands and pitch are being re-designed into 711 high-spec one-, two- and three-bedroom apartments and penthouses.

The famous marble entrance hall in the East Stand is the arrival area for the whole development.

There will be a gym and fitness centre on the lower ground level of the East Stand, plus a health and community centre, nursery and retail space.

The two-acre gardens on the former pitch will be like a typical London square, in keeping with the feel of the existing arena, with glass, water and light walls, formal hedging and trees. The scale of the stadium has been retained so the memory of Highbury lives on.

When Arsenal fans queued to buy a home at Highbury, one arrived at 1am to secure the first place. The model of the ground created to showcase the new development took six people more than a month to produce.

SHOPPING

The main store at the Emirates is The Armoury, reflecting the Gunners' Woolwich Arsenal heritage.

The Armoury's 10,000 square metres will include a Nike area, a gift area, a clothing area, a children's area and even a bed area.

Retail expert George Davies, responsible for the success of Next, George at Asda, Per Una at Marks & Spencer and other leading brands, has played a major part in redefining the Arsenal shopping experience.

A smaller shop, the All Arsenal store, is housed in the northern bridge building close to the Arsenal tube station. The Arsenal World of Sport at Finsbury Park tube will be renovated and modernised in 2007.

Emirates Stadium was completed on time to hold its first scheduled match – Dennis Bergkamp's Testimonial – 22 July 2006. Arsenal's first Premiership game in their new home will be against Aston Villa on 19 August 2006.

THE COMING SEASON

Here is Arsenal's Premiership record against each of the teams that they will face in the 2006/07 season. Almost without exception, the head-to-head stats are impressive, highlighting just what a successful era the club has enjoyed since the launch of the Premier League in 1992. We've also provided a thumbnail recollection of one of the most memorable encounters with each club since the Premiership began*. There were no hard-and-fast criteria: they might be games that saw the setting of a new record or the sealing of a title; they might be memorable for a Henry hat-trick, a sublime Bergkamp goal; or maybe they were just cracking games of football.

With no Premiership games to choose from, in the case of Arsenal v Reading we've plumped for the 2005/06 Carling Cup tie.

Above Robert Pires puts Arsenal ahead from the penalty spot in the 3–1 win against Aston Villa in October 2004.
Below Gilberto's header bounces off Cesc Fabregas's knee against Blackburn in August 2004 to make him the Club's youngest ever goalscorer in League football.

ASTON VILLA

Premiership record
W 14 D 9 L 5 F 46 A 23 Pts 51

16 October 2004
Highbury
Attendance: 38,137
ARSENAL 3 ASTON VILLA 1
The last game in Arsenal's record-breaking 49 game unbeaten streak. The old French double act of Robert Pires and Thierry Henry steal the show, with all three goals and some sublime combination play.
Goals: Pires (2, 1 pen), Henry; Hendrie

BLACKBURN ROVERS

Premiership record
W 11 D 6 L 7 F 32 A 24 Pts 39

25 August 2004
Highbury
Attendance: 37,496
ARSENAL 3 BLACKBURN ROVERS 0
A second-half goal blitz from Arsenal included one from Cesc Fabregas, who became the Club's youngest ever scorer in league football aged 17 and 113 days. Arsenal's win took them past Nottingham Forest's record of 42 consecutive league games unbeaten.
Goals: Henry, Fabregas, Reyes

BOLTON WANDERERS

Premiership record
W 6 D 5 L 3 F 20 A 15 Pts 23

13 September 1997
Highbury
Attendance: 38,138

ARSENAL 4 BOLTON WANDERERS 1

After a long drought, Ian Wright finally became Arsenal's all-time top scorer. He did so in typically exuberant style, netting a hat-trick that took his tally to 180, two past Cliff Bastin's club record that has stood for 50 years.

Goals: Parlour, Wright (3); Thompson

EVERTON

Premiership record
W 18 D 6 L 4 F 57 A 22 Pts 60

3 May 1998
Highbury
Attendance: 38,073

ARSENAL 4 EVERTON 0

Arsene Wenger clinched his maiden title, and the first half of a domestic Double. An Overmars brace won the game, but Tony Adams supplied the coup de grace in the 89th minute, rampaging the length of the pitch before firing home.

Goals: Bilic (og) Overmars (2), Adams

CHARLTON ATHLETIC

Premiership record
W 10 D 2 L 2 F 30 A 11 Pts 32

26 August 2000
Highbury
Attendance: 38,025

ARSENAL 5 CHARLTON ATHLETIC 3

Captain Vieira bounced back in style after red cards in the first two games of the season. His double against the Addicks, a delicate chip and an imperious drive, delivered an eloquent riposte to his critics.

Goals: Vieira (2), Henry (2), Silvinho;
Hunt (2), Stuart

FULHAM

Premiership record
W 9 D 1 L 0 F 24 A 4 Pts 28

23 February 2002
Highbury
Attendance: 38,029

ARSENAL 4 FULHAM 1

Thierry Henry scored twice to top the Premier League scoring charts on 20, as Arsenal intensified their title charge. Pires, as he had done so often this season, ran the show, treating the crowd to his full repertoire of runs and passes.

Goals: Lauren, Vieira, Henry (2); Marlet

CHELSEA

Premiership record
W 14 D 9 L 5 F 43 A 30 Pts 51

23 October 1999
Stamford Bridge
Attendance: 34,958

CHELSEA 2 ARSENAL 3

Trailing 2–0 after some slack defending, Arsenal looked set for defeat, when Kanu sprang to life in the last 15 minutes. A breathtaking hat-trick from the Nigerian, the third from a seemingly impossible angle, turned the game on its head.

Goals: Flo, Petrescu; Kanu (3)

LIVERPOOL

Premiership record
W 8 D 7 L 13 F 23 A 37 Pts 31

9 April 2004
Highbury
Attendance: 38,119

ARSENAL 4 LIVERPOOL 2

Resilience and flair in spades, as Arsenal bounced back from Champions League and FA Cup exits to step up their march on the title. The Gunners twice fell behind, but Henry came to the rescue with a hat-trick that included a quite brilliant solo effort.

Goals: Henry (3), Pires; Hyypia, Owen

MANCHESTER CITY

Premiership record
W 15 D 3 L 0 F 37 A 8 Pts 48

22 February 2003
Maine Road
Attendance: 34,960

MANCHESTER CITY 1 ARSENAL 5

It took Arsenal just 19 minutes to take a four-goal lead, as they put on a masterclass of fluent football. It was a performance that had City boss Kevin Keegan hailing them as the best team in Europe.

Goals: Anelka; Bergkamp, Pires, Henry, Campbell, Vieira

NEWCASTLE UNITED

Premiership record
W 13 D 5 L 8 F 37 A 24 Pts 44

2 March 2002
St James Park
Attendance: 52,067

NEWCASTLE UNITED 0 ARSENAL 2

A match illuminated by possibly the Premiership's finest ever goal. Bergkamp, back to goal picked up a return pass from Pires, instantly flicking the ball past his marker with his right, spinning on to his left, and unleashing a wonder strike from the edge of the box.

Goals: Bergkamp, Campbell

MANCHESTER UNITED

Premiership record
W 7 D 9 L 12 F 25 A 37 Pts 30

8 May 2002
Old Trafford
Attendance: 67,580

MAN UTD 0 ARSENAL 1

Having already won the FA Cup, Arsenal sealed their third Double on the ground of their main rivals. Sylvain Wiltord, on his 100th appearance, kept up the Gunners' record of scoring in every league game that season, with a cool second-half finish.

Goal: Wiltord

PORTSMOUTH

Premiership record
W 3 D 3 L 0 F 11 A 3 Pts 12

5 March 2005
Highbury
Attendance: 38,079

ARSENAL 3 **PORTSMOUTH 0**

Despite fielding a weakened team, Arsenal notched a stylish win, with Thierry Henry scoring his sixth Arsenal hat-trick. He saved the best till last – a trademark free-kick five minutes from time, delivered with trademark élan from outside the box.

Goals: Henry (3)

MIDDLESBROUGH

Premiership record
W 15 D 3 L 4 F 55 A 20 Pts 33

22 August 2004
Highbury
Attendance: 37,415

ARSENAL 5 **MIDDLESBROUGH 3**

Hopes of matching Nottingham Forest's 42-match un-beaten streak looked dashed as they went 3–1 behind. But the big Guns came to the rescue as Arsenal made a stunning comeback to clinch an eight-goal thriller.

Goals: Henry (2) Bergkamp, Pires, Reyes; Job, Hasselbaink, Queudrue

READING

Premiership record
W 0 D 0 L 0 F 0 A 0 Pts 0

25 November 2005
Highbury
Attendance: 36,137

ARSENAL 3 **READING 0**

Robin van Persie scored his eighth goal in eight games as a youthful Arsenal featuring nine nationalities made the Carling Cup quarter-finals. Italian teenager Arturo Lupoli also scored to underline just how rich a seam of cosmopolitan talent the Gunners boast.

Goals: Reyes, van Persie, Lupoli

SHEFFIELD UNITED

Premiership record
W 1 D 3 L 0 F 6 A 3 Pts 6

29 December 1993
Highbury
Attendance: 27,035
ARSENAL 3 SHEFFIELD UNITED 0
Arsenal's only win in four Premiership encounters against the Blades was delivered courtesy of a classic Ian Wright effort and two powerful headers from Kevin Campbell.
Goals: Kevin Campbell (2), Wright

WEST HAM UNITED

Premiership record
W 13 D 5 L 4 F 35 A 15 Pts 044

3 March 2001
Highbury
Attendance: 38,071
ARSENAL 3 WEST HAM 0
Arsenal raced out of the blocks to score three times in the first 20 minutes, leaving the Hammers dead in the water. All three goals came from Frenchman Sylvain Wiltord, one of only two hat-tricks in his Gunners' career.
Goals: Wiltord (3)

TOTTENHAM HOTSPUR

Premiership record
W 10 D 13 L 5 F 37 A 28 Pts 43

13 November 2004
White Hart Lane
Attendance: 36,095
TOTTENHAM HOTSPUR 4 ARSENAL 5
Nine goals and nine different scorers as the North London derby exploded into a second-half goalfest. The pick of the bunch came from Ljungberg, set up by an exquisite reverse pass from a teenage Fabregas in his first full season at Arsenal.
Goals: Naybet, Defoe, King, Kanoute; Henry, Lauren (pen), Vieira, Ljungberg, Pires

WIGAN ATHLETIC

Premiership record
W 1 D 0 L 1 F 6 A 5 Pts 3

7 May 2006
Highbury
Attendance: 38,359
ARSENAL 4 WIGAN 2
Arsenal bid farewell to Highbury in style. Cometh the hour...Thierry Henry produces a stunning hat-trick to help ensure a 4–2 victory that secures fourth place and Champions League football for the maiden season at the Emirates.
Goals: Pires, Henry (3, 1 pen); Scharner, Thompson

WATFORD

Premiership record
W 2 D 0 L 0 F 4 A 2 Pts 6

23 April 2000
Vicarage Road
Attendance: 19,670
WATFORD 2 ARSENAL 3
A classic game of two halves, as Arsenal raced into a three-goal lead before half-time before easing off the gas. A spirited fight back by the home team gave the Gunners an almighty scare.
Goals: Helguson, Hyde; Henry (2), Parlour

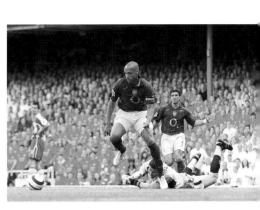

Henry rounds Mike Pollitt and scores his second and Arsenal's third against Wigan in the last match ever played at Highbury.

THE SEASON IN PICTURES

Clockwise, from above *Sunset at Highbury: Groundsman Paul Burgess carefully adds the finishing touches to the immaculate Highbury turf: The Arsenal changing room – ready and waiting: Steve Bennett blows the whistle and*

Newcastle kick-off – the final season at Highbury has begun: Thierry Henry on his way to scoring his second against Sparta Prague and into the record books – first equalling and then surpassing Ian Wright's record of 185 goals.

Clockwise, from top left Robert Pires gets the ball under control in a close contest against Manchester City, he later put away a penalty – the only score of the game: After the match Thierry Henry is presented with a golden cannon by Ian Wright for becoming Arsenal's all-time record goalscorer: Henry beats Alvaro Mejia, Ronaldo chases, but Thierry is on his way to scoring a fabulous goal at the Bernabeu to defeat Real Madrid in the Champions League.

Clockwise, from top left *A great view of goalmouth action against Aston Villa but also of the new Emirates Stadium: David Rocastle Day – the players of both Arsenal and Aston Villa clap for a minute in remembrance: Fans have* *a messsage for Dennis on his Theme Day: Walking out into the Stadio delle Alpi for the Champions League quarter-final, second leg: Fans hold up cards to create a mosaic showing the years of Arsenal at Highbury.*

Clockwise, from top left *Jens Lehmann saves Riquelme's last-minute penalty and Arsenal reach their first Champions League final: On the sidelines, Arsène Wenger and Pat Rice celebrate this victorious night: The Champions League final pre-match ceremony at the Stade de France: Sol Campbell heads Thierry Henry's free-kick past Valdés to give Arsenal a first-half lead: Sub Dennis Bergkamp waits to run onto the Highbury pitch for the last time against Wigan.*

FIXTURE LIST 2006/2007

AUGUST 2006

Tuesday 8	H/A	Qualifier 1st Leg	Champions League
Saturday 19	H	Aston Villa	Barclays Premiership
Tuesday 22	H/A	Qualifier 2nd Leg	Champions League
Saturday 26	A	Manchester City	Barclays Premiership

SEPTEMBER 2006

Saturday 9	H	Middlesbrough	Barclays Premiership
Tuesday 12	H/A	Matchday One	Champions League
Sunday 17	A	Manchester United	Barclays Premiership
Saturday 23	H	Sheffield United	Barclays Premiership
Tuesday 26	H/A	Matchday Two	Champions League
Saturday 30	A	Charlton Athletic	Barclays Premiership

OCTOBER 2006

Saturday 14	H	Watford	Barclays Premiership
Tuesday 17	H/A	Matchday Three	Champions League
Sunday 22	A	Reading	Barclays Premiership
Wednesday 25	H/A	Third Round	Carling Cup
Saturday 28	H	Everton	Barclays Premiership
Tuesday 31	H/A	Matchday Four	Champions League

NOVEMBER 2006

Sunday 5	A	West Ham United	Barclays Premiership
Wednesday 8	H/A	Fourth Round	Carling Cup
Sunday 12	H	Liverpool	Barclays Premiership
Saturday 18	H	Newcastle United	Barclays Premiership
Tuesday 21	H/A	Matchday Five	Champions League
Saturday 25	A	Bolton Wanderers	Barclays Premiership
Wednesday 29	A	Fulham	Barclays Premiership

DECEMBER 2006

Saturday 2	H	Tottenham Hotspur	Barclays Premiership
Tuesday 5	H/A	Matchday Six	Champions League
Sunday 10	A	Chelsea	Barclays Premiership
Wednesday 13	A	Wigan Athletic	Barclays Premiership
Saturday 16	H	Portsmouth	Barclays Premiership
Wednesday 20	H/A	Fifth Round	Carling Cup
Saturday 23	H	Blackburn Rovers	Barclays Premiership
Tuesday 26	A	Watford	Barclays Premiership
Saturday 30	A	Sheffield United	Barclays Premiership

JANUARY 2007

Monday 1	H	Charlton Athletic	Barclays Premiership
Saturday 6	H/A	Third Round	FA Cup
Wednesday 10	H/A	Semi-final 1st Leg	Carling Cup
Saturday 13	A	Blackburn Rovers	Barclays Premiership
Saturday 20	H	Manchester United	Barclays Premiership
Wednesday 24	H/A	Semi-final 2nd Leg	Carling Cup
Saturday 27	A	Fourth Round	FA Cup
Tuesday 30	H	Manchester City	Barclays Premiership

FEBRUARY 2007

Saturday 3	A	Middlesbrough	Barclays Premiership
Saturday 10	H	Wigan Athletic	Barclays Premiership
Saturday 17	H/A	Fifth Round	FA Cup
Tuesday 20	H/A	Knockout Round 1st Leg	Champions League
Saturday 24	A	Aston Villa	Barclays Premiership
Sunday 25	N	Final	Carling Cup

MARCH 2007

Saturday 3	H	Reading	Barclays Premiership
Tuesday 6	H/A	Knockout Round 2nd Leg	Champions League
Saturday 10	H/A	Quarter-final	FA Cup
Saturday 17	A	Everton	Barclays Premiership
Saturday 31	A	Liverpool	Barclays Premiership

APRIL 2007

Tuesday 3	H/A	Quarter-final 1st Leg	Champions League
Saturday 7	H	West Ham United	Barclays Premiership
Monday 9	A	Newcastle United	Barclays Premiership
Tuesday 10	H/A	Quarter-final 2nd Leg	Champions League
Saturday 14	H	Bolton Wanderers	Barclays Premiership
Saturday 21	A	Tottenham Hotspur	Barclays Premiership
Tuesday 24	H/A	Semi-final 1st Leg	Champions League
Saturday 28	H	Fulham	Barclays Premiership

MAY 2007

Tuesday 1	H/A	Semi-final 2nd Leg	Champions League
Saturday 5	H	Chelsea	Barclays Premiership
Sunday 13	A	Portsmouth	Barclays Premiership
Saturday 19	N	Final	FA Cup
Wednesday 23	N	Final	Champions League

Emirates Stadium – the magnificent, state-of-the-art new home of Arsenal Football Club with a capacity of 60,000.